FINDING MYSELF ALONG THE WAY

Finding Myself Along the Way

One Man's Journey on the Camino de Santiago

Michael Burnett

To write this book I relied upon my own memory of these events. I have changed the names of some of the characters in this book, and in some cases the identifying details in order to preserve anonymity.

Published by Annecy Press LLC
Zion. Il 60099
Annecypress.com

First paperback edition September 2021

Cover Photos and interior photo taken by the author
Author photo (on back cover): courtesy of Kelly Trapp
Author photo (interior): taken by a pilgrim at San Anton
Copyeditors: Doreen Martens, Kristin Davis, and Paige Lawson
Book Cover design: Anna Burrous
Map design: Khayyam Akhtar

ISBN 978-1-7378175-0-5 (paperback)
ISBN 978-1-7378175-1-2 (ebook)
LIBRARY OF CONGESS CONTROL NUMBER: 2021917771

Publisher's Cataloging-in-Publication data

Names: Burnett, Michael A. author.
Title: Finding myself along the way : one man's journey on the Camino de Santiago / Michael Burnett.
Description: Zion, IL: Annecy Press, 2021.
Identifiers: LCCN: 2021917771 | ISBN 978-1-7378175-0-5 (paperback) | 978-1-7378175-1-2 (ebook)
Subjects: LCSH Burnett, Michael A.-- Travel--Camino de Santiago de Compostela. | Santiago de Compostela (Spain)--Guidebooks. | Spain--Description and travel. | Self actualization (Psychology). | BISAC BIOGRAPHY & AUTOBIOGRAPHY / Personal Memoirs | TRAVEL / Europe / Spain & Portugal | TRAVEL / Special Interest / Hikes & Walks | TRAVEL / Special Interest / Adventure | TRAVEL / Special Interest / Religious | TRAVEL / Essays & Travelogues | SELF-HELP / Personal Growth / General
Classification: LCC BX2321.S3 .B87 2021 | DDC 263/.0424092--dc23

Printed in the United States of America

To Alyssa and Ryan—

for filling my life with light and joy.

Afoot and light-hearted I take to the open road,
Healthy, free, the world before me,
The long brown path before me leading wherever I choose.

Henceforth I ask not good-fortune, I myself am good-fortune,
Henceforth I whimper no more, postpone no more, need
 nothing,
Done with indoor complaints...querulous criticisms,
Strong and content I travel the open road.

-Opening of *The Song of the Open Road* by Walt Whitman

PREFACE

The idea for this book came to me as my walk along the Camino de Santiago was coming to an end. I felt an urgency to share my story, both of my journey across Spain, and the years leading up to my Camino. I wanted others to see the path that led me to this ancient road.

Before starting out on the Camino, I was already an experienced backpacker, having previously logged well over a thousand miles, but nothing prepared me for what was to come. My time along the Way changed how I saw the world, and myself.

This book is my way of giving back. I want others to experience the Camino—hopefully the actual physical journey, but if not, to at least experience the Way via my story. That is why this book is laid out as a day-to-day account; I want you to come along on my walk and meet the people who made my journey what it was.

Looking back now, it feels that my entire life was leading me to this walk. Once completed, it felt as though the Camino had prepared me for my life's final chapters. It was a seminal experience in my life. I feel my story can provide others with a light, not a road map, as everyone must find their own way on life's journey … sometimes a little light is all we need to help us get where we need to go. So, here is my light for your path...

ARRIVAL IN SAINT-JEAN-PIED-DE-PORT

*All men dream, but not equally. Those who
dream by night in the dusty recesses of their
minds wake in the day to find that it was
vanity; but the dreamers of the day are
dangerous men, for they may act on their
dreams with open eyes, to make it possible.*

~ T.E. Lawrence, *Seven Pillars of
Wisdom*

Rhythmic clacking and chatter fill the air as I look out onto a mountain
landscape in a foreign land and think back to my days behind a desk; a
life of not-so-quiet desperation. I wasn't that different from most people
reaching middle age in our consumer culture, but I was one who asked,
"Is this all there is?" Stuck behind that desk, day after day, I was
desperate for something more but unsure of exactly what that 'more'

was. In my mind, a storm was brewing, but outwardly I wore a painted-on smile. I would have to shed everything I had and was … to get me to *this* moment.

I know the first step in any journey is deciding to go. I look back and don't remember the exact moment, only that it took an agonizingly long time to make the irrevocable decisions that started this journey. I had to navigate a sometimes difficult course and completed it just over two years ago, when this journey began.

The clack, clack, clack of the single-car train continues as I head higher into the foothills of the Pyrenees, in the southwest corner of France.

The train stops in front of a two-story white stucco building with crimson shutters and a terra-cotta roof. A sign above a door tells me it's the end of the line: Saint-Jean-Pied-de-Port. I grab my black-and-gray Deuter backpack from above me and follow the crowd of fifty or so other pack-wearing pilgrims out onto the platform.

Pilgrim? Why do I use that term? Its simple definition is: a person who journeys a long distance to some sacred place as an act of religious devotion. I have arrived at a modern-day starting point for the Camino de Santiago, or the Way of Saint James. The Camino de Santiago is an ancient route that pilgrims have walked for over a thousand years, journeying to the remains of Saint James, a disciple of Jesus. Saint James is buried in the Spanish city of Santiago de Compostela, approximately 500 miles to the west of where I stand. While I'm not walking to Santiago de Compostela as an act of religious devotion, I am making this pilgrimage hoping to uncover what direction I should head in life; moving towards a better version of myself. Every pilgrim arriving here has their own reasons for making the journey.

The small French enclave of Saint-Jean-Pied-de-Port lies in the Pyrenees' foothills; its name translates to Saint John at the Foot of the Pass. Saint-Jean sits on the Pyrenean Mountain Range's western edge, which runs along the border between France and Spain for some 270 miles. Spain lies only a morning's walk up the mountain.

I head towards the center of town, walking with a spring in my step along a tree-lined street, every home the same white stucco topped by a red-tiled roof. Wisps of cloud float above, the temperature ideal on this early August afternoon.

While I haven't read much about the Camino, I know a stop at a local office helps inexperienced pilgrims, and I head there first. It takes only a few minutes to reach the principal street in town. This narrow, cobbled lane must be pedestrian-only, as there are no cars, only a stream of smiling faces.

A line of pilgrims extends outside Les Amis Du Chemin de Saint-Jacques, translating to The Friends of The Path to Saint James. On one of the two doors to the arched stone entranceway, the English translation is more direct: Pilgrim Office. I join the line. In front of me, a group of three women who appear to be in their early thirties are speaking English.

"Are you American?" I ask.

"Yes!" the tallest of the three replies. "Are you?"

"Yeah, from Chicago," I say. "Where are you all from?"

"Idaho," the tallest one replies.

"San Diego."

"D.C."

I find they're old friends from back home, and they've been planning this trip for some time. We talk as the line slowly moves us inside. The room we enter has a festive mood, decorated with photos, posters, maps, and depictions of someone I assume to be Saint James, the instigator for this frenetic activity. My new friends and I find a hanging scale and weigh our packs. The metric scale weighs my pack in at just under 8.5 kilograms, while one of the other's tops out at 13.2.

"Of course, mine is the heaviest," San Diego, the shortest one, says.

"Let's convert to pounds," D.C. says as she pulls out her phone.

Our packs range from 18 to 29 pounds. Mine is the lightest, probably thanks to my previous backpacking experience. I am a fanatic about packing light, a concept I recently carried over to my personal life— learning to differentiate my wants versus needs.

Posted on a wall is a chart showing the number of pilgrims from various countries who have checked in here over the past few years. The prior year, France (9,049) topped the list, followed by Spain and the U.S. (6,271), and not too far behind were Italy, South Korea, and Germany. The total number of pilgrims registering at this office last year was over 58,000. Not all who start here intend to walk all the way to Santiago de Compostela, but last year well over half did.

"Yikes!" I say. "There must be over 300 pilgrims a day who check in here during the busier summer months."

"That's a lot more than I was expecting," Idaho says.

Slowly, each pilgrim or group of pilgrims is called to meet with one of five volunteers sitting behind a long row of adjoining tables. They share basic information on the Camino and provide a multipage spreadsheet listing the accommodations all the way to Santiago de Compostela, along with a printout showing the elevation changes for each stage. A volunteer waves the three women forward. Soon I am sitting in front of Armelle, a bespectacled French woman in her early sixties with a kind smile. She asks in her accented English, "What country are you from?" The U.S. "What is your mode of transportation, by foot or bike?" By foot. "Do you need a credential (pilgrim's passport)?" Oui.

"Do you need help finding accommodations for tonight?" she asks.

"No," I say. "I've already reserved a bed, but thanks."

She points out a few things about tomorrow's walk and then, using a highlighter, marks a few of her favorite places to stay. She hands over the small stack, smiles, and says, "Buen Camino." *Good journey.*

I walk over to the three Americans, still talking with their guide. "I hope to see you again," I say, then head out to find my *gîte,* French for a hostel. Tonight's is the only reservation I have made, but now, realizing the numbers competing for beds, a seed of concern is sown. I head down the same cobbled street and cross over a bridge. A few doors down, a shell-shaped green sign tells me I have arrived at my home for tonight, Le Chemin vers l'Etoile, *The Path to the Star.*

Entering a dark, narrow hallway, I head towards an empty front desk ahead in the light. I find stairs off to my right leading up. Dark-stained wood rails climb and encircle the lobby below, with wrap-around balconies on the two floors above. I ring a bell on the desk.

"Bonjour," says a man approaching from somewhere in the back. His voice is familiar; he must be the man I spoke with yesterday.

"Passport and credential, si vous plait," he says.

I hand him my newly purchased credential and my passport. He jots down information from my passport and christens my credential with a unique stamp that has the name of this gîte, and by hand, writes today's date.

He then looks up at me and asks, "Would you like breakfast in the morning?"

"Yes, please," I say.

"Okay, that will be twenty-three euros (€), eighteen for the bed, and five for breakfast," he says. At the current exchange rate of $1.10 = 1€, the cost works out to just over $25. I hand him a twenty-euro note and a five-euro note—my supply of euros, fresh from a stop at an ATM upon my arrival in France. He hands me a two-euro coin in return.

"I will show you to your room," he says. I follow him up to the second floor on thick oak steps, evidence worn into the wood of the thousands of others who have climbed these stairs. He leads me to a room filled with ten metal bunk beds, where a couple with sleeping bags are resting on thick mattresses, packs alongside.

"You may take any bed," he says, and as he turns to leave, adds, "Breakfast will be available at 6:30."

I stick my head out a large window to find scores of people strolling along the pedestrian thoroughfare below, then stake my claim on a bottom bunk. I shower in the communal bathroom, followed by a brief nap. Then I head out to explore the town, hoping to run into the three Americans I met earlier.

I pass back through the Porte Notre-Dame, a pointed archway under a tall clocktower attached to Église Notre-Dame du Bout du Pont, *Church of Our Lady at the End of the Bridge*. I wander along this picturesque street, the Rue de la Citadelle, filled with two- and three-story buildings hundreds of years old. Lines of red, green, and white pendants hang in a zig-zag pattern above the uphill-tilting street. I make my way back past the pilgrim office and its new batch of pilgrims, past numerous shops, bars, restaurants, and at least a dozen other places where one can find a bed for the night. The tightly packed buildings are all dressed in white stucco and trimmed in crimson, with a few rule-proving exceptions. The street flattens out as I near a tall stone wall with another narrow, arched passageway at the far end of this medieval village.

A path appears next to a sign reading *Citadelle*. I follow this steep pathway that runs along the stone wall. After a few minutes, I reach an overlook, a bit winded by the climb—and look down on this quaint village, eyeing the mountains beyond. I laugh to myself when I think this short walk has left me short of breath, and tomorrow I must climb to the heights staring back at me. Nevertheless, the panoramic view from here is stunning.

Behind me lies the citadel, and I stand atop the rampart, the outer wall of the fortifications built to protect this seventeenth-century fortress. The châteauesque stronghold is off-limits to visitors, so I wander along the rampart and glimpse a dirt trail running through the grass growing between the rampart and the fortress's base. Thinking it may circle the protected center, I navigate my way down to the trail and proceed to make a large loop around this centuries-old fortification. It ends when I pass through the historic La Porte Saint-Jacques, *The Saint James Door*, the arched passageway I spotted earlier.

On my stroll back along the narrow street, I stop in front of a small outdoors shop, Boutique du Pelerin. Outside, a mannequin wearing a bright red poncho directs me inside. The store has everything a pilgrim might need, from backpacks, boots and shoes, to clothes for any condition, hats, hiking sticks and poles, sunglasses, bookshelves full of guidebooks in at least a half-dozen languages, and anything else someone who plans to walk 500 miles might possibly want.

I'm only browsing, as I feel well prepared. I won't carry a guidebook on my journey; between a mapping app downloaded on my phone and the information provided earlier today, I'm confident I'll find my way.

My next stop is a bakery. It is well into the evening, and I haven't eaten a proper meal all day. I walk out with a bag full of croissants—I am in *France*, after all. Before I reach the bridge, I turn off the main drag onto a pathway that runs alongside the shallow Nive River. Finding a low stone wall, I sit and devour my pastries, a mix of sweet and savory, before I continue my exploration of this charming town.

I pass couples and small groups either walking together or dining on the patios scattered throughout the village. There is an equal number of others who, like me, stroll in solitude. Besides French, I have heard Italian, German, and English spoken here. I am delighted by the feeling of simply being in another country, especially here, where people from all over the world gather. I had assumed most are here for the Camino but find that Saint-Jean-Pied-de-Port is a destination itself. Its history and natural beauty draw many to this quaint village, tucked away in the corner of France.

I overhear a well-dressed middle-aged couple tell a twenty-something woman in shorts and a T-shirt, "Be safe. Call often," in what I think is a British accent, or is it Australian? I watch them share long hugs before they head in opposite directions. Parents a bit wary about their child walking alone in a foreign land. I imagine they are either starting or ending their own European adventure, just not one on foot.

I'm excited to start my walk but a bit anxious about tomorrow's hike up into the mountains— the most strenuous day of hiking on the entire journey. Since arriving here, I learned there are two options when leaving Saint-Jean, elevation 594 feet. The most common, and more difficult, is the Napoleon route, which climbs to 4719 feet, meaning a gain in elevation of a whopping 4125 feet. It starts with a constant uphill climb for over twelve miles (twenty kilometers) and then descends for more than three miles (five kilometers) to the Spanish town of Roncesvalles, the most common day-one stopping point.

The other option is the Valcarlos route, where the distance is comparable but the elevation change is much less severe. This route makes its way through a valley towards the town of Valcarlos instead of over the mountain. The bulk of the climb on this route is near its end and won't reach its high point until it arrives in Roncesvalles, located at 3114 feet. I will be going over the mountain, wanting to challenge myself physically after years of rotting behind a desk in my old, sedentary life.

This journey is needed to help me rebuild after the shedding of my old self. Trusting my mid-life course change will lead to a more authentic me. I move forward, optimistic my choices will also lead to a more meaningful life.

Where will this walk across Spain take me? I know my physical destination but am uncertain of the emotional journey. How will I have changed when I board my flight back to the States five weeks from today?

Lying in the dark, I stare up at the metal springs of the bed above me; I think of Tom Hanks's character at the end of *Castaway*. After years of being lost, he returns to find his old love has moved on; now alone again, he stands at a literal crossroads in the plains of Texas, unsure of where his life will lead. He turns in one direction, then the next, imagining the possibilities with a glint in his eye and the corner of his mouth upturned. I, too, find myself in a similar situation—unsure and looking for direction, excited for what is to come.

MY JOURNEY BEGINS

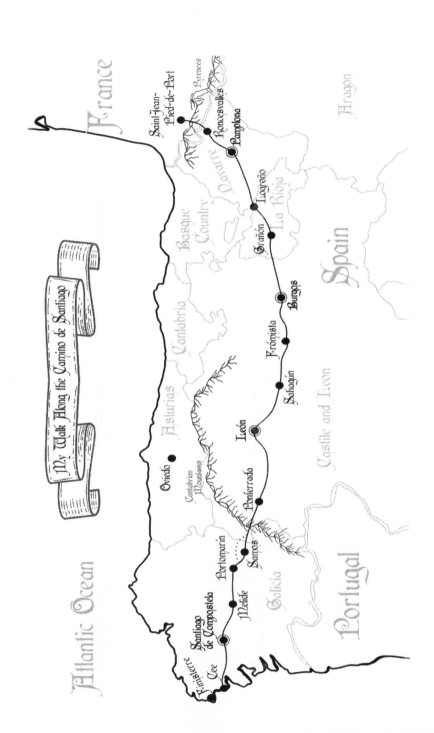

My Walk Along the Camino de Santiago

Atlantic Ocean

France

Spain

Portugal

Aragon

Navarre

Basque Country

Cantabria

Asturias

Castile and Leon

Galicia

La Rioja

Pyrenees

Cantabrian Mountains

Saint-Jean-Pied-de-Port

Roncesvalles

Pamplona

Logroño

Grañón

Burgos

Frómista

Sahagún

León

Ponferrada

Samos

Portomarín

Melide

Santiago de Compostela

Cee

Finisterre

Oviedo

DAY 1: SAINT-JEAN-PIED-DE-PORT > RONCESVALLES

If you can see your path laid out in front of you step-by-step, you know it's not your path. Your own path you make every step you take. That's why it's your path.

~ Joseph Campbell

The phone buried beneath my pillow starts to vibrate and quietly chime at 6:20 a.m. I wake to find headlamps shining down onto beds or into open packs. A few beds are empty, last night's occupants having already started their journey, but most of the room remains asleep. The shutters on the window are partially open, and I see a pitch-black sky. Quietly, I put on my shorts and moisture-wicking T-shirt, place my silk sleep sack into its small, zippered pouch, and load my pack. I grab my shoes from under my bunk and head out of the room.

After a quick breakfast, anxious to start my journey, I fill two disposable one-liter water bottles, place them in my pack's side pockets, and then lift my suddenly heavier load onto my back. The water adds another 4.4 pounds to the weight I now carry. I remove my headlamp from my pack's top pocket and head out the door.

I turn to bid adieu to The Path to the Star, but looking up, I see not a single dot of light in the blackness. The temperature is cool, but I am comfortable. A soft yellow glow from the streetlights is enough to make my way along the avenue heading west. Not sixty seconds into my walk, a light rain starts to fall. Not knowing if it will continue, I play it safe and step into a recessed doorway to dig out my rain jacket, rain pants, and pack cover. While I am putting on my gear, a few others pass, all already wearing ponchos covering both themselves and their packs. One man passes by without any protection, only a walking stick, which rhythmically clacks on the cobbled street. After a few minutes, I am ready to start again. I follow a few others out of the town center as the rain begins to fall harder and the first crack of thunder sounds. I bow my head to keep the rain from dripping into my eyes. I pay attention only to those in front of me and assume that when the road diverges and they go right, they must have seen a sign; I follow. Our route is along an asphalt street heading uphill as streams of water run down. My shoes, not waterproof, are already soaked through. Thunder cracks and lightning streaks across the sky in the distance.

I find a good rhythm and keep a steady pace. Slowly, I realize the rain has turned to hail, as I crunch tiny pebbles with each step. Soon it turns back to rain, and the sky lightens as the sun rises somewhere to the east.

My pace remains strong, and I pass several other pilgrims. I can now see a dozen or so others far in the distance in the early morning light, and I set my sights on catching up with them. Despite the constant climb, my legs feel strong, but I get winded and must slow my pace. On a particularly steep section, I stop alongside the road to catch my breath.

From this spot, I look down on the town of Saint-Jean-Pied-de-Port, now visible beneath low-hanging clouds, thinking it was the perfect place to start my journey. I feel good and am confident that my recent hiking and training on the StairMaster at Planet Fitness has me in shape to make it over this mountain.

When I first learned the Camino crossed over the Pyrenees, I imagined a mountain path like the Von Trapp Family climb at the end of *The Sound of Music*, so I am surprised the route remains on asphalt as I climb ever higher. Small delivery vans and cars pass by occasionally on this narrow mountainside road. The volume of rain lessens but doesn't stop. Will rain be a regular occurrence along the Way? God, I hope not.

Ominous clouds hover as lightning streaks across the sky to the north; its booming accompaniment follows seconds later.

When I reach a Camino marker pointing to a path leading off the paved roadway, I remember the woman in the pilgrim office yesterday discussing this exact spot; one of the information sheets even has a picture of this juncture. She recommended I stick to the pavement and avoid the more dangerous route along a mountainside path adjacent to a steep drop-off. I choose the safer route. As I pass the marker, I hear a shout. I turn to see a twenty-something guy not far behind, pointing. I wait for him to catch up and try to explain what Armelle told me yesterday. I am uncertain if he understands or even if he speaks English. He turns and follows the sign off the pavement. I walk on and convince myself that I would have taken the more adventurous route on a sunny day.

The 'safer route' is an apt way to describe how I have lived most of my life. I followed the path laid out before me; a route paved with expectations. Graduating from college and getting married in my early twenties were two markers I saw on my life's roadmap. For years, I walked with a loving wife who was also following her own path of perceived expectations.

For decades, our paths looked like the dirt ruts made by car tires through a grassy field, created by generations of others who marched on before us. Like most, our marriage had ups and downs, but we didn't soar too high or sink too low. A fitting description, given we lived in the plains of the Midwest. It was a safe journey, as neither sought a path that would lead to someplace unknown. Our walk together followed a well-beaten path, one typical for a middle-class couple in our society. Eventually, a fork in the road would appear.

After two hours of constant uphill walking in the rain, soaked and tired, I reach a refuge. Albergue (pronounced al-BEAR-gay) Orisson is a large, stone-and-timber two-story building, adjacent to the road on the mountain's side. I step in to get out of the rain and find it part bar, restaurant, and accommodation. A handful of others sit at long, heavy wooden tables in a room that probably seats thirty.

Thick wooden beams give it something like a mountain lodge feel. I remove my pack and peel off my jacket, damp with rain and sweat. I approach the bar at one end of the room and point to what looks like a frittata sliced into eight pieces, a few of which are missing, under a glass dome. The young man behind the bar says, "Tortilla?" and I nod.

I will come to find the Spanish tortilla is a staple for pilgrims along the Camino, and I guess, for all Spaniards. The only ingredients are egg, potatoes, and onion, and it comes with a slice of baguette. Sitting in this dry and relatively warm oasis, I slowly eat this delicious and filling meal as I start to dry out. The room begins to fill as more pilgrims stop in.

Many arriving later in the day will stay here, up on the second floor, where thirty or so beds await. A stop for the night in this albergue, Spanish for hostel, will break up this challenging crossing of the Pyrenees. Albergue Orisson sits seven kilometers from Saint-Jean and is the last stopping point along the Napoleon Route before reaching my destination, another seventeen kilometers ahead. As in most of the world, on the Camino, distances are measured in kilometers (1 mile = 1.6 km), and for the balance of this journey, I will follow suit.

Back outside in a steady drizzle, I lift my hood and restart my walk along the asphalt. At this elevation, the view of the surrounding mountains is beautiful but muted by the gray sky above. There are no jagged peaks like many mountain ranges; in this small slice of the Pyrenees, the mountaintops look like they have been sanded down and painted by fields of green.

Eventually, the rain stops, replaced by an ethereal mist. Fellow hikers are visible both ahead and behind when a large white dog appears and joins our ranks. I have no idea where he emerged from, as I don't remember passing a single structure since I left Orisson an hour ago. This beautiful dog, whose breed I will later identify, appropriately enough, as a Great Pyrenees, roams the grassy meadows along the route but always returns to the road and continues leading the way.

Not long after the dog appears, the clang of bells can be heard, and I soon glimpse a flock of sheep, their whiteness a vivid contrast against the lush pastures. The route has somewhat leveled off now, and I pass new flocks of anywhere from fifty to a hundred sheep every kilometer or so.

Some of the herds have a solid white coat, while others are white with a dark face and spiral horns; all communities include the odd black sheep. The big white dog trots towards each assemblage before making his return. I give him the unoriginal name of Blanco, one of only a handful of Spanish words I know.

An hour or so passes high in the mountains as Blanco comes and goes. A steady rain returns shortly before the marked route finally leaves the pavement, and I find myself walking through streams of muddy water along a rocky pathway, rock outcroppings visible nearby as the Camino again starts to climb.

Soon I reach a fountain next to an emergency HELPoint with an SOS button and a sign reading *Fuente Roland*. A red dot on a map signifying our location shows I am near the Spanish border. I stop only long enough to look at the sign before I move on. A minute later, I pass a stone marker that reads *Navarra*. I have crossed the invisible border. Blanco seems to have turned around, as I haven't seen him in a while; I decide he must be French.

I enter a grove of trees, quite a change from the treeless climb thus far. When I exit the forest, I approach a small stone building with a red-tiled roof; a wooden sign above the door reads *Izandorre*. The door to this little ten-foot-square refuge is locked; the chance of any deadly snowstorm this time of the year is remote. Still, I am sure that in the spring and fall, when the possibility of dangerous conditions is present, the door to the shelter is unlocked, saving many a hiker over the years. Off to the north, I have a fantastic view of faded green mountains and valleys, softened by a misty rain and a somber gray sky.

The route now is a wide gravel path, and soon I reach the high point of this mountain crossing, Col Lopeoder. The descent starts out relatively mild, but soon I arrive at another fork, one that my guide back in the pilgrim office also mentioned. According to a marked post, the official path goes left and is known as the forest route. It is the more direct of the two but on loose, rocky terrain and much steeper than the alternative, which follows a narrow road that switchbacks its way down the mountain.

I imagine heading down a wet and rocky path, through a forest with exposed roots to navigate, while carrying a twenty-two-pound pack. I decide again on the safer route and its extra kilometer, thinking it wise if it improves my chances of staying upright.

Glimpsing a few others ahead, I set off. While I'm on this final downhill section, the rain stops and tiny blue patches are visible in the sky to the west. I smile. I make my way down via a combination of a gravely roadway and muddy footpaths, which bisect the wide switchbacks.

Not long after I started my descent, a building far down the mountain was visible; now, as I near the bottom, I find it is a small A-framed chapel with a large cross at its side. After hours in the Pyrenees, away from any evidence of civilization, I am back. A road runs next to the small chapel, Ermita de San Salvador de Ibañeta; this roadway connects Roncesvalles and Valcarlos and continues back to Saint-Jean-Pied-de-Port.

I make a quick stop outside the chapel and then to view a massive granite monument stamped with the name *Roland*. He was one of Charlemagne's military leaders, who died in battle here in 778. Over a thousand years later, Napoleon sent his troops to fight on this same pass over the Pyrenees in a quest to expand his reach.

A Camino marker directs me to a flat path parallel to the two-lane roadway; it leads into a stand of trees. Twenty minutes later, I enter Roncesvalles. A massive three-story building with heavy stone accents and two dozen windows decorating the exterior greets me. I walk towards this grand structure and soon discover it is the Albergue de Peregrinos, the resting place for most pilgrims.

I wanted to be sure I arrived early enough to secure a bed for tonight, knowing now that I may have to compete for beds along the Way. According to the spreadsheet given to me in the pilgrim office, this is the only albergue in Roncesvalles, but it has an impressive 183 beds, the vast majority not reservable. The listing also shows a few small hotels in the village, but I don't require a room, just somewhere to rest my head. I plan to stay at the more affordable albergues on my month-long walk.

It is a little before 1 p.m., and I find a solitary figure sitting on a bench outside the albergue.

"Hello," I say to the twenty-something woman. "You made it here in good time."

"I started today in Valcarlos, so it was not a long walk," she says. "Did you start in Saint-Jean-Pied-de-Port?"

"Yes," I say as I take off my pack.

"I had planned on staying in Orisson last night, but I got nervous," she says.

"Why? The climb?" I ask.

"I guess," she says. "I admit the mountain looked much taller than I expected, but it wasn't until I heard the weather forecast that I decided to head to Valcarlos instead."

"How was it there?" I ask.

"Very nice," she says. "I spent the night at a small albergue, and stayed there this morning until the worst of the storm had passed."

"Lucky you," I chuckle.

Since 2015, the Napoleon route has been closed during the winter, from November 1 through March 31. Once the snow arrives in the Pyrenees, the path is not safe for hikers, and those walking from Saint-Jean must follow the Valcarlos route or face a hefty fine. There have been several deaths in the Pyrenees since the Camino's resurgence over the past couple of decades. A few years earlier, a Spanish pilgrim got lost in the snow in early November on the lower-elevation Valcarlos route, fell into a ravine, and died from hypothermia. No such worries in August, but death is not an uncommon occurrence along the Camino. Heatstroke and heart attacks are the biggest concerns this time of the year.

"The albergue won't open for another hour," she says.

I remove my soaked rain jacket and pants, throw them on a clothesline near the entrance, and take a seat on the bench.

"Where are you from?" I ask.

"Denmark. You?" she says.

"The States," I say as I take off shoes and peel off my socks. "Are you walking to Santiago?"

"No, I will walk as far as I can in two weeks. I'll probably make it to Burgos," she says. "Are you headed to Santiago?"

"Yeah," I say and unhook my Chaco sandals from my pack.

We sit and chat while others arrive and crash on the lawn.

"Since we have time, I'm going to wander around the town," I say. "Would you like to come?"

"I think I'll wait here," she says.

I put on my pack and head off.

I find this is not so much a town, but only a few buildings clustered around what was once a monastery. The monastery included a thirteenth-century Gothic church, the Colegiata de Santa Maria. The complex now houses the albergue, the church, a museum, and a hotel.

I stop in Casa Sabina, one of the two places I find offering something to eat, and order a Coca-Cola and a sandwich visible in a glass case on the bar. The simple sandwich, a bocadillo, consists of a few slices of meat on a small baguette: no lettuce or tomato or even the option for any condiment. I bring my meal to an outdoor table, sit under a mostly blue sky, and enjoy my cold drink and chorizo bocadillo. There are maybe ten others on the terrace, most with backpacks resting by their tables. I inhale the bocadillo and return for another, this time a slice of a tortilla, sandwiched in a baguette.

My hunger quashed, I head back. On the way, I approach a few people who have stopped on a paved pathway; to my surprise, they are surrounding Blanco. A woman with a large pack is petting this wet and muddy dog. Astonished to find him down the mountain, I rethink his nationality.

"He led me much of the way over the mountain this morning," I tell those gathered. "But I lost sight of him. He must live here."

"No," says a woman. "I work here, in Roncesvalles, and I have not seen him here before."

"I wonder if he'll head back up the mountain later," I say.

A question that will remain unanswered. I leave Blanco and return to the albergue before two o'clock and join twenty pilgrims waiting in line.

The doors open, and the line moves inside. I am surprised by how beautiful the interior is. The floors are paved with small stones, while the walls are the same stucco and stone as the exterior, giving a feeling of the past, with a modern touch. A courtyard is visible through an open door at the end of the large foyer. Soon I am at the front of the line inside the Reception Office.

"Welcome," says one of two men behind the counter. "Passport and credential."

I hand them over. I find out later that all the volunteers in this albergue come from the Netherlands. If a pilgrim arrives here without a credential, they may purchase one at the time of check-in, but one *is* required. Only pilgrims may stay in this albergue. The gray-haired Dutchman asks in perfect English, "Would you like to purchase dinner or breakfast?"

"Both," I say.

"There are two seating times for dinner, 7 or 8:30."

"Seven."

The total cost is 25€; 12€ for my bed, 10€ for dinner, and 3€ for breakfast. He hands me my bed assignment and two laminated tickets for the meals and explains where I can find my bed.

As I make my way to my designated bunk, I pass the "boot room," where pilgrims are required to leave their boots or whatever footwear got them here. My wet and muddy trail-running shoes are still drying outside, so I head up to the second floor in my sandals and find bed number 24.

Despite the vast number of beds here, I find it well organized to give pilgrims a decent sense of privacy. The sleeping area comprises four bed niches, each with two bunks separated by about four feet, along with lockers to store packs. There are about sixty bunks on each of the top three floors; the top level is the attic. Each floor has a similar layout, with a coed bathroom on one end. Tall, narrow windows line the wall near my bunk. I look out onto the large gravel courtyard, now partially covered in a colorful array of clothes drying in the sun.

I exchange greetings with those in my pod. I remove from my pack a packing cube filled with clothes, my toiletry bag, travel towel, and sleep sack and place them on the blue foam mattress on my top bunk. I shower and change into what I plan on being my 'town' clothes: clean underwear, comfortable shorts, and a soft cotton, short-sleeve T-shirt.

After a nap, I head off to explore the albergue. I pass a table covered in items others have decided they don't need—or, more accurately, no longer want to carry—but which other pilgrims may find useful. The table bears a sign reading *Free*. A pair of hiking poles, packaged food, fuel canisters for a backpacking stove, books, and clothing items are on the table at this moment. Next, I enter a large kitchen and dining area on the main floor and then find a space to do laundry in the basement. There is no need to wash my clothes today; I have a second quick-drying T-shirt, clean underwear, and socks for tomorrow.

I learn this albergue opened in 2011, after an extensive remodel from its previous incarnation, and it seems no expense was spared. It is both beautiful and practical and seems to have all the amenities a pilgrim might need. Before this albergue opened, pilgrims stayed in what was once a medieval hospital. Over a hundred pilgrims slept in a single cavernous room on metal bunks beneath massive wooden chandeliers.

The old albergue is one of only a handful of buildings in the village. Until a few years ago, it had been used as an overflow for pilgrims when the beds in the new albergue were full. Due to new restrictions limiting the number of people who can stay in the village each night, it is now closed to pilgrims. In the busy summer months, the new albergue fills up every day; fortunately, there are an additional thirty-four beds next to the albergue. Unfortunately, those staying in this overflow area don't have access to the same modern amenities as those inside the albergue. Besides the small hotels here, there may be no option for late-arriving pilgrims but to keep walking to the next town of Burguete.

I end my exploration back in the courtyard, surrounded on three sides by what was once the monastery; the end opposite the albergue opens to a small rise and a forested backdrop.

I watch dozens of others milling about, chatting with friends—I'm guessing both old and new. The courtyard is the perfect common area to meet fellow pilgrims.

"Hello," a middle-aged Asian man says with a broad smile as he approaches. "Is this your first Camino?" he asks in halting English.

Smiling back, I respond, "Yes. How about you?"

"My second," he says. "I walked the Camino two years ago."

"And you're back again!?"

"Yes, it is incredible. I could not wait to come back."

"Wow! That's good to hear," I say, surprised.

"Where are you from?" he asks.

"The U.S. You?"

"South Korea," he says. "My name in Yeong."

"I'm Michael."

Yeong is younger than me, I guess in his late thirties; he's a few inches shorter than my five-foot-eight-inch frame and has the slight body of a runner. We talk about our experience walking in the rain today and about what is to come. As it nears seven, he says, "We should head to dinner." He, too, has a ticket for the earlier seating.

I assumed dinner would be in the albergue's dining room, but Yeong leads me through an arched passageway that exits the courtyard and the monastery compound. We walk along a paved pathway, past a crowded patio, and when we turn a corner I find a familiar sign: *La Posada*. I remember this sign from a scene in the movie, *The Way*. I had first watched the film on Netflix years earlier; *The Way* was my introduction to the Camino. I watched it again after deciding to walk this storied trail. La Posada is where the main character stops to rest after his first day on the Camino, though the room where he sleeps was filmed in the original albergue across the street, with its metal bunks and massive chandeliers.

La Posada is a hotel, bar, and restaurant. We are the first to arrive for dinner, about ten minutes early, and wait in a small lobby. Soon, the entryway overflows with pilgrims. I am thankful for Yeong's guidance. If I hadn't met him, I'm not sure when I'd have figured out where dinner was.

Right on time, the door swings open and a young woman takes our laminated tickets. We are seated at one of many large, round tables, each seating nine. Bottles of wine soon circle our table, and we toast to the Camino. English, it seems, is the common language on the Camino. We chat and go around the table, sharing our home countries. Sitting at the table: my new friend Yeong, a German couple, three other solo Germans, a Canadian woman, and a Frenchman. Conversations continue as we enjoy a simple three-course meal.

"We're going to the eight o'clock Pilgrim's Mass in the church," one of the Germans says. "Would anyone like to join?"

"Sure, I'll come along," I say.

As soon as we finish dessert, a Nestlé Drumstick, three of us hurry over. We enter as the service begins and find seats on a pew in the back.

The church's interior is dim, lit by simple fixtures hanging from the soaring vaulted ceiling. With the evening light fading, the ornate stained-glass windows go almost unnoticed. Ancient gray stone columns flank the wooden pews. The golden altar glows in soft light, and the priest, robed in red, speaks in a rhythmic cadence. Not being Catholic nor able to understand Spanish, I sit quietly as my eyes wander, taking in the church and those in attendance. As mass is ending, the elderly priest calls us to the altar for the Pilgrims' Blessing. Almost all in attendance stand and approach to receive his blessing and a "Buen Camino."

After a brief courtyard conversation, I head up to my bunk before ten, when the lights go out. My head resting comfortably on the pillow provided, I review what may have been the most challenging day of my entire Camino. Relieved that my solo march across the Pyrenees in the rain has left my feet and knees no worse for wear, I doze off, excited for what tomorrow may bring.

DAY 2: RONCESVALLES > ZUBIRI

There is no greater blunder that he who consumes the greater part of his life getting his living.

~ Henry David Thoreau, *Life Without Principal*

Singing echoes through the albergue and wakes me. "Good morning, good morning, good morning," is the refrain of the song coming from somewhere. Soon, two hospitaleros (Camino speak for volunteers) in red vests, one of the men strumming a guitar, stroll by, belting out their alarm. I share a smile with those in my pod, then check the weather forecast on my phone, relieved to find a shining-sun emoji for the next few days.

I climb down from my bunk and head to the bathroom. Our morning serenade has everyone up and getting ready for the day. I quickly change into a clean walking shirt, the same shorts from yesterday, and clean socks. I grab my pack, offer a "Buen Camino," and head down to the boot room to grab my shoes. The shelves brim with, I assume, 183 pairs of footwear. At a glance, I guess two-thirds are hiking boots, and about a third are running shoes. I take my dry trail-runners to a bench in the dining room, where a handful of others are eating a breakfast of their making. I attach my sandals to the outside of my pack and fill up my water bottles in the kitchen.

Walking back to La Posada under a low-hanging fog, I don't see a soul. The doors are open, and I am seated with a few fellow pilgrims, the only others here. Of those seated, I don't recognize any faces from last night. I scarf down breakfast, eager to start walking.

Santiago de Compostela – 790 states a large road sign across the street from La Posada. I'm not sure if this represents the distance via car on highways or the distance by foot following the Camino's official route, but Santiago is a long way off, either way. A gravel path runs alongside the roadway; next to it, a shell on a blue background and an arrow point the way. I head out of Roncesvalles through a stand of trees.

The path remains in this forest landscape for thirty minutes, until the official route leaves the cover of trees and enters a town. I find myself walking along a narrow street bordered by well-kept multistory homes packed tightly together, through the small town of Burguete. This charming town, full of alpine chalet-style buildings with timber framing and ornamental details, brings a Swiss mountain village to mind. This town was a regular stop for the famed writer Ernest Hemingway before the publication of his first novel, *The Sun Also Rises*, in which Burguete is a setting for the main character, who enjoys a few days and nights relaxing and fishing in the nearby Irati River.

Most of the commercial signs in this town are composed in an unusual font. The letters are familiar yet a little quirky. The extra bold characters look similar to standard capital letters except for the letter "I," which is always lower-case with an extra-large dot. The informational signs are written in two languages: Spanish and the Basque language Euskara, with its unique font honoring the Basque population in this area of Spain. Basque is a long-lived nationality, and those of Basque descent are incredibly proud of their history and language. For thousands of years, they have occupied this corner of the

Pyrenees filled with mountains and green valleys, near the rugged coastal junction of Spain and France. They have long fought to preserve their culture, their unique language, and their land. Spain granted the Basques an autonomous region called the Basque Country in 1979. The Camino's route travels through the Navarre region of Spain, not the actual independent Basque Country, but there is a substantial Basque presence along the Camino. Its language, food, and flag are all proudly on display.

This morning's route is relatively flat, and I am walking at what I think is a brisk pace. Shortly after Burguete, in a wooded section of track, Yeong pulls up alongside me.

"How far will you get today?" I ask.

"I do not know yet," he says.

"I'll probably stop in Zubiri," I say. It's a little over twenty kilometers from Roncesvalles.

"Maybe I see you there," he says.

Yeong's pace is faster than mine, and after a few minutes of walking together, he resumes his pace and slowly pulls ahead. I notice Yeong's pack is much smaller than my forty-liter bag. What am I carrying that he's not? He must have learned a few things on his first Camino.

Soon I'm passing through another quaint little town, Espinal. The Basque influence is still evident, as is the feel of being in another alpine village. I enjoyed last night in Roncesvalles, but I think a night in either of these charming villages would have been equally enjoyable.

A gentle descent follows a short climb under a clear blue sky as the route takes me through forests and fields. Scenic views abound as I make my way ever so slowly down from yesterday's heights. I smile at frequent glimpses through trees of a valley below or views of the emerald-colored foothills as I walk across this foreign land. The weather yesterday quieted a joy that is in full bloom this morning. I am overwhelmed with gratitude to be here on this beautiful day—my eyes well with tears.

When the cover of trees fades away, the temperature heats up under the August sun. As I walk, my arm frequently reaches back for a water bottle, as I do my best to stay hydrated, and I hope this uncomfortable movement doesn't injure my shoulder or elbow. The Camino winds its way through open fields and small hamlets, each comprising a handful of homes. While walking through one such settlement, I use the hiking map app on my phone, Guru Maps Pro, to find a fountain's location to refill my almost empty water bottles.

Later, a section of forested trail empties onto a quiet highway, the route ahead visible straight across the road next to a large white van. The van's side is opened into an awning and reveals a small food truck offering various drinks and snacks. I stop and buy a cold glass of lemonade and a bag of chips. While resting on a red plastic chair in the shade next to the trailer, I watch Yeong cross the road. He takes a seat beside me.

"I stop in Espinal for breakfast. On my last Camino, I walked for an hour, and then I stop to eat. I will do that this time too," he says.

Together, we continue along a fairly steep downhill trail on loose, rocky terrain through the forest. "I will walk past Zubiri today," Yeong tells me. It is only five kilometers from the food truck. "I walked further on my last Camino, and I feel strong today," he says.

A smiling Yeong shares his excitement for the Camino and says he is sure he will come back again for the third time. As we walk, I wonder how Yeong can take a month out of his life so often to walk the Camino. I think he must be a teacher with his summers off, but I do not ask.

It seems Yeong is walking with springs in his heels, while my steps grow more solemn as the temperature climbs. My foot slips on loose gravel, and I stumble but somehow manage to avoid falling. I slow even more as we make our way down this rocky section.

"I *am* stopping for the day in Zubiri," I say, "and I am going to rest here for a few minutes. You go ahead. I know I'm slowing you down."

"Okay. Maybe I see you walking tomorrow," Yeong replies in his imperfect English. He picks up his pace and is soon out of sight.

Yeong's ability to take time off reminds me of what I wasn't able to do when I was his age. I had followed the well-worn path in my career, just like my marriage. Starting a job the month after I graduated, I worked for the same company for nearly three decades. Finance was my chosen career, and I worked the conventional nine-to-five, sitting behind a desk. Looking back now, I can see that path leading to my days of desperation decades in the future.

Growing up, I didn't have many hobbies, but I did watch a lot of TV. My expectations for adulthood were not formed by *Leave it to Beaver*, like those of previous generations; in the '80s it was Alex P. Keaton on *Family Ties* who I aspired to be. As a teenager, a job in 'business' sounded admirable and lucrative, and in my naive mind, money was the most critical factor when choosing a career. Fast-forward a few years: I left college with a business degree and began the slow climb up the corporate ladder.

The years rolled by, as did the annual raises; I was living the glorified American Dream. But life on the treadmill eventually grew stale. The days and the years ticked by with little change in scenery, empty of any exciting adventures off the beaten path. I was to learn that there is little personal growth when living the same year twenty times over.

I have difficulty explaining why I was miserable despite having a safe and comfortable life … a life most people crave. Maybe I should have been grateful and enjoyed my middle-class life, but when I had the realization that time was more important than money, my mindset changed.

Never away from my job for more than two weeks at a time, I had no opportunity for extended travel or even a long break from my routine. I grew disillusioned with the life I was living. I felt suffocated. Decades after starting out on my chosen path, I was walking in the dark, down a tunnel, and I could see no light at the end.

Crossing a bridge over a gently flowing river, I enter Zubiri. It is only 1 p.m., and I am surprised to find a dozen people lined up outside the first albergue I reach. It's just opened, and someone in line says there are only a few beds left. I stand in line for a few minutes until someone walking away says, "They're now full." I walk to two other albergues near the bridge, but neither has opened for the day. I consider moving on, but I walk to the address of yet one more on my list.

Standing in front of a row of townhomes, a familiar sign with a shell on a field of blue hangs above an open garage door, and a smaller sign above the front door reads *Albergue Segunda Etapa*, or Second Stage Hostel. An elderly man waits inside. I ask in my poor Spanish, and with the help of Google Translate, "Una cama para esta noche." He answers,

"Si." This kind man doesn't speak English, but I hand him my passport, and he enters my information in a guestbook and offers me a stamp for my credential. I pull out my wallet, and he waves his hand. I leave my shoes in a designated spot in the garage, and he leads me to a room on the second floor with five bunk beds and points out the bathroom. Two others lie in bunks. I ask, "Do either of you speak English?"

"I do," a young man says.

"What about the payment?" I ask.

"The man is the owner's father. He opens up in the afternoon while his daughter is at work," he says. "We will pay her when she arrives."

The albergue is a three-story townhouse set back from the main road running through town. The bunk room is simple and clean, with bright blue metal bunks covered in thick, comfortable mattresses. Large lockers to store our packs line one wall. After showering and changing into my town clothes, I hand-wash the clothes I've hiked in using a small container of liquid backpacker's soap and hang everything on a drying rack in the backyard.

Three backpacks with tags were in the garage when I'd arrived, and now I find a flyer about a luggage transporting service. It turns out, for a few euros bags can be sent to and from any of the accommodations along the way; your pack will be waiting when you arrive. I hadn't noticed any walkers without packs, but there are many people carrying much smaller packs than me. Now I guess that some hike with a lighter load, like Yeong, while others carry only day packs with things they may need during the day: water, rain gear, another layer, and snacks.

While I can't imagine myself sending my pack ahead, given that I am eager to challenge myself, I understand everyone must walk the Camino in their own way. The transport is a blessing for those who may not otherwise be able to experience the Camino, those older or maybe not as fit, or others simply wanting a more enjoyable walk, one with less pressure on their feet, knees, and shoulders.

While I rest in my bunk, the beds slowly fill around me. A Spanish woman who speaks little English asks if anyone in the room wants to explore the town.

"Sure, I'll come," I say.

I join Liliana, and we follow the main road heading away from the town center. We talk as best we can with my practically nonexistent Spanish and the little English she knows, but soon the translation apps on our phones are put to use. We stop and sit on a bus stop bench, and I learn that Liliana is not walking the Camino but starting a solo holiday. She lives only an hour's drive to the north in the Basque Country and will be leaving Zubiri by bus in the morning.

We meander through a town designed to accommodate the tens of thousands of pilgrims passing through each year. With a population of less than 500, it is home to at least a dozen places for pilgrims to sleep. We pass the largest, Albergue Municipal, and its eighty beds. Even with the many accommodations, there are not enough beds available to house all the pilgrims hoping to stay here during the busy summer months. Zubiri is by far the largest town the Camino has passed through since I crossed into Spain.

We turn and head back towards the town center. Once we make it to the central plaza in town, we follow along the river and find dozens of pilgrims relaxing in the sun, eating, drinking, talking, or wading into the waters of the Arga River. I recognize a few faces and wave hello, but I continue walking with my new friend. On the town square near the twelfth-century bridge I crossed earlier, an oversized food truck serving beer and wine sits on one edge of the large plaza. A temporary stage is set up on another as the town prepares for a festival honoring San Esteban, or Saint Steven.

A long table in the center of the square is staffed by a handful of teenage girls giving away cups of hot chocolate. Liliana and I join the line. An oversized crockpot-like appliance sits on the table as the girls dispense dripping ladles of thick melted chocolate into plastic cups and place a piece of a churro standing upright in it, like a flag planted in the ground. I quickly turn my plastic cup upside down, like a blizzard served at Dairy Queen, with the churro and chocolate staying in place, though, obviously, Liliana doesn't get the reference. I use my churro as a spoon to enjoy this Spanish delight. The chocolate burns my lips, but it is sweet with a hint of sugar and cinnamon. When the churro is no more, I use a finger to clean my cup. This snack teases my hunger; I haven't eaten much of anything today and am looking forward to an actual meal. Next, we each get a glass of wine and stand in the square as the crowd grows. We watch as locals get ready to shoot off fireworks from the narrow bridge.

The fireworks shoot into the sky like the bottle rockets from my youth on steroids. The explosions reverberate loudly in the square below. Pilgrims are still arriving; they cross the bridge with their packs, looking weary and a bit confused as this loud and festive crowd greets them. Shortly after the main festivities begin, I ask Liliana if she wants to find something to eat by saying, "Restaurante?" She responds, "Si."

We head back towards the main street in town, where we had passed a couple of restaurants earlier. I spot the three American women I met at the pilgrim office in Saint-Jean-Pied-de-Port. They are seated at a table, enjoying glasses of wine on a crowded patio in front of a restaurant.

"Hi there," I say with a big smile.

"Join us," the tall one says.

"That would be great," I say. "This is Liliana."

I pull an empty chair from an adjacent table and the two of us join the table. We both order another glass of wine. I find that Liliana can communicate perfectly with all three Americans, who I learn now are fluent in Spanish. The Americans and I still do not even know each other's names. All we shared at our first meeting was where we are from. I find out Idaho is Jana, San Diego is Victoria, and D.C. is Olivia.

I am glad when talk soon turns to dinner, but we find this restaurant doesn't serve food on the patio, and the inside is full. After we finish our drinks, the five of us agree to look for dinner elsewhere. We strike out at the restaurant next door as well, as there is no immediate seating available, but the hostess says, "There is another restaurant at the other end of town."

As we start walking, I notice Victoria's knee is wrapped in an elastic bandage. "What happened to your knee?" I ask.

She shakes her head and says, "I twisted it pretty bad leaving Roncesvalles. It was a big to-do, but luckily I can still walk."

"That sucks," I say. "I hope you're not in much pain."

"No pain, but I feel *something* with each step," she says.

We walk under a darkening blue sky; a whisper of orange rises above a ridgeline to the west on this sultry summer night. I stroll next to Jana, her long, light brown hair pulled back into a ponytail. As we make our way to the far end of town, we share stories of our first two days on the Camino. Olivia and Victoria are engaged in a lively, fast-paced conversation with Liliana.

We are seated right away at a large table in the restaurant, Gau Txori, which we come to find is Basque for *night bird*. This is clearly where the locals come; we are the only pilgrims here. When the waitress appears, we order a bottle of red, a bottle of white, some appetizers, and place our entree orders. Everyone else is as hungry as I am. We share stories while we drink our wine and wait for our food.

"We are staying at a smaller B&B type of place," Jana says.

"We are lucky to have found anything," Victoria adds. "We got here after four, and all the albergues were full."

"We were on our way out of town, planning to walk to the next town, when an old woman standing outside asked if we needed somewhere to stay," Jana says.

"She rents rooms in her home to pilgrims," Victoria says. "It was a Camino miracle."

We share bites of our chosen entrees and continue our conversations over a leisurely meal that includes even more bottles of wine. After dinner, we stroll back towards the town's center. I feel the effects of an evening of drinking. Loud music is audible in the distance as a live band plays; tonight's festivities are well underway.

Jana and I lag behind.

"I walk at a faster pace than my friends," she says. "I am hoping to find someone with a similar speed to walk with, so I can reach our destination earlier and meet up with them later in the day."

"I'd love to," I say.

As we approach my albergue, the two of us decide to start together at 7 a.m.

"Goodnight, ladies," I say as Liliana and I veer towards our albergue.

DAY 3: ZUBIRI > PAMPLONA

*Despite all the forces against us, we (all) want
very much to be proud of our lives. We still desire
to reach our potential. This hope, a small flame,
burns inside us and we weep for our failure to
make the changes to step into the unknown.*

~ Og Mandino, *The Greatest Miracle in the
World*

I walk towards Jana, standing on the corner where I stumbled upon the women last night, both of us smiling. Our destination today is Pamplona, where we will meet up with Olivia and Victoria this afternoon.

I hadn't paid attention yesterday, but the official Camino route doesn't cross the bridge into Zubiri, so we cross back over the bridge and rejoin the trail. We walk side by side on a wide gravel path that runs alongside the Arga River.

"So, how did you end up on the Camino?" I ask.

"Being a good Catholic, I've known about the Camino for a long time, so when Victoria mentioned she and Olivia were going, I was excited to come along," she says. "The three of us have known each other for years, from our time serving in an order together."

"What does it mean to serve in an *order*?"

"I am a consecrated lay missionary, and I belong to an order of other consecrated women. We have the same vows as a nun—obedience, poverty, and chastity—but aren't a part of the church directly."

"Wow, that's interesting," I say. "How were you able to leave for a month?"

"I'm actually on a sabbatical," she says. "I asked to take a year away, in part to walk the Camino, but also to decide if I want to remain."

"How long have you been in the order?"

"Twenty years."

"Whoa! Sorry, but how old are you?"

"Forty-one."

"What?! You don't look it." A bit taller than me, Jana is thin, with a wrinkle-free face and braces on her teeth. "There must be something about giving your life to God that slows aging." This gets a laugh. "What do you do in the order?"

"Most of my time has been in schools, teaching in cities across the U.S. and Central America."

"Sounds like fun," I say. "So, Olivia and Victoria serve, too?"

"They did, but both have left in the last few years," she says. "I figure that walking the Camino will help me decide if I want to stay. I will keep my vows until I make that decision."

We walk alongside the river, our paces similar, and I am excited to share my walk with someone today. Many others are in sight, some walking alone, others in pairs, as we move under a brightening blue sky.

"We need to switch sides," I say as I move to Jana's left. "I am deaf in one ear."

"I noticed you turning your head last night, and I thought that might be the case. Have you always been deaf in that ear?"

"No, it's been about five years," I say. "I had a non-cancerous brain tumor removed, and I lost hearing in one ear."

"That's crazy," she says. "How did you find out you had a tumor?"

"For a few years, I knew that the hearing in one ear was better than the other but assumed it was just a part of aging. One day I was at the doctor for a knee problem, and as he's walking out the door, I said, 'by the way.' Fast-forward two months, and I'm recovering from brain surgery."

"Wow," she says. "How was your recovery?"

"Initially, my balance was affected, but everything is good now," I say. "And I only notice my hearing loss when I'm walking next to someone or sitting in a restaurant," I add with a smile.

Jana and I share more stories of our first couple of days on the Camino. The three stayed at the albergue in Roncesvalles the same night I did, but they arrived so late that they were assigned beds in the overflow area. While they were happy to get beds, it was not the same experience I had.

"We took three of the last four beds," she says. "A couple walking the Camino for their honeymoon fittingly shared the last bed."

Our conversation continues as the sun peeks over the Pyrenees. An hour into our walk, the Camino passes by Larrasoaña, a town that sits across the river from the official route and was the likely destination for those who didn't find lodging in Zubiri last night.

Soon we're walking through the small hamlet of Akerreta, which houses a charming-looking hotel and little else; then we enter a forest. We walk along a dirt path in the still-cool morning air, peppering each other with questions. I learn Jana is a runner, and I'm impressed when I find she has run a marathon.

"I won't run any distance because of an old knee problem, but I can walk long distances without any problem," I say. "Or at least, I hope I can." I reach out and knock on a tree.

Eventually, our route passes a small stand operating out of either a partially constructed building or the ruins of an old building; I am not sure which. A middle-aged gentleman is offering drinks and snacks for a donation. When he learns we are Americans, he asks, "Where are you from?"

When Jana answers, "Idaho," the guy gets excited.

"Me too!" he says. "But now I spend a part of each year in this part of Spain."

He is proud of his Basque descent, and I learn there is a large population of Basque people living in southern Idaho, especially in Jana's hometown of Boise. He and Jana talk about back home. He tells us his Basque heritage led him to visit this area of Spain, and he has spent more time here over the years. Hanging on a wall is a picture of himself and Martin Sheen, taken while *The Way* was being filmed in the area.

As the kilometers pass, Jana and I discuss our lives back home.

"I am more of an introvert," she says. "I think that life in the order suits that part of me."

"I am, too," I say. "I'm not a great communicator either." Then I share with Jana, "I will avoid conflict at all costs and rarely speak my mind."

"I would think you have to communicate pretty well to be married for so long. Not that I would know, having never been in a relationship."

"I think we were together so long *because* I didn't communicate well. If I were unhappy with something, I would bury it and go with the flow."

"That's not healthy," she points out.

"I know that now," I say. "But for years, I let things build inside me and grew resentful because of it."

"I, too, have to keep a lot inside," she admits. "I don't have anyone to share things with."

"You don't have anyone in your order to talk to?"

"I have friends in the order, but we aren't close enough to share the deeper questions or issues we may be having, and my family relationships have been strained, so I can't talk to them either," she says. "What things couldn't you share with your wife?"

"Well, I brought up wanting to retire early and travel the world, and her response was, 'Why do you spend time on these pipe dreams instead of planning something we can do together now?' I learned to keep my dreams to myself, so I could keep them alive instead of having them crushed."

"You don't think she wants to travel the world?"

"Maybe she would, under the right circumstances, but we didn't have the conversation, because, like I said, I was a shitty communicator."

"What other things couldn't you communicate about?"

"Like any marriage, there are things that irked me, but I would keep quiet. I wasn't always honest about my feelings; instead, I bottled them up. Some things weren't my wife's fault, but I would still blame her."

"Like what?" Jana asks.

"Well, she's a teacher, so she always had her summers off, while I was always working. I was jealous as hell about it and would sometimes complain. She would say, 'You chose your career. If you want to change careers, go ahead.' But I didn't take any action to change things."

"I didn't have a partner like you, but I get it."

"It feels nice to be able to speak these words to another person," I say. "It's shocking to be telling my innermost feelings to someone I just met."

"Yeah, it is," she says with a smile. "Victoria and Olivia know I'm going through some things, but with a stranger, it's easier to have things spill out."

Our route this afternoon takes us through more woods, then back to crisscross the river as we approach the most populated city along the entire Camino. We cross over a bridge, watch as the river cascades lower, and soon find ourselves in an urban setting. Guided by Camino markers, mostly yellow arrows painted on the roadway or on sides of buildings, we navigate the streets. Eventually, we are walking uphill, away from the river and towards an older part of Pamplona.

Jana and I have made good time over a relatively easy twenty-two kilometers. It's early afternoon when we arrive in Pamplona.

"We are staying at Albergue Jesus y Maria, the city's municipal albergue," Jana says.

"Sounds good to me," I say.

According to my list, most towns along the Camino have a "municipal" albergue owned and operated by the town. They seem to be the least expensive option and operate on a first-come, first-served basis. Most of the smaller private albergues allow pilgrims to call ahead and reserve beds.

When we arrive, we find it won't open for another ninety minutes.

"Let's go wander around while we wait," I suggest.

We find Pamplona relatively quiet. I imagine the afternoon sun, high overhead, keeps many locals inside. We cross the Plaza Del Castillo, a huge open square surrounding a small domed stage. A tree-lined promenade surrounds the square. Gorgeous architecture abounds on all sides. We pass Cafe Iruña, and Jana says, "That's where Ernest Hemingway hung out on his many visits here." This fancy-looking 'cafe' pours onto the plaza. It was Hemingway and his first novel that first brought Pamplona to the attention of the world.

Jana and I make it back to the albergue by three, when the doors open. The large stone building sits in the heart of the oldest part of this walled city. We enter through standard-size doors carved out of two massive doors weathered by the centuries. Topping the tall archway are the words *Seminario Episcopal* and the year 1782. We claim the first two of the 114 beds. Luckily, the woman behind the front desk allows Jana to hold beds for the others, assigning them beds next to ours.

Inside the bunk room are two floors of bunks, all open to a towering barrel ceiling. The vaulted ceiling is stunning, with ornate geometric carvings, and must soar at least thirty feet high. A long row of benches fills one wall, with places for shoes and packs. It is not quite the same privacy as my first few nights, as every bed here is open to every other. Jana and I shower and change into fresh clothes before heading off to explore the city more in-depth. Jana messages her friends to inform them they have bunks reserved.

They message back, "Still a couple of hours away."

Looking at a city map we picked up from the albergue, we head towards the Plaza de Toros, the famed bullring. As we stroll through this old city, Jana says, "I'm glad to have found a walking partner with a similar pace."

"Me too," I say. "It's nice to walk with someone."

"I am glad to arrive early enough to relax and explore," she says. "Unlike my first two days, when simply finding a bed was reason to celebrate."

Pamplona is probably best known for the famed Running of the Bulls. Those brave enough are chased by six bulls through Pamplona's streets during its annual Fiesta de San Fermin, which occurs July 6–14 every year. The chase ends here at the bullring. During the fiesta, bullfights take place in the Plaza de Toros, which seats 20,000 spectators. A monument to the famous American author who helped bring this city to prominence stands in front of the bullring. A stoic-looking Hemingway glares straight ahead from an oversized bust carved from stone.

I am surprised to find there are no bullfights in Pamplona outside of the weeklong festival. Bullfighting continues throughout Spain, despite the efforts of animal-rights groups to abolish it. Traditions, in a country with such a rich history, remain important for most Spaniards. As we meander around the outside of the circular stadium, we watch as a wedding party has photos taken with the stadium as the backdrop; this is one of the more notable landmarks in this historic city.

It's difficult to imagine walking through this city a few weeks ago, when over a million people flowed through Pamplona during its annual party. Most of the albergues are closed during this time, and finding a place to sleep would have been nearly impossible. Pilgrims arriving in Pamplona during this week must keep walking to find a bed further along the Way.

"I want to find where my favorite saint was injured," Jana says.

We walk until we locate a bronze sculpture of a twenty-nine-year-old Basque soldier, Ignatius of Loyola, being carried after having his leg shattered here during a military battle in 1521.

"It was while Ignatius was recovering in Pamplona that he underwent a spiritual conversion," Jana tells me. "He went on to found the Society of Jesus, now known as the Jesuits. He was canonized a hundred years later."

"You know your saints," I say.

Returning to the albergue, we find Olivia and Victoria asleep in their bunks. Jana and I also rest before the four of us head back out into the big city. We meander through bustling pedestrian streets on another beautiful summer evening. Our wanderings lead us off the busier streets and through a small square filled with trees before we reach the edge of the old town. We look at the river valley we walked through earlier from our perch along the ancient stone walls. Later we find a tiny grocery and buy the makings for a picnic dinner.

With all three women being devout Catholics, they head to Mass at the nearby cathedral, and I join them, our bag of groceries in tow. Afterward, we circle the cathedral's stunning interior, and Victoria teaches me about each Apostle. I suppose I am Catholic to an extent, having been baptized as a newborn because of my father, but I grew up attending a Protestant church. Vaguely familiar with the Apostles from my Sunday school days, I enjoy my lesson on the background of each Apostle. I learn of Jesus's twelve disciples; two are named James and are commonly referred to as James the Greater and James the Lesser, the distinction likely due to James the Greater being either older or taller. I find out now that the Camino is leading us to the remains of James the Greater, or Saint James, which translates in Spanish from its Hebrew origins, perhaps confusingly, to *Santiago*.

We leave the cathedral in search of a place to eat; the stars are out and the temperature is ideal. We find a set of broad stairs in front of a school, long since closed for the day; the perfect spot for our picnic. We look onto yet another small plaza and enjoy our dinner of a baguette, sliced meats, cheese, tomatoes, olives, and wine as we watch generations of locals out for the evening.

We talk for hours. Jana and Olivia head back to the albergue while Victoria and I continue with my lesson. We both lose track of time and eventually make it back to our albergue at 11:05 to find the doors locked. I remember the sign about the eleven-o'clock curfew on the front desk, but I am still surprised to find it locked. We don't immediately panic.

Victoria calls Olivia and says, "We're locked out."

Thankfully, Olivia comes and opens the door to let us in. I find out later that the host reprimanded Olivia in the morning for opening the door. A security camera must have caught the illicit act.

Lesson learned.

DAY 4: PAMPLONA > PUENTE LA REINA

The purpose of life, after all, is to live it, to
taste experience to the utmost, to reach out
eagerly and without fear for newer and richer
experience.

~ Eleanor Roosevelt

Jana and I walk along glistening cobblestones, past two men hosing down the narrow streets with a power washer—cleaning up after last night's crowd. As we head out of the city, we find ourselves merging with other pilgrims beneath an early morning sky. Initially, we remain a pair in this sea of pilgrims, but eventually, we walk and talk with others as the sea of pilgrims stretches out and becomes more like a river.

I find myself walking with Robbie, a gregarious Irishman of solid build, who tells me he's walking a part of the Camino for the sixth time. He has walked the entire Camino twice before and said he tries to walk at least a part of it as often as possible, ideally every year, but takes what he can. This summer, he has two weeks to spend on the Camino. When he mentions his wife back home, I am a little surprised.

"Your wife is okay with you being gone?" I ask.

"That was part of the deal when we got married," Robbie responds in a strong Irish accent.

"How old were you when you got married?"

"I was in my late thirties when I married … for the second time," he says.

"I was twenty-two," I say. "How old were you when you married the first time?"

"Like you, in my early twenties," he says. "We grew apart and split after ten years."

"I think it's great you can travel like this. In my marriage, we never shared the same dream for travel, and my dreams got buried," I say.

"That isn't uncommon. We all have dreams when we're young, but then life takes you in a different direction."

"You seem to have things figured out now," I say.

"Not necessarily, but I find time to do things I enjoy," he says. "My wife doesn't like the walking or staying in hostels, which she knows I do, so she puts up with it."

"My wife and I didn't have the same agreement," I say. "So, I didn't pursue many solo activities."

"Yeah, I'm happy the wife is okay with it," he says. "She has her things, too."

We walk through open fields, slowly gaining in elevation. I remember not long ago looking through a journal I kept for a time during my early college days and reading about all the exciting adventures I was planning. But soon after writing those passages, I met my wife-to-be, and those dreams faded.

Robbie and I stop in front of the Iglesia de San Andres in the small village of Zariquiegui, and Robbie says, "We have a big climb ahead. I am going to stop here and take a break."

I am not tired and decide to continue. "Hopefully, we'll meet up again," I say. I look back and spot Jana a hundred meters behind, walking with another, and know we will meet up later in the day.

Robbie knows the trail well, as not long after we part the route starts a long and steady ascent, the steepest since leaving the Pyrenees. I pass a few others as I make the climb. At the summit, I am surprised to find one of the better-known landmarks on the Camino, Alto del Perdón, which translates as *High of Forgiveness*. This rust-colored metal sculpture depicts twelve pilgrims walking in a line spread out over fifteen meters, each just a bit larger than life. These two-dimensional pilgrims symbolize all those who have journeyed to Santiago de Compostela over the centuries. The first pilgrim is leaning into the wind and searching for the Way, and the following figures depict the others who would follow in later times. The last two are modern-day pilgrims, signifying the resurgence of the Camino. These metal structures sit on a ridgeline; its backdrop is everchanging, from the crops in fields below, to the position of the sun and clouds overhead. At this moment, it's an irregular patchwork of green and brown in the valley below, with rolling hills of green in the far distance, all under a crisp blue sky. It seems almost a requirement to have my photo taken here, so I join these rusty pilgrims and fight an imaginary wind. I rest atop the high point and enjoy this work of art before starting an immediate and rocky descent.

There is little shade on the gravel trail, but trees grow sporadically on both sides. Dripping with sweat as the sun beats down, I stop under a tree and use a bandana I have tied to my pack to wipe my sweat and then reapply sunscreen to my shaved head. I drink half of my second water bottle and pray I reach the next town soon.

Most small towns have a public fountain, where I find "potable" water safe to drink. I have found a couple marked "non-potable," while still others have a sign stating something to the effect that the water isn't treated, so drink at your own risk.

Not thirty minutes later, I walk into a small village and find a fountain. I feel the first few swallows of cold water course through my body; this refreshing feeling fades as I down the rest of the liter. Finally, my prayer answered, I leave with both bottles full.

Still walking on my own and hungry, when I reach the town of Muruzábal, I veer off the route to find something to eat. Stopping at the first bar, its patio filled, I go inside and buy a bocadillo and a bag of chips. Then, I head across the street for a solo picnic on the village green. Almost all the locals are dressed in white, with a red scarf around their necks and a red sash tied around their waists. Why? Resting against a tree, I recognize Jana and another walking by on the main road.

I call out, "Jana!"

Jana introduces her new friend. "This is Birte (BEER-te), from Germany." Birte, about my height, is wearing a pair of Janis Joplinesque sunglasses, her longish brown hair tucked under a buff, and is carrying a bright red pack. I throw mine on and join them. We pass several groups of locals enjoying a Sunday afternoon meal outside at long tables. I find out they are celebrating the annual Fiestas de la Virgen Blanca, a Basque tradition.

"I would like to take the alternate route, to what I've read is an interesting church," Jana says. "But it will add about three kilometers to our walk."

"Fine by me," I say.

"Let's go, then," Birte adds.

The marked detour to the Iglesia de Santa María de Eunate takes us along a gravel road through open fields as we head towards a church I hope is worth these additional steps.

Birte arrived in Spain only yesterday. This her first day of a two-week adventure.

"I will jump ahead to experience the different sections of the Camino," she says of her self-made journey to Santiago. "It was a last-minute decision" to spend her holiday walking in Spain. She is married, but her husband could not, or as she tells it, "would not" take time off to travel with her.

Iglesia de Santa Maria de Eunate is beautifully unique. The doors are locked, but the exterior is stunning. Almost a thousand years ago, masons used stone blocks to build this church in the shape of an octagon and surrounded it with an octagonal gallery composed of thirty-three archways. This twelfth-century church sits in the middle of nowhere, far from any village, surrounded only by open fields. Its solitude adds to its beauty. While our stay is brief, it was worth the extra distance walked.

As the three of us make our way towards Puente la Reina, Jana looks over the albergue options ahead. When she mentions one with a pool, the search is over, and our pace quickens. We walk through the town, pass several restaurants and shops, cross over a bridge that marks the town's end, and then go up a long, steep gravel driveway to reach Albergue Santiago Apóstol. We are the first to arrive for the day. We reserve two extra beds and order three beers at the bar, which doubles as the front desk.

For now, we have the large pool to ourselves. I swim leisurely laps in refreshingly lukewarm water. The view from the pool deck looks onto the river and town below. The sun is high overhead, and when not in the water, the temperature is too hot. After some time in the pool, we lie on our thin travel towels spread out over patchy grass under a bamboo shelter and relax in the shade.

Birte and I talk about our lives back home. She has a high-level job at a German auto company, and I find she goes by "Dr." at work, given she holds a PhD in something. Her path is seemingly set, settled in her career and marriage, while my path forward is still in question.

After an hour and a few more dips in the pool, Olivia and Victoria join us. This poolside afternoon feels more like an afternoon on vacation than a pilgrimage.

After a shower and a nap, the five of us walk down the hill to continue our lazy vacation day. Lazy if you don't count the twenty-eight-kilometer walked. I barely noticed the bridge we crossed on our rush to the pool, but now I take in this beautiful Romanesque bridge that spans the Arga River. This bridge gives the town its name, the Bridge of the Queen, named for the Spanish monarch who commissioned its construction in the eleventh century. For a thousand years, pilgrims have crossed this bridge on their journey to Santiago.

We stand on an overlook on the town side of the bridge to get a better view and discuss where to eat. The three Americans lean towards an inexpensive meal, while Birte is eager for a nice sit-down dinner and is craving a steak. While I don't have the same budgetary restrictions as the other Americans, I fall closer to their thrifty end of the spectrum.

We end up at a restaurant closer to what Birte had in mind. We have a drink outside, along the main pilgrim road running through town, while waiting to be seated. Our conversation intermingles with that of two couples from Ireland as we sip red wine. Inside, the restaurant has a rustic yet chic feel to it. We order a pitcher of sangria and feast on mostly meat dishes.

On our walk back to the albergue, we run into one of the Irish couples, seated outside another restaurant.

"Join us," the husband says.

The five of us pull up chairs, and we all order a glass of wine. We find they are walking the Camino for one week; it's their first time here. I mostly talk with the husband, who is a couple of years older than me.

"I'm enjoying it," he says. "I would love to come back and walk to Santiago de Compostela."

"It would be alone," his wife says. "All this walking is a bit much for me."

"You'll come around, Mot," he says.

The five of us agree to start together super early tomorrow. We want to get our kilometers in before the afternoon heat arrives; it's forecasted to be even hotter in the coming days. The three American ladies finish their wine and head back.

"We'll see you in the morning," I say. Birte and I continue talking with the couple.

Birte has an engaging and fun personality. Soon we, too, head back. There is much laughter on our return to the curfew-less albergue. For each of the last few nights, I have consumed more alcohol than I ever do back home, but I find drinking with new friends adds to my Camino experience—the wine helping create more intense connections. Birte and I make our way back beneath the moon's pale glow and stop at the apex of the well-traveled bridge and look up to a starry sky; from a distance, it must be a picture-perfect moment. The moment passes, and we make the climb back to our lodgings.

DAY 5: PUENTE LA REINA > ESTELLA

*The hardest thing to do is leave your comfort
zone. But you have to let go of the life you're
familiar with and take the risk to live the life
you dream about.*

~ *Tere Arigo*

It's before six o'clock when we step outside, headlamps on. I throw on
my Patagonia fleece before we set out. This morning's route has a gentle
incline; our pace slow, the five of us stay close. An hour into the walk,
we reach a small town where Olivia and Victoria take a break. With a
rendezvous point decided, we three leave them at a bar and keep
moving.

Far ahead, against a blue sky, a white mound rises above a post-
harvest landscape. It is a beautiful sight, but the closer we get, the less
appealing I find this village rising from the plain. We follow yellow
arrows up the inclined streets. The town has an abandoned feel to it this

early in the morning, and we find no commercial presence, but the three of us are hungry. We do find a small shop selling bread; a vending machine offering coffee stands outside. We go in but find nothing appealing and elect for just coffee. Jana is the first to insert a one-euro coin. Just as Birte is making her selection, Jana says, "Stop!" A split second too late, we look in Jana's cup, where a dozen ants are floating in a golden sea.

A few kilometers ahead, we find ourselves at the Olive Gard'Zen', a small stand composed of a couple of tables under a thatched roof, on one side of our path; on the other is a small forest of olive trees on a terrace, with picnic tables and chairs resting in the shade.

"Hola," says an energetic Spaniard.

"Hola," we respond.

We find he is the owner of this land and offers passing pilgrims fruit, snacks, and drinks, including wine for a donation. "The wine is made nearby," he says, pointing to the hill town we just passed. We sample his offerings to quench our hunger and leave our contributions. This friendly guy, in his late twenties, tells us he worked a typical job in Pamplona for a few years.

"But I wanted to live a different life, one on the Camino,' he says. "I bought this land two years ago and live nearby while I work on the land." He excitedly shares his dreams for the property and his love for the Camino and meeting people from around the globe.

We leave this small oasis and continue at a good pace, passing through open fields with views of rolling hills, while our walk remains relatively flat.

"Did you know Mike here is a grandfather?"

"Why, Jana?" I say, shaking my head.

"I think it's great you're a young grandpa," Jana says.

"Wow," Birte says. "I'm thirty-seven, and I'm still not ready for kids."

"But you want kids?" I ask.

"Yes, but I am not in a rush," she says. "My husband is ready, but I keep putting him off. I'll probably give in in a couple of years, but I love my job and am focused on it for now."

"What about you, Jana? Can you see kids in your future … if you decide to leave?" I ask.

"I haven't ruled it out, but it would need to be the right situation."

"Your maternal clock is not ticking?" Birte asks.

"Not really. Is yours?"

"Not yet," she says.

"Jana, your life could play out in many ways," I say.

"I know," she says. "It's a little scary ... but exciting, too."

"How old were you when your kids were born?" Birte asks.

"I was twenty-three when my daughter was born, and my son followed four years later. So, my path was set early on."

"That is so young," Birte says. "I can't imagine having kids at that age. I was still in university."

"Looking back, yeah, it was young," I say with a smile. "But I love being a dad and can't imagine life without them. But man, the years flew by when they were growing up."

"Well, now you can enjoy your grandchildren and travel when you're still relatively young."

"Yes ... relatively." I smirk. "My life played out much differently than yours, Birte. I didn't have the fun, carefree life filled with travel and adventure in my younger days, like you. But you'll probably have kids underfoot when you're sixty-five."

"I think it's hard for people to imagine living a life so different than their own," Jana says.

"Yeah, everyone has their own expectations in life, and it's hard to get past that. I was telling Jana I wasn't able to communicate to my wife what I really wanted in life, so different than her expectations."

"I think it happens a lot in marriages," Birte says. "I wish my husband and I were more on the same page, but I'm in a good place. Work has been a priority for me, and the same for my husband. But I think when we have kids, he will be the one to stay home."

"It's interesting to listen to you two talk about marriage," Jana says. "While I have no first-hand experience, I know if I do leave my order, life is going to get quite interesting."

"I think in most marriages, there are similar struggles. Marriage isn't easy," I say.

"Are you trying to scare Jana off of men?" Birte scolds.

"Of course not. I didn't mean to make my marriage sound bad. I'm the one to blame for not speaking up about what I wanted. I am grateful for everything, and my kids gave my life a purpose for decades," I say.

I fall behind the two women and think about my marriage and kids. Once our kids arrived, I no longer had the bandwidth to dwell on the dreams of my youth. Work, marriage, and fatherhood were my focus for the next twenty-plus years. My kids brought joy to my life. As they got older, I would go on adventures with them, often individually. My daughter attended a summer camp every summer from the time she was eight until she graduated college. I loved driving to the Northwoods of Wisconsin to drop her off. As she got older, we started backpacking, just the two of us—I looked forward to our annual backpacking trip to Michigan's Upper Peninsula. My wife had no interest in sharing our love of wandering through the woods.

As my son grew, he and I would take a road trip each summer; we car-camped all over the country while my wife stayed home. We did take family vacations every year, but those would always be to Florida, and while that was not my top choice, we had a good time. My wife preferred the beach; my choice would be the mountains.

The adventures with my kids would get me by and kept a flicker of my old travel dreams alive. Once my kids were older and not as reliant, my mind started to drift back to all I didn't do in my youth. When both kids officially left the nest and my purpose was no longer clear, questions arose. I had been using the idea of providing for my family to justify our lifestyle. What now, with much of the justification gone?

We pass a few hundred sheep grazing under the hot summer sun in a sand-colored meadow just off the trail. Another pilgrim has stopped to photograph the scene. He asks, "Do you know about the wine fountain ahead?"

"No," we respond.

"It is at a winery on the Camino near Estella," he says. "It is free for pilgrims."

Estella is today's destination, and the novelty of a wine fountain brings a newfound excitement to our walk. I have a vision of a large, decorative, round stone fountain with tiers of wine bubbling up and spilling down. The anticipation builds as the kilometers tick by.

We pass a flyer posted on a fence post; in English, it reads, *Taxi Company, 24 hours*, along with a phone number. All along the Camino, we occasionally pass small flyers tacked to poles or fences, advertising upcoming albergues and restaurants, but these are my favorite: taxi companies offering rides to weary pilgrims. Too hot, too tired, too sore ... relief is just a phone call away.

As we near Estella, we find the wine fountain is actually two kilometers past our albergue and getting there means walking an extra four kilometers in the heat. "I still want to go to the fountain this afternoon," I say.

"Okay, but I will continue to the next town after the fountain," Birte says. "I will be taking a bus tomorrow morning to jump ahead."

"I'm game, but let's stop for something to eat with the wine," Jana says. "I'm hungry."

Our route follows the Ega River into a city preparing for a fiesta. We pass our albergue and follow Camino signs through yet another town, one much younger than Estella, where we stop at a small grocery store to grab bread and cheese.

We stop at a unique open-air metalworking shop where the owner has many beautiful souvenirs for sale and beautiful large sculptures on display. He offers us two stamps for our pilgrim credentials, one of which signifies we have reached the 100-kilometer mark from Saint-Jean. Minutes later, we find a sign reading *BODEGAS IRACHE*, like the letters in the Hollywood sign, letting us know we have arrived.

I laugh to myself when the fountain does not match what I had envisioned. The fountain sits behind an open gate and is built directly into a large stone building. It has two taps, like a beer tap in a bar—one dispensing red wine and the other water. It was dedicated in 1991, one hundred years after the winery's founding, to pay homage to the nearby monastery's generosity.

The tenth-century Monastery of Santa Maria de Irache, only thirty seconds ahead on the Camino, provided drink to early pilgrims. The winery continues this tradition.

The monastery opened a refuge for pilgrims in the year 1054. The monastery doors closed in 1985, due to the lack of new novitiates entering the order. Fortunately, construction equipment inside the locked gate signifies it is getting ready for its next incarnation. This monastery appears in *The Way*; it's where pilgrims sleep in a cloister under a covered arcade open to the cool night air.

A sign posted at the fountain reads: "We are pleased to invite you to drink in moderation. If you wish to take the wine with you, you will have to buy it," and "Pilgrim, if you wish to arrive at Santiago full of strength and vitality, have a drink of great wine and make a toast to happiness."

The three of us pour wine into our water bottles; the only one filled to the top is mine. "To happiness and the Camino," we toast. We try to get creative with the cameras on our phones and take photos with our mouths directly under the wine flowing from the fountain. Mine is the only face that ends up soaked in wine.

We sit on our packs in the shade of the winery and eat bread and cheese while sipping our wine. While we dine, I enjoy chatting with pilgrims who stop for a few minutes before resuming their walk. One Spanish gentleman is walking the entire Camino for the sixth straight year. He says he averages more than forty kilometers a day. He looks more like a runner out for a jog, wearing silky running shorts and a minimalist pack.

After an hour filled with not-so-moderate drinking, Birte approaches me and quietly says, "You should jump ahead with me."

I am surprised by her suggestion. A few seconds later, I respond, "I would enjoy getting to know you better, but I feel I must walk every step to Santiago."

"I understand, but I was hoping to get to know you better, too," she replies with a raised brow.

I feel the need to experience the entirety of this epic trail, and even more, I enjoy walking with Jana. Soon, we all share hugs and Birte walks ahead. After I top off my plastic wine bottle, Jana and I head back the way we came.

Jana messages the others, and we agree to pick up the makings for dinner on our way to Albergue de Peregrino Rocamador. When we arrive, we find Olivia and Victoria have already checked into a private room, with four beds and our own bathroom.

I promptly pass out in my bunk.

Two hours later, I awake to an empty room and a missed message on my phone. My roommates are at the fiesta in the old part of town and have invited me to join them. It turns out that Estella has a weeklong celebration in early August every year, the Fiestas Patronales. Excited, I go and take a shower.

Somehow, I have ended up locked in the bathroom. The handle on the outside of the door is now lying on the floor. I had not yet responded to the ladies, and my phone sits on my bunk. C'est la vie. I sit patiently on the toilet, wrapped in my towel, my penance for failing to follow the simple instructions to drink in moderation and for taking advantage of the winery's generosity.

An hour later, my roommates return and burst out laughing at my predicament before freeing me from my cell.

Later, we carry our home-cooked meal from a small kitchen onto a patio overlooking a green garden. It is yet another beautiful night as the sun sets during our family-style dinner under a trellis of grapevine.

DAY 6: ESTELLA > LOS ARCOS

One of the greatest regrets in life is being
what others would want you to be, rather
than being yourself.

~ Shannon Adler

Long after the sun's rise, the four of us make our way towards the free-flowing fountain. Olivia and Victoria are both eager to experience this unique stop along the Way. The gate opens at 8 a.m., and we've timed our arrival just right. We all pour a bit of wine into our bottles and toast to our journey. We meet a handful of others who also stop, and we exchange stories of our first week on the Camino. One couple splashes wine into large white shells they have untied from their packs. They tap shells and make a toast before sipping their wine.

A shell, specifically the scallop shell, has long been the symbol of the Camino de Santiago. Signs with this shell are everywhere along the Way and are the most obvious route marker, even more than the ubiquitous yellow arrows. Most pilgrims have an actual shell attached to their pack, signifying they are on pilgrimage. While the shell has different possible connections to the Camino and Saint James, one stands out—the shell's indentations represent the numerous routes leading to Saint James's remains, just as the lines on the shell all lead to a singular point at its base. Over the centuries, the shell also served another purpose for pilgrims; it was used to scoop water to drink from water sources found along their trek. I have also seen a few pilgrims carrying walking sticks with a hollowed-out gourd attached, an emblem of those carried long ago to carry water as they walked from one river to the next on their journey west.

After our brief stop, we leave the fountain as one large group. Our pace is slow as conversations continue with those we've just met. Not long after leaving the fountain, we reach a sign that has us turning to the right.

One of the others, who has walked the Camino at least twice before, says, "There is an optional route which takes you through the trees along the side of the mountain." He points straight ahead.

As we stand in a dusty intersection, the veteran pilgrim shares, "the official route remains in a valley and passes through Villamayor de Monjardin, with a lovely church and views of a hilltop castle, while the views from the elevated route are also amazing. The paths merge in about ten kilometers."

"I'll take the higher route if anyone wants to go," I volunteer.

Olivia and Victoria immediately say they will take the valley route. Jana is the only one who joins me, and our core group agrees to end our day in the town of Los Arcos.

My breathing soon becomes labored as we follow switchbacks through an oak-covered hillside. The marathon runner slows her climb as we make our way together up the mountain before the path flattens. Our view through the trees reveals sheer white cliffs rising to a high plateau far across the mostly brown valley below.

"So, tell me about life as a consecrated woman," I say.

"It's all I've known, and I would say it can be a lonely life," she says. "Like I said before, I have friends, but we're not that close. The order doesn't want us to have tight friendships."

"Why?"

"We're only to have that close of a relationship with God."

"Really? Yikes," I say, gritting my teeth. "You said it's a lonely life. Is that one of the reasons you're thinking about leaving?"

"Maybe part of it. But I don't like the direction and hypocrisy of some of the organization's higher-ups," she says. "What I'm saddest about is, my relationship with my family has suffered over the years. I only visit them a few days each year, as the order only allows me limited time away. They wouldn't even allow me to go to my brother's wedding." I can sense the regret and bitterness in her voice.

"That's crazy, Jana. I didn't realize how little control you had."

"I have been able to heal some of those wounds since I started my sabbatical a few months ago. I have been living with my parents, and I've spent time with my siblings. My family has always supported my decision, even though I don't think they understood it. I know it hurt them, and they felt like I chose to leave them."

The route remains high along the hillside, the trail a combination of dirt and tree roots. I walk carefully to avoid twisting an ankle. After thinking about Jana and her family, I say, "When you mentioned losing touch with your family, I kind of know how you feel. After I went to college, I hardly ever came back to visit my mom and younger brothers. I didn't maintain as close a relationship with them as I should have. I'm sure they felt I abandoned them."

"I'm sure they understood you were just living your life."

"Maybe, but when I got married and had kids, I didn't do enough to build back a stronger relationship with them."

"Why not?"

"It all goes back to the fact that I couldn't communicate with my wife. I don't know if it was just the stereotypical issues with mothers-in-law, but my wife didn't like to spend much time with my family."

"It's not unusual," she says.

"Maybe, but I'm mad at myself for not pushing back. I never wanted to rock the boat at home. I have always had a relationship with my family, but not what it should have been. I didn't stand up for myself or my kids, who would have loved to spend more time with my family, especially their cousins," I say. "The words 'If momma ain't happy' did come out of my wife's mouth more than once, and I mistakenly allowed our family to operate that way."

"It doesn't sound very healthy."

"I know it sounds like I blame my wife, but I'm the one at fault for not speaking up. For years, I've felt bad about how I handled things with my family."

"How are things with your family now?"

"Much better," I say. "I've spent a lot more time with my mom and brothers, and my now-grown kids have good relationships with everyone."

In my marriage and in Jana's life, I think we both have felt the pain of not being in control of our lives. I tell Jana, "I read about a study years ago which kind of addresses this idea of not being in control of your life. Basically, it says that a strong sense of controlling one's life is a more dependable predictor of overall well-being than any other single factor."

"Yeah, I can see that," she says. "That's why I pushed for the sabbatical and am on the Camino to decide what course I want to take."

Our path leaves the cover of trees and slowly snakes its way between recently harvested hay fields. We reach a small town and find a fountain to refill. Exiting this small town, we are walking towards a bright yellow field. As we get closer, I discover it is an expansive field of sunflowers growing alongside our path. The heads of the sunflowers look at me, turning their faces to the sun high in the sky behind me.

The sunflowers fade from sight, and we merge with the official route and find other pilgrims again, but no sign of those we parted from earlier. We have been walking for a while without finding a restroom, and Jana says, "I can't hold it any longer."

She walks through a plowed field and disappears behind a stack of hay. As Jana is taking her midday bathroom break, two female pilgrims arrive and ask if I will take their photo atop the hay bales. I hesitate until I see Jana is making her way back. "Sure," I say. They reciprocate and take a photo of Jana and me, sitting together upon the bales of golden hay. It makes me feel like we're a couple. Does Jana feel similarly? I will not make any romantic overture, after her earlier comment about keeping her vows, even though I find her a beautiful soul and quite attractive.

We arrive in Los Arcos and find a bar on the plaza in front of the town's church. We drink cold beer under an umbrella while we wait for Olivia and Victoria. They arrive ninety minutes later, hot and tired after walking during the hottest part of the day. We check into the smaller of the two options we have tonight. Albergue Casa de la Abuela is a private albergue with thirty-two beds, instead of the larger municipal, which can house seventy. We are greeted by the joyful middle-aged owner of the albergue, who we find is almost fluent in five languages. She says, "I learned these languages so I can better communicate with my guests." Uniquely, this albergue does not allow hand washing of clothes, but our host will machine-wash our walking clothes for .50 euros. Quite a bargain!

After showers and naps, the four of us head back to Plaza de Santa Maria for a couple of cocktails before attending the 8 p.m. mass. As we enter Iglesia de Santa Maria, music begins, the altar lights up—and I gasp at the beautiful scene before me. The shining, golden altarpiece rises three stories and is filled with exquisite carvings and paintings, all surrounded by gold. It is one of the most beautiful church interiors I've ever seen.

I find the priest to be energetic and engaging, despite not understanding anything he's saying. Mass ends with another Blessing of the Pilgrims, after which my three friends approach the priest. He's now speaking in excellent English, and we learn he spent a few years in the United States as a priest before resuming his life in Spain. Before we leave, we peer into the attached cloister, a beautiful courtyard surrounded by the typical columned arcade. I am amazed to find such a magnificent place of worship in this small town.

After mass, we join a large group of mostly Irish pilgrims dining in the plaza out front of the church. Robbie and the two Irish couples from Puenta la Reina make up half the Irish contingent. One of the others shares a horror story for pilgrims. A middle-aged Irish woman says, "We stayed in a private albergue a couple of days ago, and I woke up and had bites on my arms and legs … bedbugs. It was miserable."

"That's my biggest fear," says Olivia.

"Besides dealing with the bites, I had to put everything I owned, including my empty pack, in a huge black plastic garbage bag and let it bake in the afternoon sun for hours to boil the little buggers," she says. "And I had to wash everything in hot water and find a clothes dryer. It cost me a whole day."

A few rules I've learned in my short time on the Camino: never place a backpack on a bed; always use my headlamp to scour my mattress for little black things; and, if on the bottom bunk, check the underside of the mattress above as well.

We eat, drink, and talk until almost ten o'clock, when we Americans leave the Irish and head to our albergue. On our thirty-second walk back, we agree to another early start.

DAY 7: LOS ARCOS > LOGROÑO

*You never really travel alone. The world is
full of friends waiting to get to know you.*

~ Unknown

We walk under a dark sky in the cool morning air for over an hour before finally removing our headlamps. A short time later, we enter a small village and are passing a bar when Olivia says, "I need to take a break."

"Okay, let's stop," Jana says.

"I think I'm going to keep walking," I say. "I'll meet you in Logroño." Which is our already agreed-upon destination. I would enjoy some time to myself.

"We'll see you this afternoon," Jana says.

The solitude this morning leads me to reflect on my life more deeply than I have thus far on my Camino. Walking under the early morning sky, I pass a small memorial alongside the Camino's route, honoring a pilgrim who lost their life while walking along the Way. My mind drifts back to another beautiful August morning in the late '70s.

It is a sunny Sunday morning, and I remember my dad arriving home after playing a round of golf with friends. He asks my younger brothers and me to help him organize and clean our garage to prepare for a joint birthday party the following weekend. I was turning thirteen, and my brother nine.

After we have the garage looking presentable, we finish by hosing down the concrete floor. My brothers and I leave to play with friends while Dad stays to install a new light fixture in the garage. Hours later, my brothers and I are inside watching *Mork and Mindy* when our mom runs into the house crying and says, "Your dad has had an accident. Stay in the house and pray for him." She leaves us in a bedroom and calls 9-1-1.

That afternoon, a combination of things changed my life—a wet floor, an aluminum ladder, and a live wire.

My father's death was the single most formative experience of my life, and the consequences of that day are still with me. My childhood went from being idyllic, with a close-knit family, to one with a huge void. As therapy wasn't common then, I didn't talk about my loss. Instead, I avoided it. It was too hard, too emotional for me to even think about. To this day, just thinking about my father brings tears to my eyes. Tears flow as I contemplate what my father would think of my life's choices.

Much of this morning's walk is alongside a roadway connecting the villages and towns on the Camino. During one of these roadside sections, a pickup truck piled high with packs passes me. It looks as though one bump would cause several packs to come flying out. There are more pilgrims sending their bags ahead than I imagined.

A lone pilgrim walks in the distance, and I gain ground on this stranger with each step. Outside the town of Viana, I catch up to a woman carrying a supersized pack. I slow my pace.

"That's quite a pack," I say.

"Yes," she says with a smile. "I was walking through the mountains in France for weeks before reaching Spain," she says.

"So, you still have all your gear?" I ask.

"Yes, my tent, cooking equipment, and a heavy sleeping bag, which is too warm for this weather."

"Wow," I say. "It sounds like fun backpacking in the Pyrenees."

"It was incredible," she says, then sips on a tube connected to a water bladder in her pack.

"By the way, my name is Mike. I'm from the States."

"Mirla, from Belgium."

She has a mop of curly hair and is wearing a headband to keep it from her face; she looks to be in her late twenties. As we walk along together, I learn she has the summer off before returning to a job at a university.

I have found that when two solo hikers meet on any trail, not only the Camino, it is easier to strike up a conversation and find a connection than if one or both are part of a group. It's not impossible otherwise, but still, I think it is probably in our nature. As a solo walker encountering a group, you are inclined to feel intrusive if you start a conversation, versus simply saying hello and moving on.

While walking the Camino, I have approached several solo pilgrims and initiated conversations, something I seldom do back home. I have found that getting to know another person, even a little bit, is one thing I enjoy when traveling solo. Not to say that solo is the only way I like to travel. Traveling with a loved one or with a group of family or friends is great in its own way, and I would never want to stop traveling with people I enjoy. But solo travel brings a different kind of joy and excitement, one I have only discovered in recent years.

As we walk through Viana, I spot a huge bird's nest constructed of tree branches atop a tall chimney. I have seen many large nests on my walk, most frequently high near church steeples, but I am unsure why they are so large.

"Mirla, do you know what those are?" I ask, pointing.

"Stork nests," she says.

"I don't think I've seen a stork yet," I say.

"Storks are common in this part of Spain during their mating season," she says. "Pairs of storks return to the same nest each year and enlarge the nests when they return. That is why some are so large. I don't think it's their mating season now."

"I don't think I could identify one if it flew by," I say. The image that comes to mind is a drawing of a stork delivering a baby. I doubt storks look like what I have pictured.

As we walk together, Mirla and I talk about a variety of subjects. We discuss our lives back home and what we will be doing once we leave the Camino.

She shares a story of meeting up with an ex on her recent travels and having an unfounded expectation of rekindling an old flame, only to find he was there with someone new.

"I was heartbroken," she says.

"Well, I booked my flight here the day after I had a relationship end," I say.

She laughs. Then says, "I came for the adventure more than anything else. I love being outdoors in nature." Walking the busy Camino is much different than her typical summer adventures in the mountains, she shares. She tells me, "I find the crowds on the Camino a bit overwhelming. I prefer the solitude in the more remote areas."

"I like hiking in the backcountry too, but I am enjoying the people part of this walk. I like the camaraderie I feel with the pilgrims I meet," I say.

"I like the connections too, but sometimes it's a bit much for me."

Everyone has their own goals and expectations of the Camino before starting. The biggest surprise for me has been the ease with which I have created connections. For Mirla, it's something different.

Later, we near a guy stopped alongside the trail, and she says, "This is Claudio, he is an *Italian*," she says, as if that means something more. "We have walked together off and on."

When we reach him, we share introductions, and the three of us follow the Camino's route as it skirts the Basque Country's border and crosses into La Rioja, a region known throughout the world for producing great-tasting red wine. Soon we enter the city of Logroño and stop at the first albergue we find.

We check into Albergue Santiago Apóstol, and I message Jana to let her know where I am staying. She messages back that they plan on staying here too, but still have ten of today's thirty kilometers left to walk.

After I shower, I wash my walking clothes in the bathroom sink. The water turns black after the first few rinsings. Once the water turns a light enough shade of gray, I deem them clean. I find the clothesline is in a small inner courtyard of the albergue. The narrow opening to a blue sky rises two stories, and the sun is not in view. I hope they dry.

I purchase a beer from a counter offering refreshment, then sink into an old but comfortable couch. My new friends join me, and we all enjoy a couple of beers before heading into the city center.

Logroño is one of the larger cities along the Camino. We find a nice restaurant near the large Plaza del Mercado and sit at an outdoor table under the shade of an umbrella to continue our 'day drinking.'

"Claudio is getting married in a couple of months," Mirla says. "He's on one last solo holiday."

"I want to have one last good time," he says with a wide smile.

A middle-aged man walking by stops when he notices Claudio and Mirla. These pilgrim friends chat, and he joins our table. We all order a four-course pilgrim menu on which there are many options for each course, not like the set menu I've had before. After finishing lunch, I leave this group and head back to the albergue. I'm not used to eating such a large meal this early in the day and am ready for a nap. When I get to my bed, I find the three American women crashed out on their bunks. Within minutes, I, too, am sleeping.

I spend the evening with my American friends, who walked most of the day with the Irish mob. The four of us have drinks on the plaza, followed by mass at yet another beautiful cathedral with an equally stunning gold altarpiece. We end our day with a late dinner, followed by a lovely stroll through the city on a wonderfully warm summer night, under a brilliant, star-filled sky.

DAY 8: LOGROÑO > NÁJERA

*The greatest thing in this world is not so
much where we are, but in what direction we
are heading.*

~ Oliver Wendell Holmes

Metal shells embedded into the concrete sidewalks mark our route through a city not yet open for the day. Our four becomes ten by the time we walk through a green space that leads us out of the city. Soon we are walking along a cypress-lined path, chatting with new faces as we walk en masse. When we arrive at a reservoir, the surface as smooth as glass under the morning light, our trail leads us around the lake and into a large park; empty picnic tables, grills, and a playground … just waiting.

We stop outside a small cafe in the park. It is still closed, but the kind gentleman inside sees our group and opens early. Most of those before me in line order a "café con leche," a drink I've heard being ordered frequently along the Camino. I am not a big coffee drinker, and I have yet to try this popular beverage. I watch the man behind his counter as he moves rapidly in front of a huge espresso machine. Loading, then locking handles filled with finely ground coffee, and placing a bright white cup underneath to catch the rich brown liquid oozing down. He pours milk from a box into a metal cup and steams the milk with a wand built into the machine. He pours the steamed "leche" into the espresso and places the cup on a saucer, where he adds a tiny spoon and a narrow packet of sugar. He gently slides the delicious-looking drink to his patron. When my turn comes, "Café con leche y tortilla, por favor."

I head outside with my breakfast to a covered patio and take a seat across from Jana. She, too, ordered a Spanish "coffee with milk." I mix in the sugar packet as I have watched others do. I lift my cup, inhale an earthy scent, and take my first sip. It is delicious!

We watch three swans chilling on the lawn leading down to the lake and talk about the simplicity of our days. We walk, we eat, and we sleep, then repeat.

"Here on the Camino, I enjoy the routine, but back in my old life, it was the routine that drove me crazy," I say.

"My life in the order is simple. I don't have much to worry about from a material perspective, and my days are pretty routine. I like it, or at least the routine doesn't upset me as it did you."

"So, your day-to-day life is good; you just want more control of your life?"

"Yeah, I guess, but it's not quite that simple," she says. "I have a lot to figure out."

"When you talk about your material needs, how does that work in the order?"

"They supply my housing and food, and I get a small stipend each month."

"Would you say you like that aspect of the order?"

"Actually, yeah. I don't have the same financial worries lots of people do."

"That *is* a big thing."

"Plus, I don't know what kind of job I can find," she says. "I'll be starting life from scratch at forty-one, without any financial safety net."

"Yeah, I can see it being scary."

"It is. That's probably my biggest concern about leaving."

"I'm lucky," I say. "I have a small pension waiting for me in my older years, but more importantly, I've already reduced my life to the bare essentials."

The larger group breaks up, as the others start walking before the four of us are ready. Eventually, we carry our empty dishes back inside, then throw on our packs and resume our walk. Jana and I walk side by side and continue our conversation.

"What was your life like before you simplified?"

"It took me a loooong time to realize the benefits of a simpler life. I got swept up in the whole consumer culture thing. I followed the expected path—college degree, marriage, job, kids, and ended up on the, quote,"—I flash quotes with my fingers—"hedonistic treadmill. Ever bigger houses, nicer cars. This despite the fact I claimed to revile consumerism. I was doing my best to keep up with the Joneses."

"It doesn't sound like a bad life."

"I must not have thought so at the time, but it came at a cost," I say. "You mentioned not having to worry about your material needs in the order, but that wasn't the case for me. Ten years ago, I lived in a big house, an Audi in the garage, and the accompanying monthly payments. Looking back now, I cringe at that life. Of course, I don't begrudge anyone for living how they choose, and I suppose I did choose that life, but it felt more like inertia as I kept on the path leading to excess."

"Were you happy?"

"At times, sure. My life may have looked ideal—a good job, a loving wife, and great kids. All the pieces of my life were fine on their own, but the whole wasn't satisfying."

"What were you hoping for?"

"I don't know. I think I am an optimistic person, but I couldn't figure out why I wasn't content. Even as I moved further down this path, I could feel the urge to get off, but I couldn't find the right path to lead my family down, so I stayed on the path paved with the latest iPhone instead. My feeling of discontent only grew."

"What finally changed?"

"Hmm," I murmur. "I guess I changed first, long before any big life changes. I started to dig a little bit under the surface. Audiobooks on my daily commute opened up my world, as did travel podcasts. I stumbled upon a book, *A Reasonable Life*, by Ferenc Máté, and some of his ideas on simplicity struck a chord with me. I started to explore different possibilities, different paths to take. I had brief discussions with my wife about some of these ideas, but she was happy with the status quo. We didn't make any changes in our lifestyle, but seeds were planted."

"Okay, so you changed. Then what?"

"Well, when my daughter graduated from college and moved out, my wife agreed to downsize our home. She could see our financial picture; despite our two ever-increasing incomes, our increases in spending took a toll. After twenty-five years, we took a hesitant step off the path we'd been following and sold our forever house."

"How did that make you feel?"

"It was a home I designed, so there was a twinge of sadness to have that dream fade into the past. Not to mention we took a big loss on the sale, selling after the market crash. Despite giving up the home I had envisioned growing old in, I felt we were heading in a better direction. We moved into a rental with half the square footage. The move started a purge, and I slowly eliminated things that felt excessive. I started to feel a lightness I hadn't felt in a while."

"It must have felt good to finally move in a different direction."

"It did," I say with a smile. "I wonder if your sabbatical is a gentle step off your path. Yours not of one of excess, *clearly*, but one without independence, and you're stepping onto a path of self-determination."

"Maybe it is."

The four of us walk in pairs through a vineyard and towards a town built on one side of what looks to be a perfectly symmetrical hill. A church's steeple rises high above the rest of town. When we arrive in Navarette, Olivia and Victoria tell us, "You two can keep walking, but we need a break. We'll meet you this afternoon."

While we walk through another of La Rioja's vineyards, we notice Robbie fifty meters ahead of us. Since we're making up ground, it's clear he's not walking at his usual brisk pace. As we get closer, we find his boots tied to the outside of his pack, and he's walking in socks and sandals with a noticeably different gait.

"What's going on with your feet?" Jana asks.

"My blisters have gotten worse," he says. "I think they're infected."

"Ouch," I say with a pained expression. With his Camino experience, I am surprised he is having problems. We continue together at Robbie's slower pace.

The three of us arrive in Nájera, a twenty-four-kilometer day now in the books. The albergue Jana was hoping for won't open for another half an hour. We search out shade and find it under an umbrella at one of a handful of bars and restaurants lining one side of a small plaza. We sip on cold beers and watch the Najerilla River flow past on the opposite side. When Robbie shows us his foot, I get a bit queasy. His foot looks raw; blisters have been rubbed open, and there seems to be pus oozing from one on his heel. We drink another beer as we wait for the albergue to open. Olivia and Victoria message they are walking with a new friend and ask Jana to reserve an extra bed.

A little after one, we head to our preferred albergue to find only three beds available. With her fluent Spanish, Jana phones a series of albergues until she finally finds one with six beds that can be reserved.

We walk along narrow streets filled with dozens of shops at street level with three or four stories of apartments above as we head to Albergue Nido de Ciguena. A gregarious guy welcomes us; his Russian-accented English is perfect. He checks us in and points out the various amenities on a city map.

This is the smallest albergue I've stayed in so far, with only fourteen beds. The lower level has an open plan with a cooking area, a dining table that can seat all fourteen guests, and a private courtyard. After our post-walk rituals are complete, Jana and I head off to shop for tonight's meal while Robbie heads to the town's medical clinic.

Jana and I walk back across the river to a decent-sized grocery store and buy bags of food for dinner and breakfast in the morning. Wine is surprisingly inexpensive on the Camino. A very drinkable bottle of wine costs 2€ or 3€ at the supermarket, and some bottles even cheaper. Walking through one of the best wine-producing regions in Spain has its benefits.

In front of the grocery store, we run into Robbie, who has come from the clinic. His foot is wrapped in bandages, and he can no longer secure his sandal.

"The doctor recommended resting for a couple of days and gave me some antibiotics," he says. "But he knew I would continue in the morning."

We tell him what we've got for dinner; then he heads inside for another couple of bottles of wine. By the time we get back from shopping, Olivia, Victoria, and their new friend, Julie, have arrived.

Our group takes six of the eight beds in our small room. I lie down to rest and find myself sweating. None of the albergues have had air conditioning, but until today I haven't been uncomfortable; regardless, I am soon asleep. I wake to an empty room and find a message on my phone: *We're drinking on the riverside terrace. Come join us.* The message was sent an hour ago. I message back, *I just woke up. Enjoy yourselves! I'll see you when you return.*

I head down to the courtyard to check on my clothes drying in the sun, and an Asian woman sitting on the patio with two children greets me. The kids look to be maybe ten and twelve.

"What led you to the Camino, half a world away from home?" I ask.

She tells me the Camino has become popular in her country over the past ten years or so. "There have been books written by South Koreans about their pilgrimage experiences, which brought awareness to the Camino. Last year there was even a TV show following one of the early K-Pop boy bands, as they reunited for a two-week trek on the Camino." She shares that the pilgrimage idea has excited her for years, and last year she thought it would be a great experience for her children. As we talk, her children quietly play a game of checkers.

"We started in Saint-Jean-Pied-de-Port and are walking about twenty kilometers each day," she says. "The kids each carry their own packs and haven't complained much at all. Physically, they are holding up better than me."

"Where will you end your walk?" I ask.

"Santiago de Compostela," she says with a smile.

"Wow! What a great adventure for your kids … and you," I say.

I find it interesting to learn what leads people from various countries to walk the Camino. The number of Americans doing the walk doubled the year after *The Way* came out. A similar story in Germany, where a popular entertainer/comedian walked the Camino and wrote a book about his journey, which later became a movie. As expected, German pilgrims flocked to the north of Spain after the movie's release in 2015.

The Camino has been the subject of popular books over the last few decades; Paulo Coelho's *The Pilgrimage* in 1987 and Shirley MacLaine's *The Camino* in 2001 were both big sellers, increasing awareness of this ancient journey of mind, body, and spirit.

Wine glasses fill as we begin preparations for our evening meal; vegetables chopped, bread and cheese sliced, a large pot of pasta put on to boil, the table set. Our dinner party soon expands to eight when a Dutch couple joins us. At the table tonight, there are people from four countries.

Over dinner, I learn Julie is a German expat now living in Sweden. With her physical appearance, light blond hair and fair skin, I'm sure she fits right in in the forested country to the north.

"While in high school, I fell in love with the culture and the people, so I decided to attend university there," Julie tells me. "After graduation, I found a job and stayed."

"It's great you can live and work in any of the EU countries," I say. "How many countries are there in the EU?"

"Twenty-eight, and yes, it is wonderful," she says. "I feel more at home in Sweden than I did growing up in Germany."

"I'm jealous," I say. "The options you have in most of Europe are not found anywhere else."

After scoops of ice cream are devoured and the table cleared, two middle-aged men walk into the albergue. They give an exhausted smile when the host says he has two beds left. These weary pilgrims tell of their difficulty finding beds; they must have checked every other place in town before stopping here. We offer them our leftovers, and they gratefully accept.

Conversations continue in the courtyard. As the last bottle of wine is emptied, we plan an ultra-early start for the morning.

DAY 9: NÁJERA > GRAÑÓN

*Take the chances a traveler has to take. In the end
you will be so much richer, so much stronger, so much
clearer, so much happier, and so much a better person
that all the risk and hardship will seem like nothing
compared to the knowledge and wisdom you have
gained.*

- Kent Nerburn, *Letters to My Son*

I join Jana and Olivia downstairs at five o'clock, our agreed departure
time. I grab an apple, banana, and two hard-boiled eggs, then pour a
glass of cold orange juice—this American-style breakfast courtesy of
yesterday's shopping excursion. Our extra early start is due to today's
destination, Grañón, being almost a thirty-kilometer walk, and the
temperature is forecasted to top one hundred degrees.

I watch as Olivia slathers Vaseline all over her feet and ask, "Where
did you learn that from?"

"I was complaining about a blister, and a guy recommended I put Vaseline on my feet each morning to avoid getting more," she says. "He gave me a tube of it. Since then, I've had no issues."

"Good to know," I say.

The three of us sit, waiting for the others to make it down. After twenty minutes, my patience wanes, and I tell the ladies, "I'm going to start walking. I'll wait for you at the first bar along the way."

My headlamp finally locates a Camino marker, and I exit the city alone. It feels a bit strange, starting by myself, but I am enjoying it. I decide to write a poem while walking to Azofra, the next town, which lies six kilometers ahead. Having written several poems over the last couple of years, I find the process enjoyable.

I periodically enter ideas into the Notes app on my phone as the sky before me slowly brightens. A little over an hour later, I reach the first bar on the Camino route and order a café con leche and a croissant. Sitting outside under the early morning sky, I start to draft my poem while waiting for the others to arrive. I order a second café con leche and drink it slowly before messaging Jana. She responds, *We didn't end up leaving until after six.* I message back, *I am going to keep walking. I'll see you in Grañón.* I complete my poem and resume my walk.

> The early morning air chills my skin, a star-filled sky above.
> The only sounds, a cricket chirping and gravel crushing beneath my dusty Altras.
> My soft, gray moisture-wicking T-shirt is already being put to work.
> My first sweet and satisfying café con leche is still kilometers away.
> Slowly, the sun rises behind me; my shadow leads the way.
> Thoughts floating; my sun-kissed legs ever moving.
> My journey has led me here, walking in a foreign land.
> My body full of vigor, my pace quickens, a smile fills my face.

My mind wanders while I continue in solitude, and I think about the events that led me here. Four years ago, my life having grown stale with little expectation for change, a time came when I was forced to make a decision that could change my life's direction—a point where the roads diverge, and I must choose.

Sitting behind my desk in Appleton, Wisconsin, my boss walks into my office and closes the door behind him before taking a seat.

"I have some bad news, Mike," he says. "The decision has been made to eliminate your position."

My jaw drops at the suddenness of this news, and I blink back tears.

"You can either accept a demotion or take a severance package," he says, handing me a folder with a few documents.

"Wow," I say under my breath. I open the folder and take out two documents. One shows the new salary and the other the severance being offered. This number, six months' salary to be paid in a lump sum, lessens the shock of the situation.

As I'm looking at the documents, my boss says, "You can give me your decision in the morning." I look up, and he says, "I know this must come as a shock."

"Yeah," I say curtly. We stand and shake hands, and he leaves.

I sit behind my desk and contemplate my options. With my family's recent downsizing, it is financially possible to live with the pay cut and still make ends meet. I think of my growing discontent, with any hopes of retiring early now diminished. Then I think about my dreams of traveling and engaging more with the world, and the possibilities life can offer. An unfocused picture appears of a different life, one not in the Midwest and its frigid winters. That afternoon, an idea forms about creating a new life, one that isn't the typical nine-to-five I have been living.

As the shock and uncertainty subside, excitement grows. This is an opportunity I never thought would come, and the timing couldn't be better. My wife and I have become empty nesters, after my son moved into his own place just months before. Our lease is up in less than two months, and my wife will soon be on summer vacation. I walk out of the building with a smile and a spring in my step.

"Let's sit on the couch," I say when I get home. My wife's eyes fill with tears as I share this life-changing news. I am unsure of what's racing through her mind, just as I am unsure of what her dreams for the future entail. "I'm thinking about taking the severance package," I say. "I've had some time to think about it—if we want to escape the Midwest for someplace warmer, this is our opportunity. The timing is perfect."

The only decision made this night: I will take the severance.

Not knowing where life will take us is refreshing. Over the next couple of days, I think of the options before us. Craving an adventure, I formulate a plan that will allow my wife and me to enjoy an adventure while developing a roadmap for the next stage of our lives. Knowing my inability to communicate effectively with her and to overcome objections before sharing my whole plan, I write a proposal to create a more exciting life. I spend days laying out my plan, incorporating quotes, basically preparing a sales pitch, so my wife can understand my vision. The plan is to end our lease, store all our belongings, and take a two-month journey out west, exploring different places where we might want to create a life. Our chance to break out of our mundane lives.

The day comes, and I share my well-thought-out plan. It falls flat. I try to convince her of how the changes would benefit her and not focus on my need to escape from our conventional life. She doesn't comprehend the depths of my angst. While I share that I need an adventure, I don't admit that nine-to-five living is slowly sucking the life from me. I keep a brave face, hiding my feelings of discontent.

My wife does agree to move out west, but only if I find a job first. Continuing my pattern of doing anything to avoid conflict, I cave to her wants instead of being more authentic to myself. I use the duty of being a good husband as an excuse, instead of moving ahead with changes that will renew my passion for life.

Through a connection with a former peer, I land a job in Portland, Oregon, and we find a three-month sublet in a nice neighborhood. The kicker is, I have to start in two weeks. No opportunity for the western adventure I was so excited about a few weeks earlier. I can already taste the bitterness of my choice.

On a dusty section of trail in the middle of a farmer's field, I encounter a young guy searching the ground for something in the dirt.

"What are you looking for?" I ask.

"I lost the rubber tip to my earbud," he says.

I help him look for a few minutes until he says, "Thanks, but I don't want to keep you."

"Good luck," I say, as I turn to go.

A while later, the Camino passes alongside the brilliant green of a well-maintained golf course before I reach the small town of Cirueña. It feels unlike any of the towns the route has passed through so far. It seems this area was constructed in the past twenty years, filled with a dozen similar apartment buildings. No history; so different after walking through villages and towns that felt like they'd been there for centuries. It's as if I am walking through an American suburb.

Before the arrows lead me out of town, I stop at a fountain in a park and rest under a small picnic shelter. A couple of minutes later, the guy I left searching catches up and tells me, "I didn't find it." Matt looks to be in his early twenties, is from England and is walking the entire Camino in less than three weeks. He says it was a last-minute decision to make this journey, as he's headed to Australia to work a six-month assignment as a nurse as soon as he finishes his walk. After topping off his bottles, he turns to head off and we share the requisite "Buen Camino." He hesitates but continues on before turning back again.

"You sounded muffled," he says. "Will you look in my ear to see if you see something?"

"Sure," I say. Using the flashlight on my phone, I make out something deep in his ear. "Yeah, I see something way down."

Now he's certain that when he took off his earbuds, the tip must have stayed in this ear, and when he put them back in, he must have switched the left and right, and the rubber tip of one bud pushed the other deep inside his ear canal.

"You don't happen to have any tweezers?" he asks.

"Sorry, no," I say.

Not sixty seconds later, four Italians—two men and two women—arrive at the shelter. Luckily one of the Italian women has tweezers. Yet another example where 'the Camino provides.' One of the Italian men attempts to remove the plastic tip from his ear but soon stops.

"It's too deep down. I don't want to hurt your eardrum," he says.

"Don't worry," Matt tells him. "Please try again."

After a couple of long minutes, the Italian pulls the object from his ear. Matt thanks him, and the Italians continue on their way.

"My hearing is still not right," he says. "I am going to a pharmacy when I get to Santo Domingo and see if they have any recommendations."

We walk together at what I think is a good pace, but soon Matt easily pulls away and says, "Maybe we will meet up again." I do the math: to cover almost 800 kilometers in three weeks, he'll have to complete almost a marathon each day.

Soon I catch up to another pilgrim carrying an unusually large pack. I slow and start a conversation with Alicia, a German, who, like Mirla, started her Camino hiking through the mountains in France before reaching Saint-Jean. Her pack, the biggest I've seen on the Camino, looks ready for a month-long excursion in the wilderness. I learn she grew up near the Austrian border, where her family would hike in the mountains every chance they got.

"I would need to drive for days from my childhood home to find any mountains," I say. "And none like your Alps."

When we take a short break, I lift her pack to check the weight. "Ugh ... If I were carrying your pack, this walk would get old, really quick."

"I could mail much of this ahead to Santiago, where the post office will hold a package, but I am used to carrying it," she says of the khaki-colored monster on her back.

"Are you stopping in Grañón?" I ask.

"No, I hope to reach Belorado," she says.

"How many kilometers?"

"About forty from where I started today."

"Yikes!" I exclaim. "I am enjoying the shorter days of walking, stopping earlier in the day and then relaxing in the afternoons."

Alicia doesn't mind long days; plus, she's on a time crunch and needs to get back home for the start of university. "I wish I was able to make more long-term connections," she says. "But I walk longer days than most." She outdistances almost everyone she meets.

I am not in Alicia's top-flight condition, but with my daily mileage walking in this heat, I feel the years melting away as I move toward Santiago. The knee and hip issues I've had to deal with in my middle years have vanished. The fact I have been hiking daily leading up to the

Camino has helped—I feel as strong and healthy as I have at any time in my life.

As we near Santo Domingo de la Calzada, Alicia says, "The cathedral here is known for giving shelter to chickens. I don't know the whole story, but I read it somewhere."

"It sounds interesting." Since I am in no hurry, I say, "I think I'll stop and check it out."

We walk along a narrow cobbled lane lined with stone buildings and soon reach the cathedral.

"I am going to keep going," she says. "I hope you enjoy your Camino."

"You too," I say. "It was nice talking with you."

I watch Alicia walk on and shake my head at the sight. It looks as though the pack has legs; her head is hidden from view.

I am surprised there is a fee to enter the church, but I pay a few euros, drop my bag in the designated area, and enter. I chuckle when I learn what 'chickens given shelter in a church' means compared to what was in my head. I'd expected to see chickens roaming amongst the pews, but what I find is an occasional clucking and a glass box on a wall. A small entryway from behind this box, located high in the church's nave, allows a couple of chickens to enter the showcase at their whim. While I entered the cathedral due to the novelty of seeing chickens, I find the entirety of the place stunning. Most impressive is yet another golden altar rising forty feet, with over a dozen intricately carved scenes. I also stroll through a small museum attached to the church, which shares the history of the chickens and other historical details of the area.

After leaving the church, I wander around the town and find it much larger than I first thought. A few blocks from the church, in a bustling commercial area, I cross a busy roadway, find a bench in a small tree-lined plaza, and enjoy a snack from a nearby grocery store.

As I make my way back to the cathedral and the yellow arrows, I find Matt chatting to Mirla outside a chocolate shop.

"Hey there," I say to Mirla. "Good to see you again."

"Matt was just sharing his recent mishap," she says.

"The pharmacist recommended some drops to use over the next few days," he says with a pained look. "I will find a doctor in the next big city if there is no improvement."

"Good luck," I say, then wish them both a "Buen Camino" and continue out of town.

The route runs alongside a busy highway for a few kilometers before heading through open fields. There is no shade this afternoon, and not even a hint of a breeze. My pace slows dramatically. I forgot to fill my water bottles after lunch, and now, an hour later, they're empty. I grab the apple from my pack and march on.

Relief finally arrives when I spy a steeple peeking above the horizon. After a short climb, I reach the village. The seven kilometers to Grañón have been the longest and hottest I have experienced thus far. I stop at the first place I find, a small trailer selling drinks and snacks.

I buy a Coca-Cola and am looking for a place to sit in the shade when, surprisingly, I spot Julie from last night. "I thought you were back with the others," I say as I take a seat across a small table from her.

"I took the bus from Nájera to Santo Domingo," she says. "I have been having a problem with my knee."

We talk for a bit, and I tell her, "I need to find a bed. I don't want the same issue as yesterday."

"There are two albergues here," she says, "one at the church, and the other a private albergue a little further down the main road."

"Where are you staying?" I ask.

"I called ahead and am staying at the private one," she says.

"Jana mentioned the albergue at the church," I say. "She said pilgrims must sleep on the floor, but there is also a communal meal which sounds intriguing. I am going to try there."

"Would you like to have lunch later?" she asks.

"That sounds great."

We plan to have lunch at a bar across from the church in thirty minutes. I head down the main road through town and find the church but struggle to find the entrance to the Albergue Saint Juan Bautista. Eventually, I find it on the backside of the church. This is a parroquial albergue, one that is run by a local church. I duck as I walk through a small archway and up a couple of flights of ancient stone stairs. I find a dozen pairs of footwear and a collection of poles lined up on a landing. I take off my shoes and proceed. I pass a large empty room, then climb a small flight of stairs and I am greeted by a sign which reads, in ten languages: *Welcome Pilgrim, make this your home.* I enter a beautifully rustic room with stone walls; in one corner, a fireplace surrounded by a small seating area, two large dining tables, and a small kitchen.

Two packs are resting on the floor and two pilgrims are seated at a table being checked in.

An Asian woman approaches. "Welcome to Grañón. Where are you from?" she asks.

"The States," I say.

"I am one of the hospitaleros," she says and points. "One of these two will get you checked in."

"Thank you," I say.

A minute later, one of the women walks toward me, her arms extended. We hug. "I will explain how this albergue works."

"Great," I say.

"One thing which makes this place so unique—we will not turn anyone away, even if we are full," she says. I smile to myself when I remember there are no beds to *fill*.

I take a seat, and she says, "Please enter your information into our register." I enter my information on ruled notebook paper with lines dividing the page into neat columns. "See those thick books?" she says, pointing to ten books, each three inches thick with a range of years written on each binding, "Those are all the registers from over the years."

"The communal meal will start at 7 p.m., when all pilgrims gather to decide on a menu, prepare the meal, and ready the tables," she says.

"That sounds fantastic," I say.

"Take one of the mats from the pile in the loft," she says, "and find a place. It will be packed pretty tight tonight."

"Thanks," I say.

I carry my pack up a sturdy flight of stairs. There is room for twenty mats when laid side by side. I need to shower and change before meeting Julie for lunch but find only one shower each for men and women. I am third in line and worry I may be late.

Eventually, I make my way to our assigned meeting place. Julie is reading a book at a table outside the bar. "I'm sorry I'm late," I say, "there was only one shower." I go into the bar and order a bocadillo. Julie and I enjoy a leisurely lunch, along with a few glasses of wine. Julie talks excitedly about her life in Sweden. While it is not required to change her citizenship to live there, she still wants to become a Swedish citizen. One of the requirements is to be fluent in the language.

"I've been studying for the last few years and am almost there," she says.

"I should learn another language," I say. "I took French in high school but don't remember much."

"Yes, you should. Americans, I find, don't usually have a second language," she says and takes a bite of some kind of pasta.

"Someday, I will," I say. "So, what book are you reading?"

"*Digital Minimalism,* by Cal Newport," she says. "I brought a couple of others too."

"What is digital minimalism?" I ask.

"It's using technology with more intention and purpose," she says. "On my Camino, I am only carrying a 'dumb' phone. I just use it to make reservations along the way."

She has eliminated all social media temptation and other mindless activities. She carries a small camera with her and says that is the only thing she misses about her smartphone. When back home, she tries to limit her digital footprint.

"I decided to go all-in while on the Camino," she says. "I want to get rid of the distractions and simply put one foot in front of the other and see where my mind goes."

"Wow, that's brilliant. I'm not sure I could do it."

"Sure you could," she says with a smile.

I finish my bocadillo and sip on my glass of now warm red wine.

While I like the ideas she shares, I wouldn't choose to walk the Camino without my iPhone. But our conversation makes me think about what it would be like to go without it. What do I use the internet on my phone for, anyway? Maps—but the route is well marked. The weather—but knowing it won't change it. Reviews of albergues—word of mouth works just fine. Maybe I *could* do without this most modern piece of technology on this ancient road.

I admire Julie's decision and appreciate the benefits of limiting technology in my life. One thing I am sure of … I spend way too much time on my phone back in the 'real world.' I hope to take this lesson from Julie and limit my attachment.

The two of us share stories, and we speak openly about the opposite sex and our past relationships. She sounds surprised when I question my appeal to women. Having never been confident in that way, I find our conversation enlightening.

While we talk, I get a message from Jana. *We just arrived in Santo Domingo. The heat destroyed us. Will be spending the night here.*

I am surprised, but I understand. Maybe it's a good thing, as I will be required to meet more new people tonight. I message back. *No worries. I'm sure we'll meet up soon.*

After our two-hour lunch, I say goodbye to Julie and head back across the street to rest before dinner.

At seven, I head down to the dining area. I find several Italians, including the four I met earlier at the picnic shelter with Matt, have already offered to cook the main course of spaghetti with a homemade sauce. I am one of many volunteers chopping vegetables for the salad: cucumbers, tomatoes, carrots, and lettuce. There will be forty hungry pilgrims plus our hosts dining tonight. More tables and chairs unfold to create enough seating.

I meet two young Italian guys from Rome who are walking the Camino together. Their names are almost too perfect: Leonardo and Lorenzo, both students at university.

Lorenzo asks, "Why are you walking the Camino?" His English is good, and his accent brings a poetic feel to his words.

"He asks this of everyone he meets," Leonardo chimes in.

I respond, "I feel unsettled, so I am taking a break, hoping to find a sign as to what direction I should head."

"You'll find more questions than answers here," Lorenzo tells me.

"Are you religious?" Leonardo asks.

"Not really," I say. "These days, I like to think kindness is my religion."

"I like that," Leonardo says.

Lorenzo tells me many Italians here tonight are on the Camino only for a fun time, while he and Leonardo seek a more spiritual experience.

I sense these two are deeply religious and wonder if they are considering a life in the church. I speak with them at length before the meal; like many conversations on the Camino, they can quickly get deep. As we talk, the aroma of the sauce cooking on the stove wafts through the air. I can't wait.

I talk briefly to several other pilgrims before dinner, including another Italian, Diana, who I learn walked to Santiago the previous year, but along a different route.

By eight o'clock, everything is ready, and the hosts introduce themselves and share a bit about their Camino experiences. This albergue is called a donativo. One of our hosts explains, "The food we are eating tonight has been paid for by the donations of the pilgrims who stayed here last night. Your donations will pay for those staying tomorrow." Each of our hosts has walked the Camino, returning to volunteer their time and share their love of it.

At dinner, I sit beside my two young Roman friends. Dinner is served family-style and is delicious. Conversations fill the room as the food and wine move around. A host takes a count of the nationalities here tonight. The Italians rule the evening, with over twenty of the forty pilgrims. Of the eight countries represented, I am the sole American. From my discussions, I learn August is the month most Italians take their annual holiday. One of the hosts says, "The percentages of nationalities who stay here varies greatly from day to day."

After dinner, large tubs of water are brought to each table, and the washing of dishes begins—another communal activity as conversations continue. With so many hands washing, rinsing, and drying, the clean dishes make their way back to their shelves in no time.

Not long after dinner concludes, we all make our way through narrow stone passageways to a balcony overlooking the church sanctuary. Everyone takes a candle, and once all have a flame, the lights go out. There is seating for everyone along the walls of the balcony, and a large circle forms. Each pilgrim is asked to share something of their Camino, in their language.

When my turn comes: "I am grateful for all the people I've met. I have shared more of myself with those along the Camino than I do back home. I have gotten to know people on a deeper level, and this has been one of the most unexpected gifts of my journey," I say. "The Camino seems to open you up and let the real you out."

As the circle continues, one Spanish couple shares a beautiful song with guitar accompaniment, the music echoing in the church below. My favorite share comes from Jonas, a twenty-something guy with hair like Fabio. Like the original pilgrims, his walk began from the front steps of his home in Germany. Today is his one-hundredth day walking, and he eloquently shares the lessons he has learned along his journey.

After we finish sharing, it seems as though we each hug every one of the other thirty-nine pilgrims before heading back to the albergue. When the lights go out at 10:30, I lie on my mat and reflect on my day. It has been one of the highlights of my Camino so far.

DAY 10: GRAÑÓN > VILLAFRANCA MONTES DE OCA

> We all want progress. But progress means
> getting nearer to the place you want to be and
> if you have taken a wrong turning, then to go
> forward does not get you any nearer. If you
> are on the wrong road, progress means doing
> an about-turn and walking back to the right
> road; and in that case, the man who turns
> back soonest is the most progressive man.
>
> ~ C.S. Lewis, *Mere Christianity*

I find myself walking alone in the dark once again. After leaving the lighted streets of this memorable village, my headlamp won't light up. It must have gotten switched on at some point while I was digging through my pack. I make do by using the flashlight on my phone, which luckily fits securely in the sternum strap on my pack and is enough to light my way. My phone is no longer in my pocket; I start to listen to music for the first time on my walk. No headphones are needed; I play an upbeat playlist through the speaker on my phone, just loud enough to hear it. I breathe in the cool air. No destination; I simply walk.

Last night's communal meal was a taste of a dream I've had for several years: to one day live in a community in union with others. Specifically, in what is known today as an Intentional Community, or Cohousing—a communal living arrangement started in Denmark in the 1960s, and a little like the hippy communes of the 1970s. Today, in these multigenerational communities, residents live in private spaces but are consciously committed to living as a community, shared meals in a 'common house' being just one example. During my days of searching for a different path to follow, I learned about these communities. However, my wife did not embrace my dream of this more communal life.

I know I envision life in such a community through a rose-colored lens. Still, my idealized vision is to one day experience life with others searching for a simple, yet more meaningful, existence. I hope there will be more evenings like last night, where everyone comes together to share a meal and a piece of themselves.

A couple of hours into my solo trek, I catch up to a woman strolling along. I slow to match her pace.

We make eye contact, and she says, "Bonjour!"

A smile spreads across my face, and I repeat her "Bonjour." Scarlett, 65, lives in Strasbourg, France. We talk as we move through open fields. This is her fourth year walking a part of the Camino. She comes back for a week each year, starting where she left off the previous year, hoping to eventually make it to Santiago.

"In past years, I have walked with my husband," she says, "but medical issues kept him home this time."

"I am sorry to hear that," I say.

"Let me tell you, I am enjoying the solitude," she says with a smile.

She is never in a hurry, is usually the last pilgrim to leave each morning, and walks for about fifteen kilometers before stopping for the day. Our conversation alights on many of the same themes as others did, as we share snippets of our lives. As we stroll side by side, many of the pilgrims I met last night pass us.

Scarlett is a practicing Buddhist, and our conversation touches on religion. She shares an analogy of waves being symbolic of our lives' stages, an ebb and flow. Our lives lead us towards the shore; at times, we retreat (the trough), but we keep moving forward (the crest). I love what she shares. An hour passes before I say "au revoir" and wish her a "Buen Camino."

As I walk on alone, I reflect on what I've picked up along my journey so far, astonished by my good fortune. I think how perfectly my life fits her analogy, the ebb and flow.

After my wife and I leave the Midwest, both excited for the change, the energy builds. Despite the fact I am jumping right back into a nine-to-five life, I am excited for a new life in Oregon. After the recent ebb, when my routine left me feeling defeated, now life is moving forward and building to another crest.

I love living in a beautiful part of the country and our small studio in a quaint old building, located in a walkable northwestern Portland neighborhood. I welcome the further downsizing in this new life. For weeks, I walk wide-eyed through our new surroundings; the vast outdoors of the Pacific Northwest is invigorating. We spend weekends exploring new places, and I start to get into better physical condition, helped by my solo walks to the Pittock Mansion after work.

But the honeymoon soon fades, and the reality of a job infinitely more stressful than my last intensifies the angst I felt before moving here. While I appreciate my wife's willingness to upend our old life, the resentment I feel about agreeing to jump back into a nine-to-five life eats away at me. The bitterness of my choice grows, and I start to shut down; my life enters yet another deep trough.

Earlier in the day, the Camino left La Rioja and entered Castillo y Leon, the largest of all of Spain's regions. The Camino will meander through this region for the next 400 kilometers. It is mid-morning when I reach the town of Belorado, fifteen kilometers into today's walk. I enjoy a store-bought breakfast while sitting under a large circle of trees planted in the town's main plaza. Three concentric circles of trees surround a gazebo, creating an umbrella of leaves, a parklike setting on a sea of concrete.

On my walk out of town, an elderly woman holds out her arm like a traffic cop to stop me. She smiles and extends a wrinkled hand and nods her head. I reach out, and she pours four fresh figs into my hand. I've learned to accept the generosity of strangers, not always for my sake but for those making the offering. I bite into one of the tiny pear-shaped purple fruits and find a warm, sweet, molasses taste accompanying the gritty texture.

Smiling, I say, "Muchas gracias." Despite speaking little English, she gives me a brief Spanish lesson before she opens her arms for a hug. We embrace.

She smiles broadly, revealing several missing teeth. I walk on; a smile remains glued on my face for at least the next kilometer.

My phone chimes with Jana's message: *Hey, how was your night? Do you know your destination for today?*

It was great. I loved the communal meal. Too bad you missed it. I don't know where I'll stop yet. You? I respond.

Belorado. If we can make it.

I just passed through there; it's a nice town. I'll stay in touch.

I enjoy walking with Jana, but I am not ready to slow down yet. I prefer walking with people, but I'm embracing this solo section, too. The axiom, "Everyone must walk their own Camino" resonates with me.

Approaching the small village of Villafranca Montes de Oca around noon, I have a decision to make. I can stop here, after twenty-two kilometers, or continue for another thirteen to the next town. Not wanting to suffer through another scorching afternoon, I stop.

The first albergue I find is attached to a hotel, San Anton Abad. At the front desk of this upscale hotel, I find the cost for a bed about twice the eight or so euros I have been paying, but it seems this is no ordinary albergue. An employee leads me through the hotel to a separate building that has all the amenities needed. No other pilgrims have checked in yet.

The first thing I do is take a long shower. It feels luxurious, standing under hot water, especially after yesterday's hurried rinsing. I shave my head, as I have done every other day, and scrub my skin clean. As I walk from the shower in my towel, I peer at my reflection in the steamy mirror and do a double take. I am taken aback by my appearance; my unkempt beard, sleeker cheeks, and tan face; an almost flat belly, and my chest and arms looking strong. I move closer and stare into eyes that remind me of my daughter's—blue-green with rings of gold. I think back to myself a decade earlier and question if that man would recognize the man in the mirror today.

After hanging my wash on a clothesline situated on a grassy hillside, I lie beneath a large tree and doze off. I wake to find a dozen others, some hanging laundry, others sitting in the grass, talking. As I head towards the albergue with my dry clothes in hand, an Italian woman I remember from last night asks if I would like to join her and her friends at the hotel bar. I gladly accept. On my way to the bar, another of the Italians also offers an invitation—so friendly, the Italians. I say, "Thanks," and follow. I find a seat at their table on the patio—actually, three tables pushed together—and join a dozen Italians and one German, Jonas, from last night. I can tell they have been at the bar for a while by the number of empty beer mugs on the table. A server appears, and most of the table orders a beer. When she returns, one of the Italians, Alessio, the one who removed Matt's earbud, picks up the tab.

There are small plates of food on the table, and someone orders more, all of which are shared amongst us all. Under a hot sun, the time for another round comes soon; I pick up the tab this time. The Italians toast 'to new friends' and thank me. Most of this afternoon's gesture-filled conversations are in Italian. I assume most of this group knew one another from back home and came here together but soon learn that everyone started their walk alone, except one married couple. This group grew as the days passed, to create this large 'Camino family.' They don't all start the day together; most walk at their own pace during the day, but they end each day in the same town. Their popular Italian guidebook lists specific stages, and they follow its recommended itinerary.

I chat with many of the Italians, at least those who speak English, while the beer keeps flowing. I lose count of how many beers I've consumed. As evening approaches, I find this group already has a reservation at the hotel restaurant. They invite me to join, and one of the women goes to add one to their reservation.

A while later, we head to the restaurant and are seated at two large tables. I sit beside Raffaella, the kind woman who first invited me, who translates for me as needed. While she isn't fluent, her English is good. I learn that Alessio, who fits the picture in my mind of a confident Italian male, travels to the U.S. often for his job and speaks perfect English. He has the month of August off, like many Italians. This year he chose to spend his holiday on the Camino.

The first of our four courses arrives, along with several bottles of wine. The food keeps coming, and the conversations continue. Someone jokes about the married guy's snoring, which they say was extremely loud last night. The snorer only laughs, reveling in their suffering. The crowd offers sympathy to his wife, who will have to deal with it long after the group sleeping arrangements on the Camino are over.

Since I was sleeping in the loft with this group last night, someone asks me, "Did he keep you up last night?"

I respond, "I didn't hear a thing." One of the benefits of being deaf in one ear is that I sleep like a baby when I put my good ear to the pillow.

When the conversation turns to tomorrow, I say, "I am headed to Burgos."

"That is way too far." One of the men shakes his head and says, "It is thirty-eight kilometers."

"I know, but I've walked almost that far before," I say. "I plan on getting an early start."

Rafaella says, "Our book recommends stopping in Cardeñuela Riopico, which is twenty-three kilometers ahead."

"It is a long way, but Burgos is a large city, and I am thinking of spending an extra day there to explore," I say. I have been thinking of stopping for a day to let Jana catch up.

The food tonight is delicious, the best yet on my Camino, and the equally tasty Rioja doesn't stop flowing. I find today's drinking has been the norm for these Italians. They are on summer vacation, and they treat every day like a party.

I stumble my way back to my bed through this three-star hotel. I have enjoyed my afternoon and evening with the Italians, but I couldn't repeat it day after day.

DAY 11: VILLAFRANCA MONTES DE OCA > BURGOS

Too often we underestimate the power of a
touch, a smile, a kind word, a listening ear,
an honest compliment, or the smallest act of
caring, all of which have the potential to turn
a life around.

~ Leo Buscaglia

I walk out the door into a light rain. I stop, dig out my rain gear for the first time since crossing the Pyrenees, and begin walking. My head is a bit cloudy, but I find walking in the fresh air and rain a fantastic antidote for my hangover. Walking in the dark, Apple's Acoustic Chill Playlist drowns out any sounds as I ascend a sloping earthen path, no headlamps ahead or behind. After this brief climb, the trail tucks into a grove of trees, and the smell of the damp earth fills the air. When a picnic table appears, I stop for a break. I sit eating cookies and a banana in the rain as the night sky begins to fade.

I turn and see a smiling face appear beneath the hood of a bright yellow rain jacket. It is a young German I met only briefly in Grañón. I remember her laughter that night and that she was quick to smile, but I don't know much more than her name.

"I love your smile, Annika," I shout, as I turn off the music. "You're always so happy." I throw on my pack and wait for her.

"Thanks! I love the Camino and so happy to be here," she says with a hint of a German accent. We step back onto the trail.

"It is nice to see you again," she says. "Did you stay at the hotel?"

"Yeah, in the albergue section," I say.

"Me too."

"Are you always so upbeat and cheerful?" I ask as we walk.

"Me? No!" she says, shaking her head. "Back home, I am not this way at all."

"*Really?*" Of all the people I've met so far, I remember you as so positive, with a contagious smile."

"That's so nice to hear," she says, her smile widening further still. "Maybe it is because I am away from home that I am so happy. "

"What? You're not happy back home?"

"Not really," she says. "I usually feel a bit depressed. I think in part because I'm still living at home."

I am surprised by her honest response and unsure of how to respond. A couple of seconds pass. "I am surprised to hear that," I say. "Do you attend university?"

"No, but I am hoping to start an art program to study photography this fall."

"That sounds interesting," I say.

"I was accepted two years ago, but I didn't start," she says. "So, I had to reapply and am still waiting on my acceptance."

"I'm sure you'll get in. It sounds like you have a passion for photography."

"I do love it, but I haven't made it a priority," she says. "For the last couple of years, I have been working at a hotel and not doing much else."

"I understand not knowing what direction to take," I say. "Is that why you're on the Camino?"

"I guess I wanted to do something different. I got my job to let me take a month off to walk the Camino. If they said no, I was going to quit."

"Good for you," I say with a nod. "I worked for decades in a job I didn't really enjoy … but it paid the bills. I wish I had found something I had a passion for when I was your age."

We continue walking beneath a gloomy sky, down a steep hill, as our path carves through a vast forest. The path climbing up from the valley below is visible straight ahead. We cross a small bridge over a fast-flowing stream before beginning our ascent.

When I start to pull ahead of Annika, I turn and say, "I'll see you at the top."

A few minutes after me, Annika arrives. "That was steep," she says on a heavy exhale. She comes to a stop to catch her breath and places her hands on her hips.

"According to the elevation chart, we have another climb later on," I warn.

For now, the path flattens out and we walk on a wide dirt road through a relatively young forest. Continuing our conversation, I say, "I'm normally an optimistic person and try to find the bright side of things, but I've had times throughout my life when I've struggled and was just going through the motions."

"What do you mean, going through the motions?"

"Working long days, followed by a long commute. I would come home, crash on the couch, and distract myself by watching Netflix for hours. A day which I repeated over and over," I say, cringing at the memory. "I wasn't sure how my life would change."

"It does sound depressing," she says.

"Yeah, but eventually, things got better," I say. "Why do you think you're not in a good place emotionally back home?"

"I think depression runs in my family. I've felt depressed for the last couple of years but don't know why," she says. "It's affected my relationship with my parents … and especially my younger sister. I have not treated them well. I hope to figure some things out on this trip."

"I'm sure if you're honest with them, are sincere, and take responsibility, they'll be understanding," I say. "You can heal those wounds."

"I hope so. I am most worried about my younger sister, as I have been the worst to her."

"It may take some time, but it sounds like it's important to you."

She nods firmly. "It is."

The rain has stopped, and when we come across a collection of totem poles carved from dead trees, we stop and pack away our rain jackets.

"One thing I have found on Camino is how we change when we're here," I say. "I think people become the kind of person they want to be … or maybe are meant to be … while on the Camino."

"That's interesting," she says.

"Soooo, Annika, that means inside you're meant to be this smiling, upbeat young woman I've met."

Annika smiles and says, "I hope so."

"Take this person you're becoming on the Camino and be that person back home." I give her a smirk and add, "Easier said than done."

I haven't glimpsed another soul other than Annika since stepping foot from the albergue. We must have been the first two to leave Villafranca this morning, and we are walking briskly.

"Are you planning to make it to Burgos?" I ask.

"No! That's way too far. I was planning on walking about twenty-five kilometers today."

After thirteen kilometers, we reach a small hamlet, San Juan de Ortega, but keep moving. Thirty minutes later, we enter the village of Agés and walk into an establishment with tables sitting empty outside. We find it part bar, part deli, with a handful of grocery items for sale.

The husband and wife, who I assume own the place, are delightful. Despite the language barrier, I walk out with a custom-made ham bocadillo measuring six inches square with an apple, orange, and chips. Unlike the other bocadillos I've eaten, this one has cheese, tomatoes, a drizzle of olive oil, and is sliced on the diagonal. Annika buys an apple and an energy bar.

Outside, we drop our bags next to a table and collapse into chairs.

"Please take half this sandwich," I beg.

At first she refuses, but eventually gives in to my pleas.

Together, we walk under a clearing blue sky along an asphalt roadway, open fields on both sides, with cars zipping by every few minutes.

"You mentioned before you had times when you struggled," Annika says. "What did you do to change?"

"Well, the last time was a few years ago. It took me some time to make changes. Eventually, I realized I had to take responsibility for my happiness and not worry about what others would say."

"Like who?" she asks.

"I guess it was just my wife," I say with a shrug.

"What did you do?"

"Well … I started out taking solo weekend backpacking trips. I signed up for classes at a local community college—and you'll appreciate this. The first class I signed up for was photography."

"Then you were happy?" she asks, hesitatingly.

"Well, ultimately, I had to quit a job I hated and took an extended solo road trip across much of the U.S., kind of like you did coming here," I say. "After that, I started a job I didn't hate, and things got better."

"I'm glad you got through it," she says. "You seem happy now."

"Thanks, I am," I say. "So, what did your family think when you told them you were coming here?"

"My parents were supportive but were worried about me going alone," she says. "What did your wife say when you left on your cross-country trip?"

"I don't think she understood why I wasn't happy. But she seemed okay with the changes I was making. Those initial changes led to more. I stopped watching as much television and started reading more and thought about the bigger questions in life."

"What big questions?"

"You know, like, what's my purpose in life? What is the meaning of life? Not that I have found any answers yet, but I finally started asking the questions, at least. But making those changes, I felt like I was growing as a person and happier with myself for doing what was best for me."

"I am not there yet," she says. "I only want to find a job I like."

"What's your dream job?"

A smile washes across her face. "Being a photographer for *National Geographic*. I like taking pictures of animals and nature."

"I love it. Follow your passion … even if it is a hobby just to start with," I say. "There's a quote I read, 'All you need to be happy in life is something to be enthusiastic about.' I've found I am happiest when I have that something."

"What is yours?"

"It's been different things, and sometimes I don't have an enthusiasm for anything—that's when I struggle. Lately, it's been travel, largely because I get to meet new people like you."

Finally, an arrow points to a narrow dirt path, and we leave the busy road and head towards a line of trees. We cross over an old stone bridge, a small creek flowing beneath, then past a small playground with several empty picnic tables. Our pace remains brisk, despite the increasing temperature, as we pass through the town of Atapuerca.

The hill shown on the elevation chart arrives in the early afternoon. We have an ankle-twisting uphill climb on rocky terrain. Next to the trail, a short, rusty barbed-wire fence is marked with signs stating that a *Zona Militar* lies on the other side. We finally reach a high plateau, where we find a thirty-foot-tall cross standing guard.

"Have you done much hiking in the mountains?" I ask.

"Besides the walk over the Pyrenees? No," she says. "It's pretty flat in the north of Germany, where I live."

"I used to live in a flat part of the States and didn't do much hiking. But then I moved to the West Coast and fell in love with the mountains. I love hiking and climbing in the mountains to challenge myself. Hey, that's something else I'm enthusiastic about."

"I do love walking here on the Camino," she says. "I need to start taking long walks back home."

"Good idea," I say. "It's said walking stimulates thinking … have you found that to be the case on your Camino?"

"Definitely. It's part of the reason I'm here. I wanted time away from my life back home to decide what I want to do."

"It's the same for me. I'm hoping to find some clarity," I say. "Though one of the young Italian guys back in Grañón told me I'll end up with more questions than answers. I guess I'll find out."

According to my calculations, Burgos is still fourteen kilometers ahead, but the city is visible in the distance on our descent. I long ago sweated through the back of my shirt, and now it feels like I could wring out an entire cup of sweat. There is little shade to be had; only the occasional cloud floating above to filter the sun's rays.

"I'm stopping for the day in the next town. I'm too hot and too tired," Annika says as we walk along a quiet country lane.

"I can't say I blame you, but I'm going to keep going."

When we reach Cardeñuela Riopico, I follow Annika as she navigates to her chosen albergue. Despite the temptation to stay when I find it has a small swimming pool, I decide to press on.

"I enjoyed talking to you," I say and give Annika a sweaty but meaningful hug outside.

"I did too," she says. "I probably won't see you again, so have a 'Buen Camino.'"

"Yes, Buen Camino." I turn to continue on.

After leaving Annika, I think of our brief encounter and her struggles back home. I wish the best for this tender soul and pray she can navigate her way to becoming the smiling, happy young woman she yearns to be.

Walking alone, my mind settles on a day just over two years ago—another of those moments that would eventually lead me here. My wife and I drive to Bend, Oregon, to visit our daughter, who also headed west a year after our move. The three of us are hiking nearby at Smith Rock State Park, a stunningly beautiful place. The weather is perfect, and we walk together and watch dozens of rock climbers clinging to the sides of the many rock faces that make Smith Rock so special. I'm enjoying our walk along a river path when we reach an uphill section with switchbacks that go up and over, leading back to the start of our hike.

"Let's turn around," my wife says. "I don't want to do that climb."

"It's less than 600 feet. That's less than the hike to Pittock. You've done that many times," I say.

"I don't want to go uphill," she says. "You two go ahead; I'll meet you at the car."

My daughter and I look at one another with looks of resignation. My daughter says, "We are not going without you." We turn around and head back. It is still a lovely walk, but I am disappointed with my wife's refusal to make an effort. It is a symbolic moment for me. If I want to challenge myself and make a climb to something more significant, it may not be with my wife.

As I near the large city ahead, I remember one of the Italians last night mentioning an alternative route into Burgos. It supposedly eliminates hours of walking on asphalt through industrial and urban areas. I spend a couple of minutes on my phone and figure out a route that runs along the Arlanzón River. I follow the official Camino as it exits the small village of Orbaneja Riopico and crosses over a major highway. After the overpass, I take a left, unmarked by any signage, while the official route continues straight.

I'm soon walking through the town of Castanares, and I navigate using the satellite view on my phone to a path that runs alongside the highway for a short time before heading into a large recreational area and a dirt path alongside the river. I pass a few people, but not one is carrying a pack. My feet feel the effects of the thirty-plus kilometers already walked, and I stop briefly at a sandy beach, where I wade into the water and cool my feet. I switch into my hiking sandals before starting out for the final kilometers. This path takes me into the heart of Burgos, and I veer off near a pedestrian bridge.

Why is this not the official route, or at least marked as an alternative? From the bridge, I have only a short walk past a stunning cathedral to the municipal albergue.

It's after three o'clock when I nervously approach the front desk— I'd heard this place fills up early.

"I would like a bed, please," I say to a gray-haired man behind the desk.

"Si. Passport and credentiale," he says.

I blow out my breath in relief.

The albergue has five floors, the top four filled with 150 beds. After getting my bunk assignment, I take the elevator to the top floor and find my friends Lorenzo and Leonardo a couple of bunks away.

"Ciao," I say. "How are you guys?"

Lorenzo, lying on a top bunk, says, "Good. It was a long walk today."

We chat before I begin my post-walk chores. Later, while I rest on my bunk, most of the Italians from last night arrive. I find out a couple of the guys did walk the entire way, but most took a bus for part of today's stage.

Burgos is an old city but vibrant, and it oozes with charm. The massive Plaza Major is where most of the action is, surrounded by many restaurants, bars, and shops. I wander alone through narrow cobbled streets bustling with locals, tourists, and pilgrims, before stopping at a bar. In a glass case on the bar, I find a wide variety of small plates offered, each only a couple of bites, and according to a chalkboard sign, these plates are called *pinchos*.

"Una copa de vino tinto," I say and point to several unknown delicacies. After the second round of tasty pinchos, I meander through the streets, stopping only when the temptation of a patisserie window filled with deliciousness is too great to pass. I walk along the river promenade, past a row of large hedges carved into intricate shapes, eating my cream-filled pastry. The temperature is perfect, and the sky isn't yet dark, but my tired feet lead me to bed long before any possible curfew.

In my days since separating from Jana and company, I have enjoyed meeting new friends. I am glad about those experiences, but I want to walk with others again. I don't feel like joining the Italian group on holiday, and Lorenzo and Leonardo are too tight a duo. It seems Jana would still like to walk together, and I am looking forward to seeing her again. I message Jana, *I will be spending tomorrow in Burgos. Maybe we can meet up when you arrive tomorrow.*

After Burgos, the Camino travels through a desolate expanse for the next 200 kilometers. The Meseta is the name given to central Spain's large, flat plains, with vistas of wheatfields lying in all directions. The distance between towns is greater, and the services far fewer. Some pilgrims have said they are skipping this barren section. I will not jump ahead; for some reason I can't quite identify, I feel an urgency to walk every step along my journey to Santiago de Compostela.

DAY 12: BURGOS > SAN ANTON

You don't meet people by accident. They are
meant to cross your path for a reason.

~ Anonymous

Sitting at one of many long tables in the albergue's dining area with my pack, I make eye contact with a familiar face from Grañón. Diana is Italian, with medium-length dark brown hair and a radiant smile. She walks towards me, and I stand to greet her. We talk briefly about our last couple of days.

"Would you like to start our day walking together?" she asks, her obvious Italian accent intriguing.

"Oh … I would love to, but I am waiting on some others who I had walked with before. I told them I would wait in Burgos, so I am planning on spending the day here," I say.

"That is okay. I am sure we will see each other again."

"I hope so!"

Diana turns, puts on her pack, and heads out.

I sit back down to finish my vending-machine breakfast of cookies and a hot chocolate and think about Diana's offer. I would have enjoyed getting to know her; she seems super friendly, and it would add to my experience on the Camino. Ten minutes later, my mind has changed; I want to walk with Diana. A sense of urgency to catch her overtakes me. Luckily my bag is already packed, so I throw it on and walk briskly out the door.

I don't know where the nearest Camino marker is, and I start walking at a hurried pace in the direction I think should lead me to the official route. I pass the beautiful cathedral that I intentionally didn't visit yesterday, thinking I would have all of today to do so. I head down a long flight of steps and zigzag through narrow streets before reaching the river I walked along yesterday. I open the mapping app on my phone to find I will meet up with the route if I keep along the river. My pace continues, and my heart races. The sidewalks are full of pedestrians, but surprisingly, no one is carrying a large pack. After twenty minutes at my hurried pace, I am still in this large city, already tired, and haven't found her. Maybe she stopped at a bar before leaving town and is now behind me.

Despite the fact I haven't found Diana, I commit to keep going. I message Jana: *I couldn't sit still and decided to keep walking. I hope to meet up soon.*

Walking through the University of Burgos along a busy road leading out of the city, I catch sight of someone a block ahead with a large pack, crossing to the other side. It must be Diana. I hasten my already brisk pace.

Diana doesn't know I am behind her, and soon, I pull up next to her. We make eye contact, and I turn my palms up and shrug my shoulders. "I thought it would be nice to get to know you. Plus, the thought of spending the day in Burgos alone wasn't appealing."

Together, we head through open fields, talking under a cloudy sky, a morning chill still hanging in the air. We walk under two busy highway overpasses before more fields of wheat. We pass through one small town and then another. As we're leaving the sleepy town of Rabé de las Calzadas, we pass Albert Einstein, Mahatma Gandhi and Martin Luther

King Jr. peering towards Santiago.

"Wow, it's beautiful," Diana says as we pass the beautifully painted mural that fills one side of a long, single-story building.

"It sure is … I am surprised to find it in this small Spanish town," I say.

Pilgrims are spread out along the route in both directions. Diana and I walk at a better-than-average pace and are soon passing others. We close in on one couple holding hands as they walk, each using one of a pair of hiking poles. Passing this young Asian couple, we all exchange a "Buen Camino." It's interesting how everyone walks in their own way, and I wonder if these young lovers are walking the entire Camino hand in hand.

In Grañón, I learned Diana had walked to Santiago before, but this is her first time on the route which starts from Saint-Jean-Pied-de-Port. While the common term for walking to Santiago is the *Camino de Santiago*, this term encompasses the many routes to Santiago from all across Spain and a handful of other countries. The path we are on is the Camino Frances, so named because of its originating point in France. Last year, Diane walked the Camino Portuguese, starting her journey in Lisbon.

"All the different Camino routes head towards Santiago de Compostela, but the terrain on each is very different," Diana says.

"What was it like on the Portuguese?" I ask.

"It went through many different landscapes, but my favorite was an alternative route I took that followed the coast for a week."

"Wow. It sounds beautiful."

"It was … the whole walk was amazing."

"So, you're back again," I say.

"This route is much more crowded," she says. "Last year, it was quieter. I liked that better. This is the busiest of all the roads to Santiago."

"Yeah, there are way more people here than I expected."

As we walk through this flat and desolate landscape, Diana says, "This time of the year, the heat can make things dangerous. That is why some are taking the bus to León."

"Do you think it could get even hotter?" I ask.

She laughs. "Maybe not, but there are fewer places to stop and rest."

"Did you consider skipping it?" I ask.

"No. I'm young and used to the heat. Did you?"

"Nope," I say as we walk under a clearing sky.

"The Meseta is the second of the three stages of personal growth which occurs along the Camino," Diana says. "The focus here is on the mind."

"What was the first?" I ask.

"The body," she says. "Before the Meseta, a pilgrim's body has been growing accustomed to walking many hours each day."

"Some bodies don't hold up too well," I say, thinking of Robbie.

"Of course, many will deal with some physical problems during the first weeks," she says.

The most common issues are blisters or sore joints and muscles. Hopefully, most are on the mend by the time they reach Burgos and can move through the Meseta with their body strong, leaving their mind free to wander and drift inwards.

But, like Robbie, many are still dealing with physical issues, most in their feet or knees. In the past week I have witnessed scores of wrapped or braced knees and far more blisters than I can count. Hopefully, a day or two of rest, and plenty of ibuprofen, a staple for many on long hikes, will suffice, and the ailing pilgrims can continue on their journey.

I ask Diana, "Have you had any physical issues on your walk so far?"

"No, but I had blisters last year when I walked in boots, so I switched to running shoes this time, and I haven't had any problems so far. You?"

"Thankfully, no," I say.

We pass through the village of Hornillo del Camino, along the only street in town. It is lined with old stone buildings, one of which has two dozen flowerpots of varying colors magically attached to its stone wall. The blooming flowers add a splash of color to an otherwise dull stretch of brown. We pass a small municipal albergue and a church, its three-story bell tower rising higher than anything else for miles.

As we walk through empty fields, Diana tells me she has one semester left to finish her graduate degree in psychology and will be starting her professional career soon.

"Travel has always been my favorite hobby," she says. "Over the last ten years, I have traveled the world at every opportunity."

"That's great," I say. "I would love to travel like that."

"So far, I've visited twenty-five countries," she says.

"Whoa. I'm impressed. Do you always travel solo?"

"Most of the time, but a few trips have been with family and friends," she replies. "I prefer traveling alone. It has helped me learn more about myself and made me a better person … or at least more open-minded."

"I like that," I say. "May I ask how old you are?"

"Thirty-one."

"Man … my life is so different from yours. I had two kids by the time I was your age, and I didn't go on any of your exciting travels."

"I may be moving onto that stage soon," she says. "My boyfriend talks about marriage and kids."

"Is he your age?"

"No, he's five years older and already settled in his career."

"But you're ready for marriage and kids now?"

Diana shrugs and says, "I want kids, but I am in no rush, but he's ready now."

"Does he like to travel too?"

"Yes, but he prefers staying closer to home."

"Are you going to miss your freedom to travel?"

"Sure, but I am excited to have kids one day," she says. "I will continue to travel, just not as much."

The afternoon sun is high overhead, and Diana takes a blue buff off her wrist and uses it as a headband and covers her hair. Its color is the same shade of blue as the frames of her sunglasses.

"Nice look," I say.

She flashes her ever-ready smile, highlighting perfect white teeth.

"As my kids got older, I looked back now and then at the things I wished I had done earlier."

"Like what?" she asks.

"Mostly travel," I say. "By the time they'd grown, I was tired of going through the motions. My wife and I had different visions for our lives."

"I can understand that … but I have always done what I wanted to do."

"It's great you've always been sure of your direction," I say.

"It will be a change to have to share decisions when I am married. I have gotten used to doing everything my way."

"Compromise is important in a relationship, but it got harder for me as the years passed. A couple of years after my kids were on their own, I felt the need to make a drastic change in my life."

"What change?"

"I imagined a life of adventure and travel and was willing to risk everything to head in that direction. Even though I loved my wife, the idea of continuing with my *normal* life was killing me."

I know now that the decision to risk everything was the first step in the journey that led me here to the Camino.

I continue, "There is a quote by an American writer, Tim Ferris; it goes something like, 'A person's happiness in life can be measured by the number of difficult conversations they are willing to have.' I agree."

"What was your difficult conversation?"

"Telling my wife I wanted to quit my job and travel full-time. It was a shock to her."

"I would think so," she says, with a raised brow.

"Yeah, I know. It took a long time to build up the courage to do it. She knew I wasn't happy with the monotonous life we were living, but she couldn't imagine living any differently."

"What did you do?"

"We got divorced. Looking back, I'm sure I could have handled it differently and found a compromise to quench my need for change, but I followed my instincts."

"How long were you married?"

"Twenty-eight years," I say. "She didn't crave adventure and wasn't willing to explore the possibilities. Maybe deep down, she may have wanted a more exciting life, but her fear of the unknown was too great."

"It had to be more complicated than that."

"Not really. At the end of this single conversation, we agreed to divorce."

"Wow! Was it difficult?"

"No ... she was understanding. Ours was a friendly divorce. It was finalized less than two months after that conversation. There were no lawyers; with no kids underfoot and no house, we spent two hours with a mediator to reach an agreement. We actually held hands and laughed, along with a few tears, as we walked away from the office after signing our final divorce papers in Portland, Oregon."

"It would not be that easy in Italy," she says.

"Ours was an exception," I say. "It's normally not like that in the States, either."

"You're lucky."

"I know. I'm grateful that she was so understanding. But guilt has followed me for leaving a caring woman who expected to grow old with the guy she met and married in college."

"Do you still talk to her?"

"Yeah, we get along. We still joke about something I told her during our difficult conversation: 'I just want you to want what I want.' Hopefully, I've become less selfish in the years since."

"Sometimes you need to be selfish," she says.

"Maybe. While I have enjoyed the freedom of doing whatever I want, it wasn't what I sought. Seeking a more adventurous life was what finally pushed me over the edge."

This afternoon, fewer and fewer pilgrims are in view; we must have outrun most of those who started the day in Burgos. There is nothing but open fields in all directions as we continue along the long, flat, straight path we have been walking on for hours. I am getting hotter and more tired with each step, when suddenly the route takes a slight turn and dips, the town of Hontanas coming into view. "Finally," I say as I wipe sweat from my brow. The town had been hiding below the horizon. It is after one o'clock, and we stop at the first bar we come to.

We dump our packs, and I quickly remove my shoes and socks— relief! My sweaty feet can finally breathe. I enter the bar in my bare feet for a Coke and a bag of chips. We sit in the shade of an awning to rest.

"This is where my guidebook suggests, but there is another place not far ahead," she says.

"I'm beat," I say. "We've walked thirty-one kilometers in the heat."

"It will be busy here. I like to stay in the quieter places along the way, and not where all the other Italians stay," she says. "But if you can't go on, I will stay here."

During our thirty-minute break, we agree on the municipal.

We walk down a narrow lane past all the other albergues in town to our chosen accommodation. We find a note tacked to the door. The albergue will be closed until next week. Diana says, "It is a sign from the Camino gods."

I laugh and say, "I agree; we should keep going." After our lengthy break, feeling cooled and rested, I am ready for another hour of walking. I have no idea what town is ahead, but I trust Diana to find us beds for tonight.

"There is an albergue located in the ruins of an ancient pilgrim hospital from the twelfth century up ahead," Diana says.

"Sounds good to me," I say.

Then she adds, "But there is no electricity or hot water." Her guidebook gives a brief description of the accommodations along the Way.

"Sure, we can check it out," I say, though the lack of hot water gives me pause.

Eventually, our route leaves the gravel path and merges with a desolate roadway; visible ahead, a large stone arch stretches over the road. As we approach, the arch seems to grow taller. When we arrive, we realize the ancient arch must reach at least fifty feet and connects to the remnants of a centuries-old structure that appears to have once been a grand church. We've reached Diana's chosen accommodation, Convento de San Anton.

"What an amazing sight," I say.

We follow an arrow to the left and find the entrance to the ruins. It looks to be three-quarters of a beautiful structure; where the roof once was, is now open to a blue sky. Once filled with glass, tall arches take up one end of the ruins, and stone steps lead to what I imagine was the altar. Inside these ruins, a low-slung roof and stone walls are attached to the original wall, creating three simple rooms.

"I'm in. Let's stay," I say, as a man dressed in all black, with long graying black hair, tied back, and a gray goatee, approaches us.

He reminds me of a gypsy, and I assume he owns the place. He speaks little English, but luckily Diana speaks some Spanish. His name is Alberto. He leads us through the middle door, and we take seats in a room with a large dining table and small kitchen area. We hand over our credentials, and Alberto points to the donation box, indicating that this is another donativo albergue. I am excited to learn there will be another communal meal tonight. He leads us to a bunk room with six old army-style bunks.

After an invigorating shower, I do laundry, then take a nap—the sleeping quarters cooled by the ancient stone wall next to me. After I wake, I find a green metal bench in the center of the ruins and read about this place's history from a book I found in the dining room. Originally built to care for pilgrims traveling to Santiago, this convent hospital sat abandoned for many generations before being turned into an albergue forty years earlier.

Sitting in the center of what feels like a huge courtyard, surrounded by ancient stone walls, I soak in the history. The ground is covered in gravel. A few large stones create a shallow ledge to account for a change in elevation. There are potted plants scattered about, a picnic table, and a campfire ring. This place is spellbinding.

Later, Alberto walks around, offering wine in clay cups to the smattering of pilgrims out in the courtyard. A second volunteer, a younger woman, also dressed for the part in flowing hippy apparel, helps by pouring the wine. I learn Alberto does not own the albergue but is a hospitalero from the south of Spain who spends a month volunteering here every summer.

Many pilgrims stop and look around, most deciding *not* to stay. It seems the lack of electricity or hot water weeds out more than a few potential guests. I am amazed at the stark difference between my accommodations last night—a large, modern place with 150 beds—and tonight's rustic accommodations, with twelve beds and no electricity.

As evening approaches, Alberto gathers the eight of us who have decided to stay. In the dining area, everyone pitches in to prepare our meal. One of those staying, Glenda from Sardinia, who cannot eat gluten, says, "I will make risotto as a course for tonight's dinner." Two other pilgrims volunteer to cook chicken on a stovetop fueled by propane. Alberto had purchased the poultry earlier today in Burgos, as there is no refrigeration here. Diana sets the table while a woman from

Amsterdam and I prepare the salad. We all share stories of our time on the Camino.

When dinner is ready to be served, I sit next to the second volunteer, Cosima (KOH-see-ma), who I find is from Germany.

She says to me, "I am walking the Camino too. I started in Le Puy (France) two months ago. I stayed here a couple of weeks ago on my walk. A week later, I contacted Alberto and asked if I could return to rest for a few days. He welcomed me back, and I have been helping with the hosting duties."

"How long have you been back?" I ask.

"Three days," she says. "I will be heading back to where I left off soon," she says.

As this is a donativo, like Grañón, we give thanks to the pilgrims from last night for our meal. Sitting around the table tonight: two Germans, a Kiwi, a Brazilian, a Dutch woman, two Italians, two Americans and Alberto, the only one from our host country. Besides myself, the other American is a young woman walking with a German guy. These two twenty-somethings met in Roncesvalles and are in the midst of a Camino romance.

As we enjoy dinner, I learn this primitive albergue is rarely at capacity. I am grateful to Diana for leading us here. We each tell a little of our story and why we are on this walk. I share a bit about my life, including, "I divorced in part when my ex-wife refused to live full-time in a camper van."

Cosima looks at me and responds, "Where have *you* been all my life?"

I am not good at picking up cues from women, but that seems a little flirty. I remain silent, not knowing how to flirt back.

Cosima, who looks to be around thirty, is attractive, with long red hair, a pretty face, and innocent green eyes.

After a long silence, I ask, "What led you to the Camino?"

"I decided to walk a Camino after my six-year relationship ended earlier this year," she tells me. Later, when she mentions that her boyfriend was almost twenty years her senior, my eyebrows rise involuntarily.

After the group cleanup, the ten of us head outside and have a fire going within minutes. Two benches, a couple of chairs from the dining room, and a large log create a large circle around the fire. We drink more wine, and the conversations continue. Diana chats with the Sardinian, the only other Italian here tonight, and I chat with Cosima and Eberdine from the Netherlands. Both women have walked the Camino before. Cosima walked for two weeks last year, and Eberdine walked the entire Camino a few years earlier.

"This desolate section of the Camino is my favorite," Eberdine says. "I came back to walk the Meseta in solitude, to contemplate my life."

After a while, someone goes inside and brings out a guitar. Francisca from Brazil starts playing a song and singing in her native Portuguese. It is a beautiful song, and she has an angelic voice. Later, the German guy sings a song in English and one in German. Someone says, "Everyone should sing a song in their language."

Eberdine sings a lovely song in Dutch with guitar accompaniment. Not everyone volunteers, but the goading gets to me.

"I could recite a poem I've written instead," I say, taking out my phone. Moments later, I say, "Oh ... I don't have any phone service."

"Then sing," Diana says from across the fire.

While I do not have a good singing voice—awful, to be honest— and have never sung solo in front of others in my life, I say, "I would sing, but I don't know the lyrics to any songs."

"No excuse. *My* phone has service," Eberdine says. "I can pull up the lyrics to any song. What song do you want to sing?"

Ouch, I think to myself. Eventually, I say, "'Colder Weather,' by The Zac Brown Band." A terrible rendition of the song follows.

It turns out I gave in too quickly, as most of the others remain silent; neither Diana nor Cosima volunteer to sing. I think my embarrassment may have scared others from taking center stage.

Cosima is quite reserved, it seems ... except for her earlier comment.

"What do you do back in Germany?" I ask.

"I am a nurse, but I am hoping to get into medical school soon," she says. "I will know in a couple of months if I have been accepted for the next class."

"What kind of doctor do you want to be?" I ask.

"A family doctor," she says. "No specialty, but I want to combine the best from Eastern and Western medicine."

"That's a brilliant idea."

More logs and wine extend this evening well into the night. Someone says, "Look at the moon, perfectly framed by one of the arches." I look up to the sky above this nearly thousand-year-old structure. Like so many times before on my walk, my head slowly turns side to side.

When I remember the poem I wanted to share is saved as an image on my iPhone, hoping to redeem myself, I announce, "I have that poem saved to my phone."

"Good, I want to hear it," Cosima says.

I recite what I had written on my travels in the year after my divorce.

MY WALK

Walking towards oblivion; On my walk that long ago begun
Numbed by the routine of life
There is a murmur of regret of the paths not taken
The whispers get louder
In time, I hear myself; I listen
The angst I feel shakes me
Understanding that action conquers fear; I step
Hesitatingly at first, Unable to find my compass, I explore
Lightening my load as my journey progresses
I wander alone, spending too much time smelling flowers
Without a map, I sometimes lose my way
With a fortunate turn in the trail, a glimpse of the mountain
   ahead
Confidently I leave the beaten path, a new trail to blaze
I find My Compass … within
Higher and higher I climb; Eyes focused on the crown
I stop, look down, and see the land through which I have
   traveled
This magnificent scene leaves me breathless
My stamina builds; it brings a smile
Dusk is approaching; I must not stop

> Watching each footfall to avoid any danger; I continue my
>   walk
> I hurry, the sun is setting; I have yet to find what I seek
> Sadly, night falls; Unsure of which direction
> Out of nowhere, lightning flashes
> In that instant, I see …

"That was good," Cosima says, looking me in the eyes. "What is it you saw when the lightning flashed?"

"It's supposed to signify the path I am to follow in my life," I explain. "But I've lost sight of it again."

As the night progresses, Cosima and I continue talking while the others slowly peel away and head to bed. Eventually, the two of us, along with Eberdine and Alberto, sit talking by the fire.

I feel a connection to Cosima. Her sincerity draws me in, and I listen to her intently. She tells me, "I don't like to make many plans—I try to do what feels right at the moment. That is why I am back here. I had not planned to return, but it felt right."

A slight touch of our hands feels electric as she refills my wine mug. I sense she may feel a connection as well. Our night ends with a knowing glance as we part. Cosima heads to the host quarters, a small metal building at one end of the makeshift courtyard. "Goodnight," she says quietly.

"Goodnight," I say.

As I lie in my bunk, another poem starts to form:

> The stars in the sky aligning
> The moon above San Anton shining
> In the ruins … a campfire, music, wine … we talk
> I look into your eyes … there is a spark

What a magical place: the majestic ruins, the quiet, the people. Today has been one of the more memorable on my journey—all thanks to a delayed "yes" to walking with Diana.

Before I fall asleep, a headlamp from outside turns towards the glass door to the bunkroom. For a second, I think it may be Cosima, hoping I will follow. Not wanting to misjudge the situation, I remain and think of her as I drift off.

DAY 13: SAN ANTON > FRÓMISTA

He who would travel happily, must travel light.

~ Antoine de St. Exupery, *The Little Prince*

After a quick breakfast of toasted baguettes, most of us gather in the courtyard, chilly at this early hour. A hazy morning light has arrived. We are saying our goodbyes when Cosima approaches me.

"You may catch up to me when I rejoin the Camino in Astorga in about a week," she says.

"I hope so," I say, smiling.

"We should exchange contact information," she says.

"Sure," I say, as I pull out my phone and find one bar of service. "What's your number?"

I enter her number in WhatsApp and send her a message: *Mike from San Anton.*

Her phone pings. "I'll let you know when I start walking again," she says. She reaches out for a hug.

After our conversation last night, I hoped I would meet her again, but that seemed far-fetched. Now, my mind races with the thought of this beautiful woman being romantically interested in me. I could be reading more into this than I should, but the prospect feels audacious.

Soon, Diana and I head out together and continue along the asphalt roadway that led us here. We walk towards a hill rising from the plains. It reminds me of Navarette, but on a grander scale. Atop the symmetrical hill, the ruins of a castle are visible through the gloom; at its base lies a town, Castrojeriz. We continue at our brisk pace as the historic fortress looks down upon us.

Not long after, we approach what seems to be a plateau rising from the level terrain which we've been walking, unsure if we will be headed up or staying in the valley. Soon it's clear; we will be making the climb.

The grade is steep, with little reprieve, and continues for what feels like a kilometer. Despite the pleading of my lungs, I march on, wanting to end this climb as soon as possible. Diana is close behind.

"Holy shit," I say as I bend over and catch my breath. "That was the hardest climb yet."

"If you had taken a break, it wouldn't have been so bad," Diana says between breaths. "I kept waiting for you to stop."

"Sorry. I was pretending I was on a StairMaster at the gym."

We find a super-long bench, partially covered for protection against the sun and wind, and a low stone wall along the edge of a sheer drop. We throw off our packs and rest them against the wall and take a seat amongst a half dozen fellow pilgrims. The view to the valley below is magnificent, a bird's-eye view of a patchwork of fields lying below, with the Camino's path cutting through on a diagonal. The grandness of Castrojeriz's hill is most evident from this vantage point.

After our break, we start again, and it is immediately evident we will not be walking on this plateau for long. Within a minute, we are walking down an even steeper descent along a concrete pathway. Paved, I assume, to avoid loose rocks from making our descent deadly. The view in front of us shows another beautiful patchwork under a clear blue sky. The expansive landscape is painted a dusty brown, a few patches of green dotted about, and the white line we will follow is visible for miles on the wide-open plain.

Diana and I often walk in comfortable silence, but when a question arises, we talk about one topic or another. Neither of us feels the need to fill every minute.

Our conversation this morning is wide-ranging. I find Diana lives in a town fifty kilometers from Venice, located near the foothills of the Dolomites. She grew up skiing in the nearby mountains, but she found her passion on the water in the nearby Adriatic Sea. While in her mid-twenties, she was invited to go out on a boat and fell in love with sailing. The stories she shares of her sailing adventures make *me* want to get on the water.

"Sounds like an exciting hobby. I wish I had found something that got me as excited about it as you are about sailing. I spent most of my life without a real passion for anything," I say.

"You said you like hiking in the mountains."

"I do, but that's new; I was fifty before I was finally able to spend extended time in the outdoors."

"So, yesterday, you said you got divorced. What did you do after your divorce?"

"I got rid of everything except two backpacks full of clothes and camping equipment, my iPhone, my iPad, and a small box of books. I quit my job, and once my lease was up, I hit the road in my Prius."

She stares at me with pursed lips, and with her brows raised, nods. "That is a big change," she says.

"Yeah," I reply with a big smile. "I remember waking up my first morning on the road near the Pacific Ocean and walking through a scene out of *The Hobbit*. The trail was even called the Hobbit Trail. I found myself alone on a remote section of beach, with tears of happiness flowing down my face."

"Why were you so happy?"

"Maybe it was more relief," I say with a shrug. "I had wanted to leave my mundane life for so long; now I finally had the chance."

"Where would you sleep?"

"Sometimes I'd camp, or I'd be backpacking in the wilderness for a week at a time," I say. "But often, if I were traveling from place to place, I would sleep in my car. I had a nice sleeping setup."

"I thought you said last night you were going to move into a camper van?"

"That was if I could get my wife to come along. When she chose not to, I didn't need anything more."

She nods. "Where would you shower?"

"I joined a nationwide chain of gyms before I took off and would shower at one of their locations if I was close by," I say. "I made a promise to myself—I would only go to the gym if I worked out. I hadn't worked out since college. Man, I got in great shape within six months of hitting the road."

"You liked living like that?"

"Hell, yes! I still love it," I say. "I'm not the only one doing it; there's a growing community of people living like this. Most *are* in a van or small RV. If you Google *vanlife*, you'll get an idea. There are websites listing places to park or camp for free."

Diana shakes her head and smiles. "What did you do all day?"

"That's a good question," I say as I chuckle to myself. "Well, If I wasn't backpacking, and I was in a city, I would hit the gym for a couple of hours, go to the library almost every day, where I'd read or plan for upcoming places to go—but every day I would find some place to take a miles-long walk."

"Did you ever get bored?"

"Sure … sometimes … but I felt like I was moving towards something greater, though I couldn't say what it was."

"Huh … I don't understand," she says, a quizzical expression on her face.

"I don't know … I felt productive in a way I didn't when I was working. I was investing in *me*, not my employer," I say. "Plus, I got to go places and do things I'd always wanted to, like a hot air balloon festival, a famous film festival, and I visited a ton of national parks. And I could visit my kids and grandkids more often. My time was all my own … it felt great."

"You make living in a car sound fun."

"It is. It's clearly not for everybody, but it is the kind of life I thought about for years."

As we walk, I think back to the day when I left my apartment in

Portland. I was as close to unencumbered as I could imagine. My kids were settled on their own; the worries of my old day-to-day life were no more. A life of possibilities lay ahead; I was starting my life anew, at fifty.

My life's footprint had become smaller over the preceding years. I happily said goodbye to the big house and grew more content as the square footage I lived in shrank. My downsizing and eliminating material things from my life took place before Marie Kondo's philosophy hit Netflix. Still, I had read her book a few years before and embraced a few of her ideas, but the book I took more from was *Goodbye Things, The New Japanese Minimalism*, by Fumio Sasaki. It highlighted for me the idea of maximizing time over anything else. At some point, I stumbled upon a quote that hit home: "Being unattached to stuff makes our lives hugely flexible." I sought to be as flexible in my life as possible, to be ready if an opportunity arose.

Reducing my possessions became a challenge I welcomed as the years passed. I focused on a few quality items that would last. Over the years, I learned a few valuable lessons as I attempted to travel through life a little lighter. I was 'all in' when I moved from a 420-square-foot studio into my Prius. I was choosing to live simply, so I could seek out adventure.

After about an hour of walking through nothing but farm fields, we approach a large stone building. It looks like nothing special; just a simple rectangular building.

"This is San Nicolás ... my guidebook says it is an interesting albergue. The Italian Confraternity of Pilgrims runs it, so all the hospitaleros are from Italy," Diana explains. "Let's go inside."

"Sure," I say as I extend my hand towards the door.

We enter a dark space, with a small window at one end of the building letting in a few rays of light—this large room is the entirety of the building. One long table fills most of this narrow room, and we find a man and a woman seated. They stand to greet us.

"Welcome," they say in unison.

Diana says something in Italian, and they chat briefly. Then the conversation switches to English.

"Would you care for water or coffee? We also have cookies," a smiling, middle-aged woman offers.

Both Diana and I take a seat at the table. I glance around and spot a stairway leading up.

"The loft is where the pilgrims sleep. There are twelve beds, in honor of the twelve disciples," the man says.

We learn these two are married, and they volunteer here together for two weeks most summers. It is still morning, so this will not be our final destination. But the couple is eager to make conversation, as they are here alone most of the day. They share their experience walking the Camino years earlier and how much they enjoy volunteering here.

"In the evening, there is a symbolic washing of the pilgrim's feet, followed by a candlelight dinner," the woman says. "Like your stay in San Anton, we have no electricity."

We say "Ciao" to the couple and are soon crossing the Pisuerga River. We head north along a gravel road leading to the village of Itero de la Vega, where we stop for lunch. After reading good reviews for an albergue, we decide Frómista will be our stopping point. We fill our bottles and head into the hottest part of the day, with three hours to finish what will be a relatively short twenty-nine-kilometer day.

We move across the shadeless Meseta at a brisker than normal pace so we may get out of the heat sooner. Eventually, the trail runs alongside a narrow canal, maybe twenty feet wide, and we pass a small pier with a sign stating something to the effect of 'experience a boat ride for part of your Camino.' However, there is no boat. We march on, albeit at a slower and slower pace, the afternoon heat draining our energy.

Finally, an arrow directs us over a narrow dam. Its gate is closed, and the water level on the opposite side is a few feet lower than the canal. We cross over and into Frómista and navigate towards our albergue, in this, the largest city since Burgos. We find out the albergue is directly across from a beautiful old church in the city's center. The entrance sits under a covered arcade that runs an entire city block.

Diana says, "The name of the albergue means *The Light of Frómista*."

"Welcome!" says a vibrant man with a smile. "I am Gabriel, your host." He leads us into what looks more like a beautiful home than an albergue. A grand staircase lies ahead, but we turn and enter an office, its walls filled with beautiful artwork.

"San Anton!" Gabriel exclaims when he catches sight of the stamp in one of our credentials, "It was amazing, no?" He asks about our walk as he checks us in. Then leads us upstairs to one of several rooms, ours filled with ten or so beds. "We will talk later," he says before heading back down.

After completing our post-walk activities, Diana and I agree to cook dinner in the small kitchen here. Conveniently, there is a small grocery store across the street where we purchase pasta, vegetables and two bottles of wine.

While we are eating in a large dining area upstairs, a familiar face appears; Eberdine has just arrived.

"That smells delicious," Eberdine says as she inhales deeply.

"It is," I say, "Our Italian friend here knows how to cook."

"There is still some pasta left downstairs," Diana says. "It's yours."

"Thanks, that would be great," she says, "but, first, I must shower."

She is soon back and joins our table. We learn that she left right after us this morning, but she walks at a relaxed pace and makes frequent stops throughout the day.

After dinner, I enjoy a long conversation with Gabriel. He tells me he opened this albergue about a year earlier, with his wife, Anita, and their teenage children. Gabriel is from the south of Spain, and his wife is from the Netherlands; they settled in Spain when they married long ago. Gabriel shares with me the incredible story of how they came to find this property.

A few years earlier, he and his family were living hundreds of miles away in Spain's Galicia region, also near the Camino. Significant problems arose on their property, and because of a crooked contractor, they lost a big chunk of their savings. The issues eventually led them to sell that home, inexplicably, to the shady contractor. On the same day he agreed to sell, he found this place online, in a city that had special meaning to him and his wife.

Before they married, they had walked the Camino together and stayed a night in Frómista. "It was a sign," he says. "We had long dreamed of creating a life on the Camino." I find the fact that Gabriel and his wife shared the same dream inspiring; it was something I felt was missing from my marriage.

They had purchased this place a little over two years ago and had a lot of work to do to convert the property into today's "Light of Frómista." The building rises three stories and has a lovely small courtyard in the back. Gabriel explains problems with his initial contractor (another shady contractor, yikes!), who failed to get the proper permits or insurance for his workers. Gabriel had to have all work stopped and deal with the permitting himself.

On the day he was finalizing things with the municipality, a woman who lives above the municipal office ran in, shouting, "My husband is dying." Gabriel ran upstairs with the woman and found the man choking. Serendipitously, the week before, he'd watched something online about the Heimlich Maneuver and was able to save the man's life. Gabriel says, "I knew then, regardless of any obstacles, we are meant to be here." Eventually, the construction came to a completion, and the albergue opened.

Gabriel and his family all live on the third floor, while the albergue fills the lower levels. Despite the typicalities of staying in an albergue, like sleeping in a bunk room with a dozen others or waiting in line to shower, my time here feels more like staying in a friend's home.

DAY 14: FRÓMISTA > CALZADILLA DE LA CUEZA

Don't be too timid and squeamish about your
actions. All life is an experiment. The more
experiments you make the better.

~ Ralph Waldo Emerson, *Journals of*
Ralph Waldo Emerson

Walking under a night sky along empty streets through this small town, chilled to the point of shivering, provides a refreshing start to my day.

The warnings of fewer places to stop along the Meseta will be most evident today. Diana's guidebook says we will reach a decent-sized town in nineteen kilometers, but then nothing for the next seventeen. "Except the possibility of a trailer offering food and drink midway through the long stretch of nothingness," she says. Diana and I plan to walk thirty-six kilometers versus the shorter alternative.

As the sun slowly rises from behind, I learn more about Diana's life. While completing her graduate studies, she has continued serving as a swim instructor during the school year at the local pool where she has worked since she was a teenager. She works in unison with the school year, so she has traveled almost every summer and winter break. I enjoy hearing about Diana's trips around the globe, and I share some of my travels.

"How can you afford to travel without working?" Diana asks.

"Cashing in on my retirement," I say.

"What will you do when you are older?"

"I plan on living frugally now … and when I'm older."

"I don't know that word … frugally," she says, shaking her head.

"It means cheap. I don't need to spend a lot of money to live."

"Okay," she says, nodding. "I understand."

"When I divorced, I knew I was giving up a more secure life, but it felt urgent to live a more adventurous life now."

"Your life of travel wasn't expensive?"

"No, not compared to a more conventional life. I had no rent or utilities. I had vehicle expenses, my gym membership, cell phone, and food," I say. "I don't think you have the same issues with health insurance, but I planned on going without, due to the unbelievable cost."

"I read about health care in your country, and it seems crazy."

"It is, and going without it is a risk, but I'm in good health," I say, and I hold out my hand with crossed fingers. "I was planning to live this way until I was sixty-five."

"Why sixty-five?"

"It is when I can collect a pension from my old job and social security."

"It is a long time away," she says.

"I know, but, at the time, nothing was more important than leaving my conventional life behind," I explain.

"I understand the need to travel and take a break," she says. "I am fortunate enough to go on holiday several times every year, but I can't imagine living like that."

"For me, it beat the alternative. I thought mine was the only life which made any sense, a life of adventure over one of security."

"I like adventure, too, but I need to earn money," she says.

"I'm lucky I can access the money I saved during my almost thirty years of employment. I remember reading a quote from Paulo Coelho,

'Travel is never a matter of money, but of courage.' And I added it to my collection of quotes. I'm trusting things will work out."

After three hours of walking, we stop for something to eat when we reach Villalcázar de Sirga. We enjoy café con leche and slices of tortilla on a small plaza in front of a huge Gothic church while chatting with others parked on the plaza.

"It amazes me these small villages on the Meseta, like this one, have such grand churches," I say.

Diana says, "My book recommends a visit."

After we finish eating, we climb a long flight of stairs but find the doors locked. The church won't open for another hour, so we move on.

I am enjoying the rhythm of my days on the Camino: leaving the albergue early and walking for a couple of hours as the sun rises; stopping at a bar for nourishment; then walking until noon and stopping for a bocadillo before continuing; reaching an albergue around three; shower, laundry, and a nap, followed by dinner. The short breaks throughout the day are re-energizing, and getting to know new people is both fun and enlightening.

We reach Carrión de Los Condes before noon, my shirt already soaked with sweat. I sit outside in the shade of yet another impressive church while Diana goes into the Pilgrim Oasis, a shop catering to pilgrims, to buy more sunscreen and pick up a headlamp battery for me. I message Jana about the special albergue from last night and recommend they stay if it syncs with their daily mileage.

This city is a popular stopping point for pilgrims preferring to walk the long stretch in the morning. While I'm waiting outside, a few of the partying Italians stop nearby, in a small, grassy plaza. I am surprised to see them, as I expected they would be far behind.

I walk over to Rafaella. "How did you get ahead of me?" I ask.

Smiling, she says, "We took the bus for part of today's stage. The others are still walking."

It seems some of the Italians are walking each kilometer, while others jump ahead. Bus routes connect many of the small towns all along the Camino. Taking the bus allows pilgrims with a physical ailment (or those simply wanting to avoid walking in the heat of the afternoon) the opportunity to keep up with their Camino family.

Before heading into the long void, we stop at Dia, a Spanish supermarket chain, and buy food for lunch and salty snacks for this afternoon. I also buy a liter of a Gatorade-like sports drink, Aquarius, which I hastily consume. Lastly, we search out a fountain to top off our water bottles; we find one next to a small playground. We sit on a bench and slowly eat our store-bought sandwiches.

"Shall we," I say. We rise and head into the desolation.

Long minutes are spent in silence as we move through this barren expanse. Thoughts bubble up as my mind quiets. I think of all the choices that led me to this point in my life. Life is simply a series of choices, many not easy to make. I imagine life as though it was a convoluted flow chart—if I choose this, it will lead somewhere and to yet another choice—realizing all along there are consequences for each decision I make. When I think of those choices, like dots, it reminds me of the Steve Jobs quote, "You can't connect the dots looking forward; you can only connect them looking backwards. So, you have to trust in something—your gut, destiny, life, karma, whatever." Looking back on my life, some of these dots are blinking brightly, while others are barely visible as I recreate the path that led me here.

A couple of hours into our afternoon walk, we pass what looks like a storage container masquerading as a bar and find a dozen pilgrims sitting at umbrellaed tables. We both have plenty of water and food left and agree to keep moving. Not even a hundred meters ahead, I notice a bus parked where our route intersects with a road. How many pilgrims will be getting on it? Or maybe have gotten off and will continue walking from this point?

The sun's rays are draining; the view is never-changing. We walk under a bright, blue sky along a wide gravel path between barren fields. Our route heads straight as an arrow towards our final destination, somewhere beyond the vanishing point.

Much too long after we started this afternoon, I glimpse the outlines of buildings rising above the horizon, but they are still a way off. I am desperate to get out of the sun. As we get nearer, visible on one of the buildings, *Albergue Municipal* is painted in large letters. We find adjoining albergues: one private, with a small pool, and the municipal, with a courtyard. We choose the municipal.

After completing our post-walk necessities, we head to the patio. We meet a mother and daughter from southern Spain who are walking the Camino for two weeks. The daughter, in her thirties, speaks a little English, while her mother doesn't speak a word. The four of us sit in the albergue's courtyard, drinking a cold beverage. Later, we all head across the street for dinner.

While we're dining, an exhausted Eberdine walks into the restaurant. It is after eight o'clock, four hours after we arrived, and she has just now pulled into town. She covers the same ground Diana and I do, but walks the Camino in her way.

We make eye contact, and I wave her over.

"I am lucky they have a bed for me," she says. "All the others are full."

"Join us," Diana says.

"I *will* have a drink," she says, pulling over an empty chair.

We compare notes from our day over one last glass of wine. Earlier than usual, we call it a night, after another long, hot day on the Meseta.

DAY 15: CALZADILLA DE LA CUEZA > BERCIANOS DEL REAL CAMINO

*Purpose is the reason you journey. Passion is the
fire that lights your way.*

~Unknown

Diana whispers, "I will meet you outside," as she walks past, heading downstairs. I respond with a raspy, "I'll be down in five." I slept soundly but am finding it hard to get up this morning. A few minutes later, I climb down from my top bunk, hurriedly pack and head down.

I walk around the outside of the albergue, but don't find Diana. I message, *Where are you?* and wait a couple of minutes but get no response. A couple more minutes pass, and I start to think she may have already started out. I message again, *Maybe I misunderstood. I am headed out now.*

Guided by my headlamp, I walk on a path alongside a deserted roadway when Diana messages, *I didn't leave without you. I was in the bar next door. I'm walking with some others now. I want to reach Bercianos del Real Camino and stay at the parroquial albergue.* I check my spreadsheet and find it means a thirty-four-kilometer day. I message back, *I'll see you there if we don't meet up before.*

The darkness lifts as the sun peeks above the horizon behind me. As the minutes pass, my long shadow slowly starts to shrink on the gravel path. As I walk alone, my mind takes me back to the night in San Anton and Cosima. It was a mystical place, and our interaction seemed tinged with a sexual charge. I imagine a romance with her along the Camino and am tempted to message her, but I decide it best to let her be the first to reach out.

An hour into my walk, I am approaching a building with a mural showing a pilgrim walking on a path through fields of green. The building is the Albergue Morena in the village of Ledigos. I find several tables on a patio outside the entrance. I stop.

I carry my café con leche and chocolate croissant onto the patio and take a seat.

A middle-aged man with a full beard at the table next to me asks, "Where did you start out today?"

"Back in Calzadilla de la Cueza," I say. "How 'bout you?"

"I stayed here last night," he says.

The two of us talk about our walks thus far. I learn Jerome is from France and is forty-four. When I finish my breakfast, we start out together.

We walk side by side along a narrow road that exits the village and pass a concrete tennis court, the net gone, the green paint and white lines both faded by years of the beating sun. Jerome towers over me. He's at least six-feet-two, with short brown hair and a deep tan, and he looks to be in excellent shape.

"I only have three weeks to walk the Camino this summer," he says, "and I have walked some long days."

"I gave myself plenty of time to walk, so I'm in no hurry, but I like to put in a decent number of kilometers each day," I say.

"I have walked forty-five a few times," he says. "But I pay for it the next day."

"I haven't even made it to forty. I've been starting early and trying to end in the early afternoon."

"I normally start later and walk until I need to stop for dinner."

My pace is a bit faster now, to match Jerome's longer stride. We talk about our lives and what led us to the Camino. I learn he, too, divorced a couple of years earlier. He shares that it has been a difficult transition for him. He is now a practicing Buddhist, but like many, his religious beliefs have been ever-evolving.

I find it interesting to have stumbled upon two Buddhists in the last week. What attracts Buddhists to the Camino? I answer my own question—regardless of religion or walk of life, serendipity can put anyone on this consequential journey.

Jerome worked in many different fields before his latest career change. He is now a high school teacher.

"I am surprised how much I love teaching," he says. "I struggled to find something I was excited by, and I finally found it. It's the most purposeful job I have had."

"You're lucky to have found a career that provides meaning," I say. "I'm still searching for that."

"It has been a long journey for me over the last few years, but I'm finally in a good place," he says.

"I've met a lot of people along the Camino, and it seems many, like myself, are looking for something," I say. "I have made progress, but I am still hoping to find something I love to do."

"You should read the book *The Seeker*. it is written by an American author, Terry Dodd," he says. "I read it and found it helpful after my divorce."

As we walk, I take out my phone. I locate the book online and add it to my list to purchase later.

"I love the title. In my search, nothing has clicked. Travel and hiking have been my only passions since my divorce, and while I love it, it doesn't give me the meaning you've found in teaching."

"Finding something to be passionate about can be just as hard as finding something that provides meaning," he says.

As we walk, I think about people in my life and try to identify their passions, but find it's not easy. My kids, my ex, my mom, and brothers … I have no idea. What are people passionate about? Do they keep it to themselves, or are people simply lacking passions? Should they be spoken of or obvious to family and friends? Yet one more question to answer.

There is a difference between passions and meaning. I now have a passion for travel but don't necessarily find meaning in it. My kids provided my life with meaning when they were younger, but they are now living their own lives. I think of those I've met on the Camino. Jana may have found passion and meaning in serving God when she was twenty but is now searching for something new. Diana's passion seems to be travel and sailing, but she likely doesn't find meaning in those things, though children will soon fill that void.

Both passions and what people find meaningful seem to me to change over time. I'm guessing both are important for a contented life, yet both seem elusive. Finding both of these at the same time may be the key. But it's not an easy puzzle to solve.

As we approach the town of Sahagún, two fifteen-foot-tall markers flank the Camino's path. Each holds a life-size carved statue, one of the twelfth-century king who protected the Way, and the other one of the founders of this town. These markers signify the halfway point of the Camino as measured from Roncesvalles to Santiago, so it's not quite the halfway point from the more common embarkation point of the Camino Frances.

"There is a church in Sahagún offering a *compostela* for completing half the Camino," a woman who has also stopped tells us. A compostela is a completion certificate. Our journey ends in the symbolically named city where pilgrims will receive a compostela signifying that they have traveled at least a significant portion of the Camino.

Jerome and I weave our way through the city, not knowing where to find the church mentioned. Eventually, a local who speaks little English directs us, sensing what two obviously lost pilgrims may be in search of. We make it to the Santuario de la Virgen Peregrina, located at the far end of the city, and enter what I can best describe as a welcome center for the church and attached museum. A straight-faced woman behind the desk robotically asks for our credentials and collects 3€, and a printer spits out our compostela. A small cardboard tube, purchased separately, may keep it from being destroyed in my pack. Pilgrims not making it to Santiago may find this a meaningful souvenir, but this is not a required stop for those who will reach Camino's terminus.

An hour later, we reach Bercianos del Real Camino. "This is my stopping point for the day," I say.

"I have at least another seven to go," Jerome says. "I'm not yet sure where I'll stop."

Given the distance he covers, it's unlikely we'll meet again. We hug goodbye on a quiet street in the middle of a seemingly deserted village. My day is complete, and I'm happy to have put another chunk of kilometers of the Meseta behind me.

A sign reading *Bar* points to an open door; I enter and find a half dozen empty picnic tables lined up under a partial roof. I throw off my pack, sit down in the welcome shade and peel off my shoes. I am in what seems to be the courtyard of the bar.

"Hola," says a young woman walking from inside.

"Hola," I say, "Coca-Cola y calamares, por favor."

"Si," she responds and heads back inside.

A large sidewalk tent sign out front showed pictures of some food options. The picture of a plate of calamari was too tempting to ignore.

A minute later, she brings out a glass of ice and a bottle. Coca-Cola is not something I drink back home, but after long, hot days, it tastes amazing. I don't feel a bit guilty about the sugar or calories. I haven't worried about anything I've consumed here, as calories are burning at a crazy rate. While waiting for my food, I message Diana, *I've reached Bercianos.*

A minute later, she responds, *One hour away.*

While eating lunch, I reflect on my good fortune along the Camino and the many meaningful interactions I've had. These encounters are not typical in my life back home. It's a matter of chance whom you'll meet, but most pilgrims are open and welcoming, seeking the same connections I've enjoyed. Is this why so many people return time and again?

My journey here is vastly different from my solo travels back home. I met many people on my travels, but loneliness was an issue. On the rare occasions I was in a city with a hostel (not common in the U.S.), I would stay for a night to meet new people. An evening of board games and drinking at the occasional hostel would provide some of the human interaction I craved. One of the more interesting results from such a stay resulted in a twenty-something guy from Australia and I hiking the Grand Canyon and road-tripping to Colorado together. Hostels, like albergues, are great places for solo travelers to meet and mingle.

Here on the Camino, I'm finding you never walk alone—unless you choose to.

After lunch, I find the Albergue Parroquial Casa Rectoral. I'm excited to find it another donativo albergue with a communal meal. Just as I finish checking in, Diana arrives.

"How was your day?" I ask.

"Hot!" she says with a smile and crashes into a chair. "The group I was walking with stopped an hour ago. How was yours?"

"Good. I walked with a Frenchman for most of the day, but he kept going," I say. "Another communal meal tonight!"

"Yes," she says, "it is why I wanted to stay here. I always search for places like this."

Again, I feel a rush of gratitude. So thankful for Diana's planning and company along the Way.

The two hospitaleros are both enthusiastic about being here; their energy is contagious, even to weary pilgrims.

At 5:30, everyone gathers in the kitchen and dining room to prepare for dinner. I volunteer for vegetable duty yet again. There are about thirty pilgrims gathered to contribute to tonight's meal. While I don't recognize most here tonight, getting to know new people enhances my time spent slicing tomatoes and cucumbers. Everyone's smiling and ready to enjoy another evening on the Camino.

At seven o'clock, a gregarious German man fills wine glasses at our table, and then grace is offered by everyone singing a song in Spanish, the lyrics posted on a wall. While we are eating, one of the hospitaleros stands at the front of the room. "Everyone is invited to an after-dinner reflection to watch the sunset," she says. "We will gather in front of the albergue a little before nine."

When the hour arrives, fifteen of us gather out front, then walk to a small playground on a hill with a view to the west and of the low-hanging sun. A guitar plays, and songs are sung. Two other native English speakers and I sing Leonard Cohen's "Hallelujah." Despite my qualms about singing, I am more comfortable in front of a small crowd as part of a trio. Our host passes out lyrics to a final song that everyone sings together. Most of us don't speak Spanish, so our version of the song, sung to the tune of "La Bamba," is all over the place. The song is titled "Cancion de Peregrino," *The Pilgrim Song*, and the refrain is "Peregrino, Peregrino, Peregrino." The lyrics are apparently humorous, as those who understand Spanish are laughing. Later, I translate the lyrics and find they are about a pilgrim's life, good shoes, sore feet, snoring pilgrims keeping us awake, sleeping under a tree if no donation is offered, and remembering everything that happens along the Way.

When the singing stops, Diana and I sit on large blocks of stone at the edge of the park and watch the sun fall below the horizon. Even though we didn't walk in tandem today, it is nice to end the day with Diana.

DAY 16: BERCIANOS DEL REAL CAMINO > LEÓN

If we don't offer ourselves to the unknown, our senses will dull. Our world becomes small, and we will lose our sense of wonder. Our eyes don't lift to the horizon; we don't hear the sounds around us. The edge is off our experience, and we pass our days in routine that is both comfortable and limiting. We wake up one day and find that we have lost our dreams in order to protect our days.

~ Kent Nerburn, *Letters to My Son*

Diana and I sit outside a bar, enjoying a café con leche two hours into our day, when I see Jerome approach.

"I thought you would be further ahead by now," I say.

"The heat got to me. I stopped here last night and then got a late start this morning."

I introduce the two, and Jerome removes his pack and joins us for a quick hit of caffeine. Jerome and Diana talk, and I interject occasionally. When I find out he started four days after I did, I say, "Damn, you are walking long days."

"I think they've caught up to me," he says. "Today is my latest start yet."

This is Jerome's first time walking in Spain, but he says, "I will be coming back, whether or not I reach Santiago."

He shares how easy it was for him to start his Camino. "I ate breakfast at home, drove four hours, had lunch in Saint-Jean-Pied-de-Port and dinner in Orisson."

"I'm jealous," I say. "I wish there were walks like this in the States."

"I thought you did have long hiking trails. I know the Appalachian Trail and the one in the movie with Reese Witherspoon," Diana says.

"Yes, *Wild*, that's the PCT, the Pacific Crest Trail. It runs from the Mexican border to Canada. We do have long-distance hiking trails, but they are almost entirely in the wilderness, where you make it to civilization maybe once a week to resupply your food. Nothing like you have in Europe, where you can find a bed and food every day."

Diana collects the empty cups and saucers and takes them inside. She also uses the bathroom. Bars are an essential part of the Camino, and not just for the coffee and wine.

We throw on our packs and head west. "Do you know the Via Francigena?" I ask.

"I know of it but haven't walked any of it," Diana says.

"I've heard the name but don't know where it is," Jerome adds.

"It runs from Canterbury in England to Rome. It's also a pilgrimage route, but not popular like these routes in Spain. I walked it last summer," I say.

"How long did it take you?" Jerome asks.

"Three months. It was much more of a solitary journey."

"How did you decide to walk it?"

"I kind of stumbled upon it. When I was on my post-divorce travels, I was doing lots of backpacking, but my hikes were only for a week at a time. I wanted an extended hiking adventure. Initially, I was going to walk the PCT, which takes about five months, and was planning to start the following spring."

"That is crazy long," Diana says.

"Yeah, and I was getting nervous about some of the more difficult mountain sections," I say. "Over the winter, I Googled long-distance hikes in Europe and learned of the Via Francigena. I thought a walk across France, Switzerland, and Italy sounded amazing and not as physically demanding as the PCT. So, I booked a flight to England instead."

For the next couple of hours, the three of us continue along a familiar landscape. After we pass through Reliegos, our route follows a first along the Meseta—a tree-lined pathway. It is still before noon as we walk along this surprising section of today's route. The intermittent moments of shade provided by these trees must feel heaven-sent for those walking here in the heat of the afternoon.

When we reach Mansilla de las Mulas, having already walked twenty-five kilometers, Diana and I agree to take a break.

Jerome says, "I am going to keep going. I need to make it well past León today if I'm going to make it to Santiago."

Hugs are shared. I watch Jerome head off and think we may have been slowing him down. Jerome is a genuine and friendly guy; after he's gone, I wish we'd exchanged contact information.

The two of us park ourselves next to two tired pilgrims relaxing under a large stone cross in the center of this small town. Our tired neighbors ... part of a sculpture built upon tiers of stone featuring these two modern-day pilgrims resting on its steps. We don't stop long as we have planned this as our longest day yet, forty-four kilometers, to reach León, the second-largest city along the Way to Santiago.

We stop for a quick bite. I find this is one of my favorite small towns on the Meseta. It is not as worn and faded as most others, and it has all the necessities.

We still have three hours before reaching León as we head into the hottest part of the day.

"Tell me about the Via Francigena," Diana asks.

"Well, the section through France is not well-traveled," I say. "During my first two weeks, I was completely alone. I met only two others walking the route during the entire month."

"Was walking all day by yourself tough?"

"Nope," I say. "It was at the beginning, so I was excited to just be on an adventure. Plus, it was what I was expecting."

"Were there hostels?" she asks. "Where did you sleep?"

"Occasionally, but not like there is here," I say. "Eventually, I learned that if I arrived at the Mairie, the town hall in the small towns I passed through, before they closed for the day, they would usually have a place for pilgrims to stay. I once slept in an empty school classroom, but many had a city-owned house or apartment where I could stay for a few euros. But there were also many nights I wild-camped in a bivy sack. It was sometimes challenging, but it was fun."

"What was it like in Italy?"

"That was my favorite," I say with a big smile. "Lots more people, especially Italians. Still nothing like here, but at least there were more places to sleep."

"Hostels?"

"A couple, but lots of convents and other places offered by churches."

"Was it easy to find your way?"

"Yes. It was very well marked. When I reached Rome, I didn't want to stop walking. I loved the simplicity of my walking life."

"I had the same feeling after the Camino Portuguese, and it's why I came back."

"I remember leaving Rome on day ninety of my ninety-day visa, not wanting to return home. While I appreciated that my lifestyle allowed me to go on a European adventure, I wasn't excited to return home to my solitary life on the road."

We walk for some time alongside a busy roadway, then pass through a few small towns before we reach the outskirts of León. We make our way through some not-so-lovely industrial and commercial areas along a protected pathway next to a major highway. After a few more kilometers of urban walking, we reach tonight's resting place, the Albergue Benedictinas Santa Maria de Carbajal.

"Hello!" says one of two friendly hospitaleros sitting behind a small table set up outside.

"Hi," I say as he collects our passports and credentials. We discover that this parroquial albergue separates pilgrims by gender, with the men in one large room upstairs and the women in a room on the lower level.

Diana and I agree to meet at the large plaza in front of the León Cathedral in two hours and then head to our sleeping quarters.

I find this my least favorite albergue so far, but I am happy to rest my feet after my longest day yet. The beds are typical, but the room is dark, and the smell reminds me of my grandparents' seldom-used attic. There is no common area, just a large courtyard shared with parked cars. After a shower and laundry, I relax on my bunk and message Jana, *How are you doing? Where are you stopping today?*

Just as I'm about to fall into sleep, my phone pings. I check the message. *We are two days from León. We will be staying in Sahagún tonight. Victoria will be ending her Camino in León as planned, and we are planning on spending a rest day there. I don't think we'll see each other again.*

You're probably right, I message back, as she will be three days behind. *I'll stay in touch and let you know of any interesting accommodations.*

Deciding to explore the city for a while before meeting Diana, I find the city bustling with a mix of locals and pilgrims, some with their backpacks on, and others like me enjoying the city without lugging a heavy pack. León is a beautiful city; many buildings look like they've been here for at least a hundred years. I stop at a bar bordering a small plaza and order my new favorite beer, Estrella Galicia. Sipping my drink under a blue sky, I watch the scene around me. Groups of people laughing and talking; I assume many are pilgrims with friends they met along the Way.

I head towards the cathedral, walking along narrow pedestrian-only lanes, inhaling the scent of cooked meat, passing numerous bars and restaurants whose customers are standing at tables outside, enjoying food and drink. When the narrow street opens onto a large plaza, my eyes widen, and my jaw drops. At least a dozen spires reach skyward; the cathedral is breathtaking. A large circle of stained glass is the centerpiece of the front facade; the windows are laid out like a rose. A large plaza spreads out along two sides of this Gothic masterpiece. At the edge of the plaza, large metal letters spelling out *LEÓN* are proving popular for photos, with the subjects standing, sitting, or in one case, jumping from atop the letters.

I notice Diana sitting with a couple of the women from the large band of Italians. I head over to join them.

"Ciao," I say. "I remember Raffaella's name, but I have forgotten yours," I say to the other woman, whom I know only as the wife of the snorer.

"Paola," she says with a smile.

"Where are the others?" I ask.

"Still walking," Raffaella says. "We took the bus again. We are tired, and our feet hurt."

The four of us head off to get a drink. We find a table outside a bar on a small square and order. The elderly gentleman who comes to help us points to a menu on the table for tapas.

"We choose one with our drinks," Diana says. 'It is included."

When my turn comes, I say, "Estrella Galicia, y morcilla," pointing to the menu.

"Do you know what you ordered?" Diana asks.

"Of course not. I don't know what any of those are."

"You ordered blood sausage," she says with a hint of a smile.

A minute later, our drinks and tapas are set before us.

The morcilla looks like a black sausage filled with rice and is sliced into bite-size pieces. I hesitatingly take my first bite and find it has a smokey taste, and I think I taste paprika.

"It's fine," I tell a staring Diana, "but it has a metallic aftertaste. I'll try something else with my next drink."

I am sitting next to Raffaella, and our conversation turns to what led us here.

"I quit my job to walk here," she says with a distinct accent.

"What was your job?"

"I was working at an art gallery in Milan," she replies. "I will find something different when I return home."

"You didn't like your job?"

"It was good, but I want to try something new. I was bored."

Rafaella is simply taking a break from her life's routine. I've been surprised to find people from all over have some of the same frustrations I've felt. I had believed this angst was more of an American phenomenon, but I'm finding that not to be the case. There is a quote by Emerson: "To believe your own thought, to believe what is true for you in your private heart is true for all men … that is genius." Is that true? Does everyone think like I do? That it's crazy so many people spend the majority of their lives working just to get by. Is this why we're here?

After two more rounds and a variety of tapas selections, Paola gets a message. "They are checking into the albergue now," she says. "I'm sending our location, and they will head over after they shower."

When the others arrive, we move tables together and order more drinks. Most of the conversation is now in Italian, as a couple of the guys don't speak English and I am the only non-Italian here. When the next round comes, I order a Coke. I am already feeling the effects of too much beer and wine.

Talk soon turns to dinner. Around eight o'clock, we head to a well-reviewed restaurant in their guidebook, only to find it doesn't open until nine. So, we head to the nearest bar for more drinks and free tapas. This pattern repeats until just after ten.

"We must head back to our albergue," Diana says to the crowd. "We are not in a private albergue; we need to return before our curfew."

The Italians wish us a "Buonanotte." We respond in kind and leave this fun-loving crew.

On our walk back to the albergue, zigzagging through darkened streets, we lose our way. I chalk it up to the fact we are in an unfamiliar area, but the alcohol we've consumed doesn't help. Tonight is the second time I am feeling a little more than a mellow buzz, and both times were with this same group of Italians. While it's been another entertaining night, I will think twice about joining this festive crowd on holiday for another evening of drinking. Thankfully, Google Maps guides us back, and we arrive before the doors are locked.

DAY 17: LEÓN >
SAN MARTÍN DEL CAMINO

Travel isn't always pretty. It isn't always comfortable. Sometimes it hurts, it even breaks your heart. But that's okay. The journey changes you - it should change you. It leaves marks on your memory, on your consciousness, on your heart, and on your body. You take something with you...Hopefully, you leave something good behind.

~Anthony Bourdain, *No Reservations: Around the World on an Empty Stomach*

The sun peeks above the horizon from behind the spire-laden cathedral; a line of wrought-iron streetlamps dangling globes of yellow light perfect this early morning scene. Diana and I turn and head down a wide boulevard lined with beautiful three- and four-story buildings; the only shops open are those offering coffee or croissants.

Before leaving León, we pass a pair of yellow arrows painted on the stone walkway near the Plaza de San Marcos. One points to the left, to Santiago de Compostela, the other to the right and Oviedo. Oviedo is a town 120 kilometers to the north, over a rugged mountain range. It is the starting point of another popular route, the Camino Primitivo, the most physically demanding route to Santiago. It travels through the Cantabrian Mountains, with challenging changes in elevation throughout.

On one side of the Plaza de San Marcos, standing proudly is the massive Parador de León, a five-star hotel with an intricately carved facade. Not too long ago, an ambitious hotelier converted this incredible structure, a sixteenth-century convent and hospital, into luxurious accommodations. As we make our way across the grand plaza, we admire the ancient bronze pilgrim resting against a stone cross before we pass over the Bernesga River and leave the resplendence of old León behind.

Our walk continues along the pavement for some time. Eventually, we reach an uninviting industrial section of the city, where we stumble upon a small stand under a pop-up canopy in front of a large warehouse.

"Wow," I say, as we peruse a variety of fruits, juices, chocolates, and other snacks here for the taking—an offering to passing pilgrims. A small metal box accepts donations. A professional-looking gentleman greets us with a smile. "This is a gift to pilgrims from a circle of friends. It is our way of giving thanks for what the Camino has provided us."

At least a dozen other pilgrims are assembled here, everyone picking from the bounty before us. In addition to our few euros, we leave our mark in the form of a pin on a large world map and join the countless other pilgrims who have stopped and marked their hometown. This brief respite makes up for the last hour of unglamorous walking.

The next hour is more of the same. Slowly, the buildings turn more commercial before we find ourselves walking near a busy highway. I witness the most traffic I've seen since beginning the Camino, and it reminds me of the daily commute during my old nine-to-five life. A rush of relief flows over me, grateful that those stress-filled days are behind me.

Eventually, the storefronts fade away, replaced by open fields. When we reach a sign pointing to an alternative route, Diana checks her book.

"It says the alternate is a little longer but more scenic, rejoining the official Way in about twenty kilometers."

Tired, we continue on the shorter official route and return to a bland walk through a rural landscape next to a mostly quiet roadway.

"So, have you had any relationships since your divorce?"

"Yeah, one," I say. "I started dating a woman who I had exchanged emails with during my walk to Rome."

"Did you know her before?"

"No, we met online just before I left and had yet to meet face to face. We were modern-day pen pals for months."

"Where does she live?"

"She lives near Chicago, which is where I was in the weeks before I left for the Via Francigena."

"Were you still living in your car?"

"No." I laugh. "I was at my mom's house near Chicago."

"So, what happened?"

"I decided to stay around the area to see if things with Kelly—her name is Kelly—progressed."

"Did they?"

"Yeah ... quickly. Our first date lasted three days," I say. "Both of us were recently divorced and in search of something, though neither of us knew exactly what."

"Did you move to Chicago?"

"Yeah, I stayed and started driving for Uber to earn money and keep myself busy. She has three kids, so she has a busy life."

"Did you miss your life of adventure?"

"Not really. I found myself content living a life that allowed me to spend as much time with her as possible."

"What attracted you to her?"

"Initially her smile, and then the fact she was able to be vulnerable with me, despite being a strong woman. I also liked that she's athletic and likes backpacking."

"She sounds perfect for you."

"I'm not sure about that. We were at two different points in our lives, but it felt good." I continue, "So, I never asked you about Luca. What attracted you to him?"

"He is a kind man, and he is good to me. I like that he is honest and caring," she says. "I can picture starting a family with him. He will be a good father and husband." She smiles.

"I am sure you'll have a great life together … with many bambinos."

Just past noon, our route having never left the side of the road, we reach the outskirts of a small town.

"Do you want to stop here?" I ask.

"Sounds good to me," she says. "We've walked almost eighty kilometers the last two days."

San Martín del Camino seems a bit depressing, but today's relatively short twenty-five kilometers will at least allow us an afternoon of rest. There doesn't seem to be much to the town, and we aren't sure where we will stay. We passed a sign earlier mentioning an albergue "under the water tower." When the first albergue we reach looks a little iffy, Diana says, "Let's try the next one." We continue towards the ball hovering above the small town.

The Albergue San Martín is the municipal albergue, and as the sign said, it sits directly beneath a water tower. The door is open, and we walk through a beaded curtain but find there is not a soul here. A sign shows the cost of drinks and snacks offered, and we grab cold drinks from the fridge. Thirty minutes later, the hospitalero arrives. "Hola," he says.

Javier is probably in his late sixties, has a kind smile, and speaks no English, but Diana deciphers he had driven to León to shop for tonight's dinner. Since this is not a donativo albergue, the optional dinner is an extra charge, but Diana and I respond with a smile and 'Si.'

After my post-walk necessities and a lengthy nap, I wake to find a dozen pilgrims either lying on bunks or relaxing in the front yard of the albergue, with more arriving still. I take a seat at a picnic table and read on my phone. While I prefer reading a physical book, I chose not to carry one on my walk due to the extra weight. The Kindle app makes reading while traveling super easy, and I downloaded a couple of books from my local library before leaving on this trip. While I haven't read more than a couple of times on my Camino, the app comes in handy when traveling by plane or train.

The book I'm reading, *The Razor's Edge*, was written by W. Somerset Maugham and published in 1944. This is my third time reading it, and if I were to choose one book that had the biggest impact on my life, it would be this one. It was eye-opening when I first read it in my late thirties. It forced me to reflect on how I should live my life. Do I follow the masses or trust my inner self?

The story follows one man's search for meaning after returning to America after the First World War, but the idea of nonconformity was what took the deepest root in me. I ruminated on the ideas in the book for more than a decade, feeling relieved I wasn't alone in my feelings of discontent.

Living a life that didn't mesh with society's expectations of my generation grew more and more appealing as my nine-to-five life slogged on. By no means have I modeled my life on the main character in the novel, but by coincidence, Larry Darrell returned to the States after his travels seeking to answer the bigger questions and started working in the 1930s equivalent of Uber.

The Razor's Edge made an appearance in my generation when the actor Bill Murray wrote a screenplay based on the novel and later starred in the film. This was a departure from his usual comedic roles and it was therefore challenging to get studio backing. Eventually, Murray agreed to star in the film *Ghostbusters* in exchange for the studio funding the production of *The Razor's Edge*, a remake of one made in the '40s. The movie was a passion project for Murray, who attended Loyola Academy, a private Jesuit school outside of Chicago run by the order founded by the Basque soldier, Ignatius, who was injured long ago in Pamplona. The book's themes of spirituality and social nonconformism were what attracted Murray, as they did me. While the movie wasn't a box-office hit, I imagine it opened a few minds when released during the 'greed is good' decade.

Dinnertime arrives; Javier has spent the afternoon preparing everything himself. Picnic tables are pulled together for tonight's al fresco meal, dishes are brought out, and the table is set. There are sixteen of us chatting under the stars when a delicious aroma wafts over the table. Javier carries out a large metal pot filled with a hearty stew.

One by one, we walk up and fill our plates.

Conversations fill the table as the sky turns from blue to orange. Several pilgrims are fluent in Spanish and English, and I learn that Javier volunteers here for a month each summer. Dinner is not a tradition at this albergue; it is simply his, and many locals are not happy with his cooking. The local bars and restaurants lose business during his time here, and they have asked him to stop, but he refuses. Translated, he says, "I enjoy feeding pilgrims on their momentous journey."

At tonight's table, Diana's is the only familiar face. I am sitting next to a quiet young woman, Rebecca, a Canadian. "How is your Camino?" I ask.

"Today was my first day," she says.

León is a common starting point for many with time constraints, as one can experience the Camino and reach Santiago within two weeks.

"Let me tell you, today's walk was not typical. In fact, it was my least favorite day of the Camino," I tell her.

She laughs. "That's a relief. I was disappointed. I was expecting beautiful scenery, not walking next to a road all day."

"I was disappointed, too," I say. "Did you meet many people?"

"No. I walked the whole way by myself," she says quietly. "You are the first person I've really talked to. I spent much of the day wondering what I had gotten myself into."

"Yikes! That is a rough start," I say sympathetically. "Did you stay in an albergue last night?"

"No, I had reserved a hotel room before I arrived."

"Don't worry, it will get better, I promise," I say with a smile. "I've walked solo a few days since Saint-Jean, but the people I've met and walked with are what has made my time here so great."

As we devour Javier's lovingly cooked meal, talk around the table is a combination of days past and what lies ahead. During dinner, my phone vibrates. I smile when I read: *Message received from Cosima.* I tap the screen and find she resumed her Camino today in Astorga and is staying in Rabanal del Camino tonight. I message back my location and tell her I will keep in touch. I figure out she is forty-three kilometers ahead. Will I catch her before Santiago?

Later, as I am headed back into the albergue, I smile when I spot

Rebecca talking to a young Dutch guy and learn they are starting out together in the morning.

I lie in bed thinking of Cosima and wonder again if she is interested in something romantic.

DAY 18: SAN MARTÍN DEL CAMINO > MURIAS DE RECHIVALDO

Have faith in your journey. Everything had to happen exactly as it did to get you where you are going next.

~ Mandy Hale

Javier has cooked dozens of over-easy eggs for breakfast and has them in a shallow pan on the stove. This home-cooked breakfast is a first for me at an albergue. Diana and I sit around a small table in the kitchen with a few other early risers.

"What a kind man he is," says one of the others.

"You can tell how much he enjoys providing for those he meets," Diana says.

After eating, and before we head out of the kitchen, we each give Javier a quick hug as he smiles to us all. We grab our packs lined up outside the door and head out for the day, the sun already low in the sky.

Diana and I approach the village of Hospital de Orbigo, which gets its name from a hospital founded along the Orbigo River to care for medieval pilgrims. We will be crossing over a beautiful thirteenth-century bridge spanning almost 200 meters, supported by twenty arches. Today, most of the bridge spans dry land, the river no longer what it once was after a dam was built upriver, centuries after the bridge's construction.

This ancient bridge is famous for the story of a knight, Don Suero de Quiñones, whose unrequited love led him to challenge any knight wishing to cross, to joust him atop this expansive overpass. Those not brave enough would need to ford the river below. Decades later, a book was published inspired by the knight's life and his story of unanswered love. The book is *Don Quixote*.

Our *uneventful* crossing leads us to a charming village along a stone-paved avenue, following the same route as an ancient Roman road from León to Astorga. We pass a beautiful church, small shops, several albergues and signs directing pilgrims to still others. This town would be a lovely place to stop, but our day is just starting, so we keep moving. Minutes later, we come to a fork in the road, with arrows pointing in two different directions. After yesterday's walk, we choose what seems like the more scenic route through a couple of small towns instead of walking alongside a roadway. Clouds appear as we pass through Villares de Orbigo, and eventually, the pavement recedes. We now tread on a red dirt road through a slowly changing landscape. More trees than we have seen in a week, and gentle climbs and descents replace the ironed landscape of the Meseta.

We reach the last of the three sections of personal development along the Camino. After the Meseta and the long days of desolation, my mind having ping-ponged from my life's events, the Camino is said to be taking a spiritual turn as I near the end of my journey. But as my legs continue to move, my thoughts continue to flow.

High on one of the hills, as I start my descent, I spot five solo pilgrims walking ahead, each separated by fifty meters or so, all with their own thoughts. What is swirling in their minds? Are they thinking of their lives after returning home? Of past or current relationships? Dysfunctional family dynamics? Struggles with drugs or alcohol? Or are they simply thinking of the beauty all around? Maybe it's just about their sore feet and whether they'll make it to Santiago. I follow the others, and my mind settles on Cosima and what might be.

Our walk continues along a wide gravel lane. Seemingly in the middle of nowhere, a small stand appears next to the path. This kiosk offers a wide selection of food and drinks at no charge to passing pilgrims. We spend ten minutes talking to David, a handsome Spaniard with a manicured beard and deep tan who looks to be in his late thirties. We find he owns this property and makes his offering to pilgrims 24/7, 365 days a year. Next to the stand, he has built a small two-sided hut with a wood-burning stove to keep himself and passing pilgrims warm during the colder months. A single-story red clay building sits back twenty meters, young trees and bushes growing in front. There is a small can hidden where he accepts donations, yet he says, "the Camino provides." His generous offering to those passing by comes with no expectation of anything in return. As we walk on, I wonder if David's own experience on the Camino led him to settle on this ancient road.

"What are you going to do when you finish the Camino?" Diana asks.

"Long term, I have no idea," I say. "But for now, I'll keep driving Uber. Hopefully, I'll stumble into something I find more meaningful."

"Are you still going to travel?"

"Yeah, I expect to," I say. "After I met Kelly, I reverted to a life of routine. The same kind of life I'd grown tired of before I divorced. This time, I was sitting behind the wheel instead of a desk."

"I don't think it's routine you hate. I think you need something that excites you." Diana says.

"Maybe," I say as I think over her words. "You're right. I wasn't planning for my next adventure or trying to unearth new passions. I was content to be in a relationship, happy for the companionship of a sweet woman."

"Do you love her?"

"Yes, and I was definitely in love. She had become like a drug, and I was always looking for my next fix."

"You're on the Camino now, so something must have happened."

"Yep … she broke it off. She told me she didn't think I was done with my wanderings and didn't see a future with me. I was heartbroken. I booked the flight to come here the day after."

"So, you are on the rebound."

"No, no. It's been like eight months now," I say. "When I look back, it was clear I was relying on her for my happiness, and she felt that pressure. She didn't want to be my addiction. She wanted a man who was following his passions. I think she fell for me because I had found a way to live differently and was adventurous."

"You stopped being adventurous?"

"Maybe, but I sure wasn't focused on myself or my reason for being, only her. I was no longer the guy she fell for. I gave up too much of myself."

"It sounds like she was smart to break it off … for both of you."

"You're right," I say. "When it ended, she shared a wise analogy of two sets of trees growing side by side in a forest. One pair stands tall and straight, with their roots tangled beneath the surface. The other pair had grown twisted together, neither able to grow tall into the sunlight. With Kelly, I had twisted myself around her, and it was stunting us both."

As we near the city of Astorga, the sky darkens and an ultrafine mist appears. We catch up with another pilgrim and start talking. He has walked this route before.

"I am excited to eat a meal you can only find in this area, the Cocido Maragato," he says. "There are several courses, and it includes a wide variety of meats."

"It sounds delicious," I respond.

We part from our culinary guide and soon spot Astorga rising high on a hill, two large towers dominating the view. As we make our climb, the mist turns to a steady drizzle. We shelter next to a building and throw on our rain gear.

We walk through glistening streets, stopping every so often to soak in the amazing architecture. The Bishop's Palace, designed by the famous architect Antoni Gaudi, reminds me of every fairy-tale castle in the princess books I read to my daughter. This surprisingly picturesque palace, constructed of white granite blocks, its turrets topped by spires rising skyward, stands next to the grand Cathedral de Santa Maria. The cathedral has its own dramatic appeal. Built over centuries, it combines numerous architectural styles; its two Baroque towers, visible from afar, flank the original Gothic edifice. I stand for a few minutes in the rain, staring in amazement at the stone carvings that surround the massive cathedral doors, before we continue our stroll through the city.

We enter a plaza and find a large crowd peering in one direction. We turn towards a beautiful building with an ornate facade; its three towers face the plaza, the middle tower housing a large bell with two figures standing guard, a small clock face below. After a minute, we move on. Only later do we learn that every hour, on the hour, the two mechanical figures "standing guard," the Maragatos, move and strike the bell with mallets to signal the new hour. We must have left just before the Maragatos struck.

We pass upscale restaurants and luxury hotels in this touristic city as we wander about. Many restaurants are advertising the regional dish we learned about earlier. We decide 'when in Rome,' as we both want to try this meal. Remembering a fancy-looking restaurant near the cathedral, we head back.

We enter the Hotel Gaudi, directly across from the Bishop's Palace, and remove our packs and wet rain gear in a small reception area. We approach a younger gentleman in a suit behind the desk.

"Hola! We would like to eat; we are excited to try the Cocido Maragato," I say, hoping he speaks English.

"I am sorry," he says, "the cafe doesn't offer this meal … only the restaurant, but it will not open for another forty-five minutes."

He senses our disappointment and says, "Please wait here. I will be right back." A few minutes later, he returns and asks us to follow him. He leads us into the empty restaurant and seats us at a large round table for six, and says with a smile, "Your server will be right with you." Yet another example of how the Camino provides.

I can best describe the restaurant as elegant, with dark stained wood throughout and tufted walls of gold; stylish sconces encircling the room light the space, creating a beautiful ambiance. This will not be a typical pilgrim meal on the Camino.

A lovely middle-aged woman with a big smile approaches. "Hello! I hear you want to order the Cocido Maragato."

What must she think of two wet pilgrims in shorts and T-shirts? Our appearance is quite the contrast to our environs.

"Yes," Diana says. "It was recommended to us. What are the courses?"

After listening to the description, we think we should split an order, only to find this meal is only offered family-style.

Our waitress comes back a few minutes later with a bottle of Rioja and says, "Your first course will be out shortly." Diana and I toast to our good fortune.

Our server and another young woman walk towards us, each with a large platter. On one is a wide variety of meats, and on the other, two dozen slices of tomato drizzled with olive oil.

"Whoa! That's a lot of food," I say, thinking there is no way to finish all this—and this is just the first of many courses. All Diana and I can do is laugh. We cannot identify many of the meats, seven in all, but on closer examination, we do identify one: a pig snout. We try *everything* and eat almost all of what is on both platters.

Thirty minutes after the first course was brought out, the next arrives—a platter of garbanzo beans and sauerkraut, along with another bottle of wine. Again, we manage to almost clear the silver platter. By the time the third course arrives, other diners have arrived and been seated. There are two large groups, both families spanning multiple generations, all dressed in their Sunday best. I have to think; yes, today is Sunday. It is easy to lose track of the days when they all feel the same.

Next up, a large crock of a tomato-based soup with vegetables. Why is the Cocido Maragato served backward? Typically, in Spain, large meals like this start with soup and end with a meat dish. But in this region, they follow the tradition of days long past, when many locals in this region were employed in transporting goods from one place to another, I suppose the equivalent of today's truck drivers. After cooking all their foods together in one pot on their travels, they would eat the best food, the meat, first, before it could get cold. The tradition of eating in this order remains, and of course, it makes an interesting way to attract tourists and pilgrims to try this culinary experience.

Our meal ends with a delicious custard dessert, and by then we are both ready to explode. We pay for our most expensive meal of our Camino, each paying what we think is a reasonable 25€. We grab our packs and step out onto the street, happy to find the rain has stopped during our ninety-minute lunch.

We had passed a large albergue with 150 beds when entering the city, but since Diana prefers not to stay at crowded places and it is not yet three, we keep walking. The clouds slowly vanish as we move west, and the sun brings its accompanying afternoon heat. Five kilometers after leaving Astorga, we reach the small village of Murias de Rechivaldo and check in at the small municipal. This albergue is the most basic of all so far. A small foyer acts as a reception area with two small bathrooms, and it opens to one large room filled with beds. There will be only three others staying here tonight, which leaves most of the fourteen single beds empty.

We rest for a couple of hours before walking several blocks under a darkening sky to find an open bar. Diana and I order beers in the nearly empty establishment and split another regional specialty, a bowl of garlic soup. Neither of us feels much like eating after our extravagant lunch. It's a quiet night in this quiet town. Clearly, most pilgrims choose to stay in Astorga.

As we take turns dipping our spoons into the soup, I say, "Cosima, the volunteer from San Anton, messaged me. She's walking again, and I hope to catch up to her at some point."

"Where is she now?" Diana asks.

"I'm not sure, but she started from Astorga yesterday," I say. "I hope to walk a couple of longer days, but I'll take it day by day."

"Sure," she says, nodding her head.

It is a bit awkward talking to Diana about Cosima, but I want to meet up with her again. Despite the fact I am enjoying my time with Diana, the possibility of a romantic interlude on my Camino is too great to pass up.

We finish the soup and our beers and head back, calling an early end to our evening.

DAY 19: MURIAS DE RECHIVALDO > EL ACEBO

It's important to let go...to feel free from burdens we are keeping in the mind... it's important to move on...from what we were yesterday... it's important to leave things behind...because it's the only way forward.

~ Varima Ranjan Gautam, *Tea with a Sprinkle of Love*

As we walk beneath the stars, the cool morning air chills my bare legs; we quicken our pace to warm up. We slowly gain ground on a pair of lights dancing in the distance. As we get closer, we find the pair is a woman and a child.

Our headlamps alert them to our approach. "Hola," I say when we reach them.

Looking over at us, she says, "Good morning." Then adds, "This is my son, Liam."

The boy looks up at us and quietly says, "Hello."

"How old are you?" I ask.

"Twelve," he says.

We learn they are from England and are spending a week walking the Camino. While not a big hiker, the woman has long known of the Camino and asked her son if he'd like to go on a walking adventure in Spain. He thought it sounded fun. Now, just weeks later, here they are. It reminds me of my travels with my son. One-on-one time with a child to create memories and deepen connections is valuable, be it a day together exploring a new city or a week walking across a foreign country. Diana and I wish them a "Buen Camino" before pulling ahead.

Today's route is to be a slow and steady climb up a mountain to the village of Foncebadón. If we are gaining in elevation this morning, it is barely perceptible. No other pilgrims are in sight as the sky ahead starts to brighten. I turn my head every few minutes to see if the sun's rise is worthy of a photograph.

Walking all day, every day, in one direction is the norm on the Camino, but I have learned to turn around occasionally to see the view behind—it could be incredible. It's also a wise lesson for life; unless you look, you'll never know the perspective of those not headed in your direction.

After three hours on the road, we enter a small village, Rabanal del Camino, and find a table next to a small green space. At a small shop across a narrow lane, we find food to fuel our climb to Foncebadón. We hang out for an hour and chat with other pilgrims who make brief stops. This grassy field is a makeshift campground where pilgrims carrying tents can sleep.

I have passed a couple of campgrounds along the way, but they do not appear frequently enough that one could camp every night. Many pilgrims carry sleeping pads and a tent, but maybe, like Mirla and Alicia, they are on a much longer journey, or perhaps they just prefer to sleep in the wild. I love backpacking and sleeping outdoors, but here on the Camino, I would miss the interactions in the albergues. But everyone must find their own way.

As we head out of the village, the number of pilgrims has multiplied.

Over a dozen others walk solo or in groups within a hundred meters of us. It seems that with our lengthy mid-morning break, many of those who stayed in Astorga last night have caught up. Shades of green dominate my view, made up of foliage alongside the trail and rolling hills in the distance. The wide gravel road narrows to a dirt path, and we march in single file. The rise in elevation is now obvious but doesn't yet slow our pace. The landscape is evolving the higher we climb; both the evergreens and mountains in view grow taller. Our path pulls alongside a roadway, and several pilgrims on bikes pass, following their own route to Santiago.

A yellow arrow appears and directs us away from the roadway. We veer into the woods and climb a steep dirt hillside; large rocks and tree roots help secure our footing. Our ascent continues, and my breath becomes increasingly labored. When Foncebadón finally comes into view, I give Diana an exhausted smile. We cross over the same roadway we left down the mountain and walk on an incline into this small hamlet on high. We pass ruins of long-abandoned buildings and then a few old stone buildings, now restored. One such restoration is the Albergue Monte Irago, named for the mountain we just climbed.

The village consists of maybe twenty buildings, many renovated over the last twenty-five years. This hamlet lost most of its residents to the larger nearby cities in the '60s and '70s and fell into disrepair. By 1990, only two citizens remained, a mother and son. With the Camino's resurgence in the '90s and the return of pilgrims passing through, the town rose from the rubble to help provide for those making their way to Santiago.

The road continues to climb, and we walk past another albergue, a bar, a small shop, and surprisingly, a pizzeria.

"I think we should stay at the parroquial albergue," Diana says. "There is a communal meal."

"Fine with me," I say.

We arrive at Albergue Domus Dei, the last building along this sole passage through town. It is just past noon, and there is a line of pilgrims running from the porch onto the street.

"There are only eighteen beds," she says.

We count the waiting pilgrims in line … sixteen. But we learn the doors do not open until two.

Though I know it would be another memorable experience, I say, "I don't want to stand in line for ninety minutes. I think I am going to keep walking, but I'll understand if you want to stay."

"I'll keep going … *if* we head back to the pizzeria for lunch first," she says with a smile.

The pizzeria is named L'Isola che non c'e, which Diana tells me is Italian for Neverland, from *Peter Pan*. A large sign out front, the actual hood of a car, is red and filled with a colorful painting of Neverland and Peter Pan's silhouette. Diana starts a conversation with two twenty-something Italians behind the counter. The three speak in their language. Later, I find these two longtime friends, along with a third, had walked the Camino a few years earlier and agreed to make a life somewhere along the storied trail. I am finding this life choice not uncommon. Together, they decided on Foncebadón to open a pizzeria serving authentic Italian pizza. The restoration and creation of the restaurant and attached living space was quite the project. The three opened this place last spring and are doing well. The pizza, of course, is delicious.

Thirty minutes after leaving the restored village, we arrive at one of the most iconic landmarks along the Way, the Cruz de Ferro, or Iron Cross. This marks the high point of the Camino, at 4,934 feet (1505 meters). A cross has been standing atop this mountain for centuries. Only a few others are here, as many have stopped for the day in Foncebadón. Diana and I learn many pilgrims will walk here for sunset (with a bottle of wine) and then walk back to the village to sleep. While it sounds like a beautiful night, our choice has been made.

The monument here is the epitome of simplicity: a tall wooden pole, twenty feet tall, topped by an iron cross. The pole rises from an ever-increasing pile of stones left by pilgrims on their way to Santiago. There is no consensus on how long the Cruz de Ferro has been standing in this spot, nor the exact reason for its construction. The wooden pole and cross standing here today are copies; the originals are on display in the Museum of the Way, housed in the Bishop's Palace back in Astorga.

Tradition holds that those on pilgrimage carry a stone from their hometown and drop it at the Cruz de Ferro to signify leaving their burdens behind. Like the cross, this ritual's origins are also unknown, but most modern pilgrims honor this custom, as evidenced by the growing mound before us.

I climb over the burdens left behind. Many stones have writing on them, and the languages are varied. Pilgrims from all across the globe stop here and contemplate the burdens they carry and pray they can move forward carrying a lighter load in life, just as they move from here with a slightly lighter pack. Resting my hand on this simple wooden pole, I drop a small stone that has been in my pack since I started my journey.

Leaving this symbol of the burden carried, I hope to walk from here unencumbered by the guilt I have been carrying for years. Guilt for not being the son and brother I should have been in the years after moving out of my childhood home—guilt for selfishly asking my wife of twenty-eight years for a divorce.

Diana and I begin our descent of Mount Irago and soon approach a colorful oasis alongside a quiet lane, still high on the mountain. It is a curious sight, with various flags waving in a gentle breeze, dozens of aging wooden arrow signs giving direction and distance to sacred destinations—Jerusalem and Machu Picchu—and some I assume are previous pilgrims' hometowns, such as Budapest and Bonn. An official sign directly in front of this collection of small buildings makes clear we are in the village of Manjarín. This compound is one of the few habitable places in this remote area, as we have just passed the ruins of many ancient stone homes.

Diana and I follow a short dirt path and enter an old structure with rays of light seeping in from the walls and roof.

"Hola," says a thirty-something man with a big-time hippie vibe.

This is the Encomienda Templaria, a refugio where pilgrims can sleep and enjoy a communal dinner in the Knights Templar tradition. I hesitate to call this an albergue, given its extremely rustic nature; no running water, no electricity, and an aged roof unable to keep out the elements. While I am sure it would make for a memorable night, we keep moving.

The views are incredible as we walk along a gentle downhill section on a narrow, rocky path, mountains as far as I can see. Steep ravines separate our mountain from its neighbors. A small stone hamlet with a handful of stone houses balances on the side of one. Amazing!

As we move in silence, an indescribable feeling surfaces. I smirk and slowly shake my head as I follow my lovely Italian friend. The blue sky above, filled with white fluffy clouds drifting not too far above our heads, the emerald green of the tree-covered mountains, the dusty brown of the trail beneath our feet. Breathing in the smell of juniper and dry earth. I snap an image to memory, and the words that first come to mind are French: *joie de vivre*. And the next word: *grateful*.

When the trail turns, a vista opens to show a broad valley and the large city of Ponferrada in the distance. I have grown used to the heat of the afternoon, but today, up at elevation, the clouds give brief respites from the sun, and with a gentle breeze, the temperature is ideal. We stop for a short break before a steep section of trail. My pack makes for a comfortable seat. I gaze past the city to the mountains we will be crossing in the coming days. Diana pulls out her guidebook, and again we decide on a destination, the village of El Acebo.

We still have a way to go, and the trail becomes steeper and rockier. My pace slows as I take each step with care. Eventually, a mild twinge in my knee appears with every step, and I worry what that might mean.

When a small village appears farther down the mountain, I say, "I sure hope that's it."

When we arrive, a sign reads *El Acebo*, and a sense of relief washes over me. Like most places on the Camino, it caters to pilgrims. We walk the length of the village and find the newest and most modern of all the albergues I've seen so far. It is more like a hotel in both price and feel: a pool, a spa, a restaurant, and rooms that are shared by only six. Our choice, however, is the Albergue Parroquial Apóstol Santiago, when we learn there will be a communal meal.

Our hospitaleros are two American men from Los Angeles, the first American hosts I have come across. After checking in, we must leave our backpacks and shoes downstairs, so we dig a change of clothes and toiletries from our packs and head up solid wooden stairs to our bunks and showers.

After I complete my daily chores, I wander along the only street in this quaint village on the side of a mountain. On a patio outside a two-story stone building with a cafe and rooms available, I order a Coke.

This morning's stop at the Cruz de Ferro has me thinking. I've read that childhood is when we develop the lens through which we see the world and how we cope with pain. When I reflect on my life's choices, it seems I will do anything possible to steer clear of painful events, by searching for something to distract me from them. I've always been a dreamer, thinking about the future instead of dealing with the issues at hand, ignoring the work of addressing the root of the problem, the shard of glass causing me pain.

Examples that come to mind include: failing out of college—blow off finals week and take a month-long road trip. Passing through a vigorless midlife—get divorced and travel solo for a year. My relationship with Kelly ends—book a flight to Europe and walk the Camino.

Always running. Have I learned nothing?

At least a dozen pilgrims are gathered on the patio. A few, I find, are staying in the fancy new albergue, but most have just arrived and haven't yet found accommodations.

"There is a communal meal at the parroquial albergue," I say.

"What … you cook together?" a guy at a table of four asks.

"Kind of. Everyone helps out in some way, and then everyone shares a meal," I say, surprised no one at their table has yet experienced my favorite element on the Camino. "You should experience it at least once."

Later, in the albergue's courtyard, I chat with David, one of the hospitaleros. I'd guess he's in his mid-sixties and find that he and John, the other host, have been volunteering at this albergue the past few years.

"How did you become a hospitalero?" I ask.

"A pilgrim association in the States holds a weekend training session. The only requirement is to have walked at least a part of a pilgrimage," he says. "Most other countries have a similar system." David is effusive about his time spent helping pilgrims. It seems the most important prerequisite for volunteers is to like people, and I haven't met any who didn't tick that box. These volunteers are different than the small handful of those staffing some of the large municipal albergues, who seem to view the job as their own nine-to-five grind.

The preparations for tonight's feast begin as American music from the '70s plays in the background. My habit of chopping vegetables for the salad continues, and soon the elder half of the Spanish mother/daughter duo from a few nights back joins me at the sink. Our communication, reduced to smiles and hand gestures, is more than enough to complete our task. Our host, John, prepares the main course tonight, while others make sangria, slice bread, set the table, or pour glasses of water.

When we finally all sit down to dinner, someone asks to pass the sangria, only to discover the glasses on the table are all filled with water.

"It's our way to ensure pilgrims get enough water in their bodies after the day's exertions," David says with a grin.

I give a nod and smile at two of the pilgrims I spoke with earlier, who are seated at the table. Before the food comes out, we are asked to share something about our Camino. My share tonight: "I feel more like myself on the Camino than I do back home. The openness of those I've met on this walk has led me to be more open with them and myself. I have formed more meaningful connections here on the Camino in two weeks than I have back home in the last two years."

There's something about gathering around a physical table that unites people. No matter who you are, where you're from, and whether or not you recognize it, eating together encourages us to bond. Halfway through the meal, two more pilgrims arrive and join us to share what food is left.

Before dinner is over, David stands and says, "Everyone is welcome to join us for sunset at the edge of town."

A bit later, ten of us gather out front of the albergue and find it has turned quite chilly. Most of us run back in to add a layer. Together we walk a hundred meters to a large wooden cross sitting atop a layered concrete platform. It creates a perfect place to sit and reflect. The view is stunning—the valley laid out below, against a backdrop of low mountains and a pink and orange glow. Conversations continue as the sun drops behind a veil of clouds.

"There is an excellent photo opportunity from a certain spot, maybe twenty meters back," David says.

John leads a few of us over to it. "Amazing," I say. The setting sun in the center of the intersecting wooden beams, a bright yellow ribbon of light crossing the sky created by the gap between clouds and the mountains on the horizon, and the silhouette of pilgrims sitting beneath the cross. The shutter on my phone's camera engages ... snap.

The perfect ending to my day.

DAY 20: EL ACEBO >
VILLAFRANCA DEL BIERZO

You have the freedom to be yourself, your true
self, here and now, and nothing can stand in
your way.

- Richard Bach, *Jonathan Livingston*
Seagull

This morning, we are only two among a large pack of pilgrims walking
out of town as the route follows the sole roadway leading to this
mountain haven. Slowly the pack thins out as we make our way down
the mountain. After passing through a small town, Riego de Ambrós,
the trail steepens. I've worried about my knee after yesterday's descent,
but so far today, it feels fine; the twinge is gone.

   Walking through woods on a rocky pathway, the trail switchbacks
to soften our descent. Diana and I find ourselves the only two in a
narrow valley. Leaf-filled trees covering the hills, crossing a dry creek
bed, the rustling of leaves, and the quiet chirping of birds the only

sounds. My steps slow and my head slowly turns to survey this serene tableau—yet another unexpected moment of bliss here on the Camino. After the steepest section of the morning, the trail drops onto a road leading to the town of Molinaseca. A steepled church towers above the small town, visible as soon as there is a bend in the road. We make a quick stop to fill our water bottles next to another church, this one built into the hillside, and then cross over a bridge into the heart of Molinaseca along a picturesque, cobbled walkway. Our route soon rejoins the same road that led into town as it now heads out.

We are both in need of caffeine after two hours of walking. As we're not finding a bar, our morning pick-me-up drops from a vending machine inside an upscale albergue we happen upon. Properly fueled, with the downhill portion of the day behind us, we sail along at a good clip. Our route turns south and meanders through a small village before crossing over the Boeza River. We enter Ponferrada, the last large city on the Camino before reaching Santiago de Compostela.

Diana will be meeting up with two Spanish friends from her previous Camino about an hour outside this city. It is not yet ten, and Diana has a few hours before meeting her friends. We find the huge medieval Templar castle here and elect to spend our spare time exploring it. The castle's exterior looks exactly as I picture a medieval castle. We climb a ramp and cross over what was once the moat-spanning drawbridge. Entering the gates between two stone towers, we stop and pay the reduced pilgrim entrance fee and drop our packs behind the small ticket kiosk.

We follow a self-guided tour, with English translations, through the castle, which I find fascinating. We walk along the fortress walls. Up and down the stairways in the guard towers. Then across the large grass-and-gravel plaza in this ancient fortress's center. The views from the castle are spectacular, with mountains in all directions. There are many displays throughout that explain life in this castle. The restorations completed are amazing, and more work is in progress. Our time is well spent.

The route leaving Ponferrada gets a bit sketchy, as we walk on the side of a busy road with cars zipping by every ten seconds. We are relieved when we finally reach Camponaraya and walk along a sidewalk.

Diana's friends live about an hour away and are driving here to have lunch and catch up. "I'm planning to stop in Villafranca del Bierzo, about fifteen kilometers ahead. That will make it another forty-kilometer day," I say.

"I'll meet you there. I shouldn't be too far behind you," she says.

When we arrive at their rendezvous point, a horn sounds and Diana leaves to meet her old friends. I keep following the yellow arrows.

A few minutes later, I cross over a major highway, and the Camino bisects fields of recently harvested crops as the sun beats down. An hour into my afternoon walk, I arrive, overheated and exhausted, in the town of Cacabelos. After finding provisions in a small market, I search for shade to enjoy a picnic lunch and find the perfect spot in a tree-lined park next to the Cúa River.

A steady stream of pilgrims passes by as I stretch out on the grass, my head resting against my pack. As my body cools down, my thoughts drift back to the decision to come to Spain.

I know now that my breakup with Kelly was a needed wakeup call; it forced me again to think about what I want to do with my life. After my divorce two years earlier, the answer to that same question was simple: adventure. I had found it. But I took a step backward during my time with Kelly, giving up too much of myself.

Thinking of Shakespeare's words in *Hamlet*, "to thine own self be true," I understand that travel and adventure are important to me; I can't lose those pieces without losing a part of myself.

I start a long climb on the shoulder of the highway before coming to a fork in the road. A sign has an arrow pointing to the right, but common sense and Google Maps says continuing along the highway is the fastest and most direct route to my destination. The pilgrim in me, who wants to experience the official route, wins out over the near-exhausted me, and I turn right.

Soon I am walking on a wide gravel path through dusty fields of almost-ripe grapes; harvest season is fast approaching. I eat a stolen grape and feel my face pucker at the taste, but the juice is refreshing. I pick another handful and keep walking. When I reach the deserted hamlet of Valtuille de Arriba, I don't see a soul. I pass an interesting building with a low-slung roof and empty tables outside. It's likely a bar, and a cold drink is enticing, but I want only to reach Villafranca and rest my feet. I follow yellow arrows painted on decaying stone houses and am soon heading back in the general direction from which I came. A couple of short uphill sections along a dirt road lead past more vineyards and a picturesque scene that makes up for the extra distance. A crisp white house on a hillside covered with vines sits under two towering trees beneath a cerulean sky. I snap a picture and keep moving.

Somewhere along the Camino, I learned of a 'hippie-ish' albergue in Villafranca Del Bierzo, and the gypsy spirit in me wants to stay there tonight. I remember the name *Felix* and Google the lodgings in the city as I get close. I find an Albergue de Peregrino Ave Fénix, and it turns out to be one of the first buildings I come to upon entering the city along the official route.

The albergue has a different vibe than most; it seems to be mostly younger pilgrims staying here. When checking in, I am asked, "Would you prefer the quieter room?" I'm guessing this is where most of the older pilgrims are staying.

"No, the main room is fine," I say.

"Would you like dinner tonight or breakfast?

"Yes, both please," I say.

Besides the indoor dining room, which houses one long table, all the common areas are outside, on two levels, most protected from the elements by the roof's long, overhanging eaves. There are stone-paved pathways, small trees growing in the courtyard, and a gazebo-like structure in the garden. It is reminiscent of my summers as a kid in Wisconsin's Northwoods; there is a definite summer camp feel. My sleeping quarters are in the attic of this near century-old building, beneath solid timber beams.

Diana arrives an hour or so later. "There is supposedly a beach along the river that runs through town," she says.

"Sounds great! Let's go," I say.

I throw on my quick-drying walking shorts and stuff my travel towel into my pocket. We head out to find it.

We zigzag our way through streets descending towards the center of this bustling city; we walk along a riverside path and spot a narrow pedestrian bridge. We cross to find hundreds of people lying about in a large, grassy field, about the size of a football field. This green 'beach' abuts the river, a mountain rising steeply from behind. Dam-like walls have been built both up- and downstream to create a large swimming area. Large boulders line the other bank, and kids are jumping from them into the river.

I wade into the barely flowing river; the cold water is refreshing. I submerge and swim towards the river's center before climbing out on steps fashioned out of rocks. I scan the crowd and think there must be a handful of other pilgrims here, though I'm unsure.

While I'm excited to be staying in this town tonight, I think it would make a great place to break up a long day walking under the summer sun. Neither of us had been aware of this oasis until Diana learned of it from a woman she met on her way. I message Jana, send a picture of the beach, and tell her this is a must-stop.

After an hour of riverside sunbathing, we wander through this beautiful town. Tour buses are parked in the city center, and I can understand why. Villafranca del Bierzo sits in a small valley at the edge of the Cantabrian Mountains, with plenty of nicer hotels, restaurants, historic churches and palaces, all in a beautiful locale.

"Should we stop for a beer?" I ask.

"Great idea," she says with a smile.

We sit on a patio on the main plaza in town, people-watching and drinking beer. There are loads of people walking about; some are carrying bags of groceries, a mother walks with two toddlers, a man in a suit carries an expensive briefcase, and of course, there are many wearing large packs.

We make our way back around dusk, just in time for dinner. This is one of the oldest continually operating albergues along the Camino. It has been in the same family for eighty-two years. One of the descendants, Jesus, in his seventies, cooks a delicious meal that includes vegetables from their garden.

Over our meal, I chat with siblings, both in their thirties, from Scotland, walking the Camino for two weeks.

The woman says in her accented English, "I had to twist his arm to get him to come along."

"True, but I am now glad I came," her brother replies.

"We start and end each day together, but he walks at a much slower pace," she says.

"We live a couple of hours apart back home, and I don't see her too often," he says. "It has been good spending time together."

"What a great idea, to walk the Camino," I say.

"He complains about the walking," she says. "But I think he likes it more as the days pass."

The Camino is a great way to make new friends, but I am finding it is also an excellent way for family or friends to strengthen longtime bonds.

While at dinner, I get a message from Cosima. *Where are you tonight?*

The hippie albergue in Villafranca del Bierzo after a 40 km day.

I knew you would stay there. You must want to catch up to me?

Is it that obvious?

We are in La Faba tonight.

I have another big day in me. Maybe I'll walk 50 km tomorrow.

The gap has been closed to twenty-three kilometers. At this point, it seems clear I will indeed catch her. I do wonder who the "we" in her message refers to.

DAY 21: VILLAFRANCA DEL BIERZO > O CEBREIRO

*Because in the end, you won't remember the
time you spent working in the office or
mowing your lawn. Climb that goddamn
mountain.*

~ Jack Kerouac, *The Dharma Bums*

Diana and I retrace our steps from yesterday as we weave through
narrow streets squeezed by beautifully restored two- and three-story
homes in the early morning twilight. We reach the city center, not
finding a single soul. Then back along the promenade, the only sounds
our footsteps, and the quiet babbling of the river.

A larger-than-life stone pilgrim points the way, and we cross a bridge
and head out of this memorable town. A minute later, we find a sign and
arrow for an alternate route, the Camino Duro.

Diana checks her guidebook and says, "This route is not much
longer but has a lot of elevation change before connecting with the

official route in Trabadelo."

"I'm fine with either," I say. "But we have a climb to O Cebreiro to end the day."

"The alternate should have some amazing views, but I don't want to kill ourselves before we have an even tougher climb," she says.

"Fine by me," I say, a bit relieved.

Diana and I leave Villafranca del Bierzo, our walk relatively flat through a narrow valley beside a highway but inside a protective concrete barrier. As the sky brightens, the traffic zooming past increases, and the tree-covered hills draw my eyes as we make our way higher. After two and a half hours of walking on asphalt, my feet feel as if they've been beaten. We crash outside a bar when we reach the small village of Trabadelo. Diana heads inside. A few minutes later, she walks out with a café con leche for each of us.

"This is going to be a long day," she warns. "I am already tired, and it's not even noon."

"My feet hurt," I say as I massage a bare foot. "They've gotten progressively worse over the last few days."

We soon return to our roadside walk, passing through small villages every few kilometers. When we reach Las Herrerias, ten kilometers since our last stop and the last place to refuel before we start our longest climb since crossing the Pyrenees, we take an extended break and relax in the shade of a large beech tree.

The route continues along the road and starts to gain elevation faster as the sun glares down upon us. Finally, an arrow points to a path in the woods and off the asphalt. It is good to be out of the sun, but immediately the effort needed to make our way intensifies. After a few switchbacks on rocky terrain, we head straight up, the grade much steeper than any climb along the Camino so far. I am faster on the uphills than Diana, and when we stop for one of our frequent breathers, I say, "I'm going to keep going. I'll see you at the top." I push on.

The constant climb continues, and I pass many pilgrims on the ascent. My breathing is labored, but I make my way ever higher. Despite my road-tested legs and cardio training, this section is a struggle, but I don't stop.

I have always loved climbing a mountain as an analogy for life. In a college philosophy class, I wrote a paper about finding happiness. I based it on a story told by the French philosopher and Catholic priest Pierre Teilhard de Chardin, about three men heading up a mountain. The first man turns back after the climb becomes too challenging; he is the pessimist. The second climbs higher and finds he is content frolicking in a meadow with beautiful views of the valley below; he is the hedonist. The third is the enthusiast, and he must continue for the sake of the climb; he is seeking something more.

For much of my life, I was the second, seemingly content with what I had. But as I slowly passed through the middle of my life, I spotted something higher on the mountain and felt a growing need to resume my climb. After my divorce, I gained in elevation but eventually lost sight of my path. Still determined, I hope to blaze my own trail to reach heights still unknown.

There are as many paths to 'finding happiness' as there are people on this earth, and, as on the Camino, there is no right or wrong way. I hope, for everyone setting out on their own journey, that they will find *their* way.

I am confident my inner compass will lead me, but I know that much effort will be required to reach the peak, just as in today's climb.

Clanging bells wake me from my thoughts, and seconds later, three large latte-colored cows and a dog barking directions at them pass by. A middle-aged man follows as they all head down the mountain. I turn and watch them veer off the path, through a gate and into a grassy hillside meadow. Minutes later, my path leaves the forest's cover and enters the small hamlet of La Faba, where Cosima started her day.

Finding a fountain as soon as I walk into this hilltop village, I refill my bottles and then sit in the shade of a building as I catch my breath.

I make my way to El Refugio, combination bar and albergue, and order a sandwich and an Aquarius. Young, friendly, hippie-ish volunteers run this place, and like last night's accommodation, it has quite a cool vibe. A garden across a narrow street provides much of the food for the vegetarian cuisine they serve here. They also provide shelter for up to eight pilgrims each night. Sitting at a table out front while eating my lunch, I expect Diana to walk up any minute. When she doesn't, I continue on.

No longer protected by the forest that shaded me lower on the mountain, my head is now beaded with sweat. I walk through a lovely mountain meadow, the long grasses swaying in the breeze, and watch as a hawk floats at eye level, far above the valley below. The expansive vistas of the surrounding mountains and a brilliant blue sky overhead make this one of the most beautiful scenes on my Camino so far. I experience what is becoming common on this walk: a brief bout of euphoria.

While the hike since La Faba has not been as difficult as it was getting there, the route becomes more challenging as the afternoon passes. Eventually, I reach a five-foot-tall graffitied stone marker signifying the Camino's entrance into the Spanish region of Galicia.

Galicia comprises the northwest corner of Spain; it is bordered on two sides by the Atlantic, and to the south, Portugal. Galicia is known for its green landscape of rolling hills and is the rainiest region in Spain. Even in the summer months, rain is not uncommon here. Luckily, this afternoon there is not a cloud in sight.

Reaching O Cebreiro winded, I collapse onto a low stone wall, alongside a roadway that found its own way to this mountaintop village. The views from here are stunning. I look out over a sea of green, a valley with dark-green patches of evergreens and a patchwork of faded green fields along the slopes, leading down to an unseen stream. In the distance, tree-covered mountains reach towards the horizon.

As I enter the village, off to my right I find a beautifully preserved church, Santa Maria la Real, built in 836. It is here I learn the history of the ubiquitous yellow arrows along the Camino. The parish priest here in O Cebreiro, Elías Valiña Sampedro, a Camino scholar, dedicated much of the last part of his life to bringing the Camino back to life. He led the effort to revive lost stretches of the ancient route and map out a modern-day route to Santiago de Compostela. In 1984, he began painting yellow arrows marking the route now known as the Camino Frances. When asked why he was painting the arrows, he responded, "I am preparing for an invasion." Elías Valiña died in 1989, before his prediction came to fruition. He is buried here at the church he presided over; a bronze bust of this visionary stands outside to honor his contribution to bringing back what was almost lost. Just as he predicted, millions of pilgrims have walked at least a part of this man's legacy.

I wander around and find only about a dozen ancient stone buildings, surrounded by cobbled lanes that run through this mountaintop refuge. Fieldstones in every shade of brown dominate my view. It seems that long ago they constructed every building and pathway with this abundant resource. I love the monochromatic esthetic it creates in this picturesque village.

I find a seat in front of an oval-shaped stone building with a rounded, thatched roof to wait for Diana. I learn that the building is a small museum honoring this type of traditional dwelling, called a *palloza*. While I'm waiting, my phone pings.

I open a message from Cosima. *My brother and I are staying in Fonfria tonight. Where are you?*

Her brother!? I now assume she has been walking with her brother since her return to the Camino. With this news, I wake from my dream of a romantic ending to my walk across Spain. She is only twelve kilometers ahead. I message back, *I am sitting in O Cebreiro now. I should finally catch up to you tomorrow.* She messages back a smiley-face emoji.

Diana arrives about thirty minutes later. "The walk was beautiful, no?" she says with a tired smile. "I thought it would never end."

"I know, I loved it. This place is amazing, too," I say.

We wander around together, passing a couple of restaurants, a gift shop, a small hotel, and a few smaller places with rooms to let, then walk to the municipal albergue on the far edge of the village. This modern structure contrasts with the rest of O Cebreiro and is the only albergue.

We find a line of pilgrims outside waiting to check in. We claim the 64th and 65th beds of the 104 available.

Upon the advice of the woman who checked us in, we walk back to the village center and find a restaurant to reserve a time for dinner. Diana and I agree to meet outside the albergue just before our reservation, and I head to my bunk for a needed rest after today's exertions.

I climb down from my top bunk onto sore feet. I must look like a ninety-year-old man as I shuffle ahead, taking tiny steps. My funny walk and accompanying grimace are now the norm whenever I am off my feet for an extended time. Luckily, the pain recedes after a few minutes of movement. While waiting for Diana out front, I find there are no more beds available, here or in any other accommodations in the village. Any pilgrims that arrive now must continue to the next village … eight kilometers ahead.

Two such pilgrims walk away from the albergue, both looking tired, but they smile as they continue their walk, which will end well past sunset. I don't think I would have taken the news with such grace.

Diana and I are seated in a large dining room with windows overlooking the green rolling hills, on the opposite side of the mountain from which we arrived. Dinner, as expected, is a pilgrim menu with options for each course. Thirty others, primarily pilgrims, were already seated when we arrived. Somehow, two smiling servers work efficiently to get everyone fed promptly.

The sky slowly turns dark as we eat a typical, yet tasty meal. Over dessert, I say, "I think I'll catch up to the woman from San Anton at some point tomorrow." I assume Diana knows I hope for romantic entanglement with Cosima, but it remains unspoken. We started walking together ten days ago, the same day I met Cosima, and we have grown close, sharing our true selves.

"There is an alternate route tomorrow that leads to a historic monastery in Samos. I am planning to stay there tomorrow," she says.

"I don't know if I'll be headed there or not," I say. "It will depend on if I reach her before the detour."

After dinner we meander through this dimly lit hamlet high in the Galician mountains under a sky blanketed by stars, our heads a bit lighter after sharing two bottles of wine. There is a chill in the air at this elevation, and we soon head back to the albergue for a good night's sleep.

DAY 22: O CEBREIRO > SAMOS

It is the possibility of a dream coming true
that makes life interesting.

~ Paulo Coelho, *The Alchemist*

A light in front of the albergue illuminates a haze; the temperature is the lowest it's been yet. We head out with several others and find an unexpected climb to begin the day. Headlamps guide our way.

The sun's rise becomes evident, but it remains hidden from view, our elevation fluctuating after leaving O Cebreiro. When we reach the apex of one brief climb, we find an impressive ten-foot bronze statue, depicting a pilgrim from centuries ago battling the wind atop Alto de San Roque. This morning, high in the mountains under an overcast sky, Diana and I are likewise headed into a substantial wind.

After a few hours, we encounter a steep hill leading to yet another peak. The hike up to Alto do Poio reaches 4386 feet, even higher than O Cebreiro. As is usually the case, I start to pull ahead, my goal of catching Cosima now front of mind. I turn and say, "I'm going to keep going. I will wait for you before the detour to Samos."

When I reach the top, I keep walking despite my lungs' pleas. Once my breath returns, my objective clear, I accelerate my pace.

Uncertain what a reunion means, I think again of our single evening and a handful of texts. Am I reading something into it that isn't there? Maybe it's simply a younger woman finding an older guy interesting, and maybe she finds him attractive, so she flirts and strokes his ego. If that is the case, it will be disappointing, yet getting to know someone from another foreign land is still an intriguing prospect.

Sooner than I expect, I reach Fonfria, a small settlement consisting of a few homes. I make my way along a concrete pathway, trying my best to avoid what the village cows have left behind on their way to and from the surrounding fields, though I cannot escape the stench. It is not yet ten o'clock when I pass an albergue, Cosima's starting point.

Continuing at my hurried pace, the trail now on a descent, I pass many other walkers, but none with the long red hair I remember from San Anton. At one point, I pass two guys gingerly descending a particularly steep section. What has caused them to slow to a crawl?

An hour has passed since I walked through Fonfria, and I sense Cosima must be getting close. Will I instantly recognize her face? Or have the intervening days clouded my memory? The trail takes a turn and heads down into a tiny village, or, more precisely, a handful of buildings crowded around the intersection of two narrow gravel roads. I pass Albergue Fillobal and then a bar but don't stop, despite my growing hunger. A few steps past the bar, I glimpse, standing alone under an ancient oak, the back of a woman with long, red hair. I walk towards her, then past, stop and turn.

As I stand in front of her, smiling, we make eye contact. "Cosima?"

"Hi!" she says, as she reaches out for a hug.

"It took a while to catch you," I say, grinning sheepishly. "When I left that morning, I wasn't sure I'd see you again."

"I knew you'd find me," she teases, her German accent prominent.

"I have thought of you often," I say with a smirk.

We stand alongside the trail as others pass by.

"I met my family on the northern coast for a few days—my brother,

Till, said he'd like to experience the Camino for a couple of days," she says. "We took the bus back to Astorga, and he's been with me ever since."

"Where is he?" I ask.

"He's behind on the trail," she says. "He hurt his knee on his second day, coming down from Foncebadón. He still has trouble going downhill, and he's walking with a friend he met on the Camino. I am waiting here to let them catch up."

"I know them. I flew past them about thirty minutes ago, and yeah, they were going slow."

"Are you taking the route to Samos?" I ask.

"Yes. Are you?"

"Well … I am now."

Cosima laughs. "That is why I am waiting for Till. I want to make sure he knows which way to go when the route splits."

We are still standing in the same spot talking when Diana walks towards us.

"You remember each other," I say. They both nod and exchange greetings.

"I am headed to Samos, too," I tell Diana.

We talk for a couple of minutes before Diana says, "I'm going to keep walking. I'll see you there."

"Have you been walking together since San Anton?" Cosima asks.

"Yeah," I say, "we walk at a similar pace and get along well."

"I can tell she does not like me," she says.

"Why?" I ask. My brow furrows.

"You should have seen the look she gave me."

"What? No, I'm sure you're reading into it."

Cosima responds by raising her eyebrows.

Diana and I enjoy each other's company, but I am eager to spend time with Cosima, who has been on my mind for days. If Diana feels jilted—not the right word, but you get my meaning—I am saddened, but am glad I'll see her later in Samos.

After waiting another five minutes, Cosima messages her brother to remind him of the detour in Triacastela and to meet her in Samos. We throw on our packs and start walking.

Cosima has an emerald-colored Kelty brand pack, wears a navy blue skort, a black tank top, and well-worn hiking boots. Her hair is pulled back into a long ponytail, now hidden under her pack. She walks with a wooden walking stick, which moves in unison with her strides. On her wrist, a couple of bracelets dangle as her arm propels it forward. "I'm bringing this stick to Santiago, to return it to a friend who forgot it at an albergue the day he left our little Camino family," she says. "Santiago is his childhood home."

"I left it at our albergue this morning and had to backtrack twenty minutes to retrieve it," Cosima says and looks at me with a smirk. "Why did you think you caught up to me so easily this morning?"

I smile back and think she has been just as excited about seeing me again as I have been about seeing her.

We walk at a leisurely pace, talking more about our adventures since our evening by the fire. Time flies by, and in no time, we are entering the town of Triacastela along the main road. As we approach a bar, a guy sitting at a table outside waves. I don't recognize him, so clearly, he is waving to Cosima.

"This is Cameron. He too is from the States," she says.

The two of us shake hands. "This is Mike," she says.

We all settle at the table.

Cameron looks to be around thirty and lives in California. I learn they met in Astorga, where Cameron started his walk, and their small 'Camino family' has been walking together for a week now. Cameron only has two weeks of vacation but wanted to experience the Camino, so he is walking a shortened version ending in Santiago.

I am happy to get off my feet after walking seventeen kilometers, with only the one brief stop, but I am taken aback by Cameron's presence. The uncertainty of Cosima's feelings towards me resurfaces.

"Altras!" Cameron says.

I look down at Cameron's feet and laugh. "You're only the second person on the entire Camino who I've met wearing them," I say.

"You're the first I've seen," he says.

This brand of shoes is popular in the States for long-distance hikers. I have owned several pairs of these same shoes since I discovered them years ago. Cameron is also loyal to this brand and tells me he hiked the entire PCT in them. I'm impressed he completed this legendary hike.

Cosima leaves us and goes into the bar to use the restroom. The first thing Cameron says when she leaves is, "So you're the famous Mike that Cosima has been raving about. She has been worried you would accidentally pass her."

"Really? I have to admit I wasn't sure what to expect. We only talked for one night," I say. "But it seems she is a kind and generous soul."

I sense he may have a romantic interest in Cosima. He is attractive, and they are much closer in age. There is a chance Cosima may reciprocate Cameron's feelings, but what Cameron shares gives me hope for a more intimate connection.

Cosima walks out of the bar smiling, carrying three bottles of beer. "Cheers!"

Cosima and Cameron both work in the medical field and have worked as EMTs. As we enjoy our cold beer, they share a few amusing emergency-room stories, and I learn of the unusual things people come to the ER to have removed from their rectums.

The three of us resume our walk, and after one hundred meters, the route comes to a T. We turn left while the official route heads right. Samos is ten kilometers ahead, and this detour will add six kilometers to our total distance traveled.

It is a beautiful afternoon, not nearly as uncomfortable as the afternoons along the Meseta. Often, two of us walk side by side, talking, while the other trails behind or walks ahead. When Cameron and I walk together, I learn he is recently divorced and that it wasn't his choice.

"It's been rough. I still love my ex, and I know I always will," he says. "She was my best friend. When I hiked the PCT, it was with her."

"I'm sorry to hear that," I say sincerely.

"We did everything together, so when she asked for a divorce, I was devastated."

"I can't imagine being in your shoes," I say. "When I divorced, it was my decision, but I know it's hard being in love and having to say goodbye."

"I want her to be happy," he says. "But it hurts to see her in another relationship already."

"Yeah, that would be tough."

"I want to move on, but it will be hard to find someone I feel as connected to as I did with her. I don't know what she was looking for."

"I don't know what women want, either," I say. "But I think having something that excites you, something that gets you up in the morning, will translate to all areas of your life. I think women like that, or at least I hope so, because if it's about the money, I'm out of luck."

"I'm kind of lost at this point. Which is why I decided to walk in Spain," he says.

"Me too."

"Cosima is the kind of girl I can see myself with," he says. "She loves the outdoors, is fun to hang out with, and she cares about people."

It seems Cameron is holding out hope for a deeper connection than they have had thus far. I respond, "Yeah, I can tell in the time I've spent with her, she has an empathetic heart. I can't believe she's walked almost a thousand miles."

"I haven't found many like her back in the States," he says.

I can sense he's thinking of his wife. It seems, when he is describing Cosima, he is hitting on the qualities he loved about his ex. "Yeah, it's hard finding a person you connect with on every level," I say.

"I wish us both luck finding the right woman," he says.

There are fewer people on our route to Samos, most pilgrims having stayed on the official route, but this is still a popular detour. We walk through beautiful landscapes, shades of green dominating our views. The time passes quickly as we make our way at a leisurely pace, passing through small villages along quiet roads and along dirt paths through the trees. Our conversation eventually turns to food; none of us have eaten a proper meal all day. Cosima talks of finding someplace to enjoy a picnic dinner, while Cameron is eager for a hot meal at a restaurant. I am open to either.

The three of us find ourselves staring down at a picture-postcard scene. We have a bird's-eye view of the immense monastery resting in a narrow valley below, a backdrop of tree-covered hills rolling beyond.

"It's beautiful," Cosima says.

"This sight alone is worth the extra kilometers," I say.

We descend into the village of Samos and stop at the first small market we pass. I grab an Aquarius, and Cameron buys a box of chocolates. "Please take some," he says as he holds out the box. "I can't possibly eat all these."

We cross a bridge leading to what is the main road through town and stop at a bar across from the monastery. Sitting under a blue sky, the three of us enjoy a cold beer, and then another.

"This place is awesome," Cameron says.

Cosima laughs and asks me, "Do you use the word 'awesome' frequently?"

"I don't think so. Why?"

"Because Cameron says it constantly. It's an easy way to tell he's from the States because Americans always use this word."

Cameron shakes his head and says, "I don't say it that much!"

"I'll be careful not to be the typical American," I say.

Cosima stands and begins waving her arms. Her brother, Till, and his friend approach our table. The two pull over empty chairs. "Nice to meet you both," I say and shake their hands. We order another round.

Till is much younger than Cosima, and tall, his long, blond hair covered by a forest-green baseball cap with a Bitburger Brewery logo. He is also wearing a weary smile. Max, his new friend, also from Germany, is gangly, with an unkempt mop of dark hair and a sparse beard. Till tells of his rough day walking. The many ups and downs of today's route were not easy with his bum knee.

Over our drinks, we discuss dinner options. The consensus is a picnic meal around six. After one last beer, Cameron, Cosima, and I leave Till and Max at the bar and head over to the albergue located on the back side of the monastery.

Cosima and I find lower bunks next to one another, while Cameron takes the bunk above Cosima. Diana is already here and is resting on her bunk. I walk over to her.

"How was your walk this afternoon?" I ask.

"It was good," she says. "Did you visit the monastery yet?"

"No. Have you?"

"Yes. It is beautiful inside," she says. "The courtyard is amazing."

"Do you want to join me and the others I met for a picnic dinner later?" I ask.

"Thanks, but I am having dinner at the restaurant with a couple of others I met on the way here."

"Nice," I say. "We'll talk later. I need to shower."

We don't talk about tomorrow, but everyone must be out of the albergue early, and I assume we will all start out together.

The thick stone walls keep it comfortably cool. There are beds for seventy pilgrims in this one cavernous room. A large unisex bathroom is at one end. When I return from hanging my laundry outside, Diana is no longer on her bunk.

I chat with one of the hospitaleros, who tells me, "There is a 400-year-old cypress tree close by. Those who hug it will be granted good luck." He points out a window in the direction of the tree. Apparently he also talked of this tree and a nearby chapel with Cosima. "Let's go," she says, and we head out to find this luck-inducing cypress.

We cross the street that runs in front of the albergue, past the clotheslines and their colorful array, and walk fifty meters along a quiet street before spotting a gravel path to our left. A towering cypress stands guard next to a small stone chapel, with a stream flowing behind.

We walk in silence along a paved pathway that runs beside the shallow stream, which glides along in the shade of trees lining both banks; the only sounds are the flowing water and the twitter of birds darting past.

A barefoot Cosima wades into the water while I stand back, watching her. She pulls up her flowing gypsy pants to keep them out of the stream. She's wearing a burgundy top with skinny shoulder straps, and a pink gemstone necklace hangs from her neck. She glances back at me, grinning, as speckled sunlight dances on her shoulders. My heart is racing, astonished to be here with this woman.

We step through a small arched doorway into the chapel, Capela do Cipres, built in the tenth century. Walking around each other in this empty but still tight space, I ache to touch her bare skin. My arm involuntarily reaches out as I stand behind her, but my head shoots down the urge to even brush her arm with my trembling hand.

I'm not sure of her feelings towards me, but the possibility of a more intimate connection is exciting. I don't want to risk being told she is not interested in anything physical. *Not risking, so I can keep this hope alive.* Here in this ancient place, it could be a romantic moment to touch her, to hold her, but simply being here is enough.

We stroll back to the monastery's albergue, its available beds dwindling, and expect to find Till and Max checked in. They are not. We decide to find them and to shop for dinner. Cameron opts not to come along and says, "I think I'll find a hot meal before our picnic."

Cosima and I walk along the main road and find Till and Max still drinking. "You should go now and reserve a bed," Cosima tells them. "All the beds will be taken soon."

Samos is a small village dominated by the monastery but has the basics needed to support the pilgrims and tourists who visit this historic site.

Cosima and I walk the length of the main road and notice stairs leading to someplace unknown. We make our way up and find ourselves on a dirt pathway that soon merges with an empty road, where we peer down onto the village below. This quiet lane eventually leads us back down to the main road.

We wander down a narrow alleyway behind buildings that line the street and discover a faded blue Juliet balcony overlooking a small courtyard. On a door that opens onto this small space, a sign says, 'Pension – Double Room 25€.'

Gazing up, Cosima plays the part of Romeo, her arms outstretched, but whispers Juliet's famous line, "Romeo, Romeo …" In my head, the line ending "O that I were a glove upon that hand, that I might touch that cheek." How intoxicating would it be to stay the night here, together.

Back to the task at hand, we locate a decent-sized market and find the makings for our picnic: bread, cheese, salami, cucumbers, tomatoes, three bottles of wine, and a large bottle of beer (for Till). Unfortunately, we aren't able to find any disposable cups for the wine.

"The only other shop in town is the small market we stopped in earlier," I say. "Let's head back there."

I walk up and down the two narrow aisles in this dimly lit shop, to no avail. I grab another bottle of wine and ask the owner, an elderly man behind the counter, for "cuppas," not knowing the Spanish word for cups, and act it out, pouring the bottle into my hand. He pulls out two plastic cups from behind the counter. I return his smile and say "cinco," and he nods. I hand him three 1€ coins for the wine, and he hands me five cups at no charge.

Cosima puts our food and two bottles in a cloth bag she brought along. I transport the three remaining bottles. On our way back to the albergue, we scout out the perfect location for our picnic. A river runs through the town and along the monastery's opposite side. A large meadow spreads out next to the river. We take a stairway next to the bridge and tramp through tall grass to reach the river's bank. In addition to an assembly of ducks, we find a large round slab of concrete, covering something unknown.

"It will make a perfect table for tonight's meal," she says.

We bring our groceries back to the albergue and find all three guys resting on their bunks. Cosima and I do the same. Sensing I will soon drift off to sleep, I set the alarm on my phone.

Around 6:30, the five of us walk past groups of pilgrims sitting outside the restaurant and bars along the main thoroughfare, heading to our riverside spot. I look for Diana but don't see her. We reach our destination, and Cosima tosses out a large, gold-colored, tie-dyed sarong and uses it as a picnic blanket to cover the circle of concrete.

The three Germans all have knives and quickly slice the baguette, salami, cheese, and vegetables. I pour the wine and Till's beer. We raise our plastic cups and say "Prost," the typical German toast. I learn the most important part of the toast is looking each person in the eye when you clink glasses. I am told that, on most evenings along the Way, this small group has dined out as we are doing now.

"My feet are hurting," Cameron says.

"Give them to me," Cosima says.

Cameron moves his legs so Cosima can massage his feet.

"She is too nice to you," Till tells him.

I learn that Cosima tending to Cameron's feet has been a regular occurrence in the evenings. To me, this is an intimate act, but maybe it's her way of showing compassion. I chalk it up her empathetic heart. After all, her goal in life is to become a doctor.

Tonight's picnic fare is simple, tasty, and inexpensive. The total cost was less than 20€, or 4€ each, for a filling meal and a seemingly endless amount of wine. Our engaging conversation lasts well into the evening. As our 10:30 p.m. curfew approaches, we gather the remnants of our meal and stumble and laugh our way back to the albergue.

Opening the door, we find the cavernous room dark; the other sixty-five pilgrims are already in bed. We make our way to our bunks, then head to the bathroom with toothbrushes in hand. Soon, Cosima and I are the only two in the bathroom, standing next to one another. We glance at one another, and our eyes lock. I step closer, caress her cheeks, and lean in for a kiss. We are soon wrapped in an embrace, kissing passionately, both well aware someone could walk in at any moment.

Taking Cosima by the hand, I lead her into a shower stall. We continue kissing, our tongues probing, my hands roaming over her body. This brief make-out session ends before things go any further—and before anyone else enters. Cosima exits the bathroom, and I follow seconds later.

I lie in my bunk in a state of hazy euphoria, ecstatic to know this beautiful and kind woman is interested in something romantic. The poem I started in San Anton continues:

> Finally, I see you again, standing under a tree.
> My plans are changed; I am heading to Samos with you.
> We walk and talk and are soon joined by another; it leaves me uncertain.
> Later we visit a chapel and hug a large cypress.
> Our first picnic is planned as we stroll through the city.
> We stop, your arms outstretched under a blue balcony.
> Simple food and much wine.
> Late that night, our lips first touch.

Soon, the long day of drinking catches up to me, and I fall into a heavy sleep, still grinning—of that I am certain.

DAY 23: SAMOS > SIVIL

You have to take risks. We will only
understand the miracle of life fully when we
allow the unexpected to happen.

~ Paulo Coelho, *By the River Piedra I*
Sat Down and Wept

My alarm sounds. A dull ache fills my head, and it seems to intensify when I smile, remembering the night before. I roll out of bed and put my feet on the floor, my back hunched over. Cosima is standing in between our bunks; I glance up, and we exchange smiles and a "Good morning."

The albergue is a hive of activity. Dozens of pilgrims are loading their packs or making their way to and from the bathroom. A buzz of conversations about finding coffee or breakfast and today's possible destinations fill the room. I search for Diana, but her bunk is empty; her pack gone. I fear she feels I have abandoned her. She could have joined the group I now seemed to have attached myself to, but it would have been awkward after it was just the two of us for so long. It was a blessing to have spent time with Diana. I enjoyed walking with her, opening up to each other, and getting to know her. I am happy to have shared a part of my Camino with her and hope we meet up in the days ahead.

My new party of five is almost the last to depart. We walk out of the albergue just after 7:30.

"I'm going to stop for a coffee. I'll catch up to you soon," Cameron says. He heads into the same bar we visited yesterday as we keep walking. Our route merges with the official route in ten kilometers; it is well-marked with signs and yellow arrows. We move at a leisurely pace. Cameron catches up quickly and has brought a new friend: a German woman, Caroline. The six of us make our way along the roadways and pathways through woods and quiet hamlets.

Eventually, our group spreads out due to our differing pace. Cameron and Caroline lead the way, while Cosima and I fall farther and farther behind, at a leisurely stroll. Last night, Cosima shared that she is meeting her best friend from back home in Sarria tomorrow and will be walking with her for a twenty-kilometer stretch.

"Sarria is only fifteen kilometers ahead, so we are not in any hurry today," Cosima says.

"That's fine with me," I say. "I'm not in a rush." I don't plan on leaving Cosima's small tribe, after all the effort it took to catch her. I am hoping to walk with her for a while.

About an hour into today's walk, Cosima and I find ourselves walking through a valley between rolling Galician hills, surrounded by moss-covered trees; feathery green strands hang over the deserted road that is our path. We move quietly, next to fields covered in an early morning mist; a shallow river flows next to the base of the steep hill, its height blocked from view by the trees overhead. We walk through this mystical forest and have it all to ourselves. The sun, low in the sky, shoots rays of light through the trees. Cosima, her shoulders covered with her golden sarong, stops and looks towards the sun, her shadow mixing with those of the trees. It is a scene I will etch into memory. My head slowly moves from side to side as we drift through this magnificent landscape. Cosima says she could live in this place and walks off the road, to a small patch of dirt leading down towards the river, and stops. For the first time today, I reach out to touch her and gently kiss her lips. Our steps slow as we soak in this paradise. For more than half an hour, there is not another soul, only the beauty Mother Nature provides.

When a building finally appears through the trees ahead, my response is "Shit—civilization." We hesitate but continue walking, deflated that our time in this special place has come to an end.

When we reach the building along the tree-covered road, we find Till and Max waiting—Cameron and Caroline having continued on. The building is an old farmhouse with a few outbuildings and a sign out front reading *Comida y Bebidas*, or food and drink. We learn this place, A Fonte das Bodas Pension, is a kind of B&B.

We find a few long tables sitting out front of the beautiful home, with a flowering blue passion vine climbing its two-story stone walls. The four of us find an empty table that can easily seat six—a handful of fellow pilgrims are sipping café con leches and one eating a slice of tortilla.

A smiling woman delivers coffee to a couple sitting nearby, then walks over and says, 'Hola!" and points to a small laminated menu listing a few items. She doesn't speak English, but we all order a café con leche. I also order tortilla.

In two minutes, the woman is back with our coffees and my food. The tortilla is deliciously different, as the potatoes inside are crispy, which I have found is not usually the case. I make the other three try it, and they agree it is the best yet. Max and Till each ask for a slice.

This kind woman is Isabel. She and her husband, Enrique, own and operate this lovely property. I watch her provide excellent service, accompanied by her warm smile, to each pilgrim who stops. Enrique comes and goes and chats with many who stop. He speaks with a heavy accent, but his English is good.

Isabel comes back and refills our cups. We are enjoying this extended break, and I find Cosima speaks a bit of Spanish when she helps translate Isabel's Spanish for a British woman who stops.

A couple of thirty-something Italian men are being rude to Isabel because of the language barrier. Enrique overhears what is said and gets upset and raises his voice to the Italians—and, for no reason, to Isabel. This minor ruckus makes Isabel get emotional and tear up. Cosima, standing near, rubs Isabel's arm to comfort her and talks gently, in her limited Spanish. Cosima brings the smile back to Isabel's face.

We accept more coffee and continue to soak in this place. At some point, each of us wanders alone on the property, a perfect little country estate. There is a renovated outbuilding near the front of the house, a large garden, an orchard off to one side and, behind the house, a large field with horses. Someplace unseen, chickens are clucking.

We chat with many who stop. Our party of four remains while others leave, replaced by more who stop for a brief respite before they too move on. Well over an hour into our stay, I approach Cosima and look into her eyes. "We should all stay here tonight," I say. "This place is amazing." She doesn't respond. I continue, "You said before you learned to do what feels right, and to me, this place does."

Cosima doesn't verbalize a response, and as if she's being saved by the bell, Isabel walks out of the house with a platter of croquetas de jamón. These small, lightly battered, fried ham fritters melt in my mouth and burst with a creamy flavor. No one ordered these. She simply brings them out to share; we are the only guests here. After our mid-morning snack, I find Cosima in the garden and ask what she is thinking.

"I want to stay," she says, "but it is too expensive. The double rooms are 44€, so it would be 22€ each."

I don't know how she knows this, but I'm happy she wants to spend the day … and night. I know Cosima has been careful about her budget, as she has been away from home and walking for over two months and plans to continue her journey for another month or two. I say, "I'll happily pay the difference between the cost here and a normal albergue for all of us."

"No!" she says, shaking her head.

"It was my idea. I want to stay. I want us all to," I say.

The thought of spending the day with this sweet and beautiful woman is exciting, but I will not push any harder. Cosima and I head back to our table and help finish the platter of croquetas.

"Cerveza?" Till asks Isabel. She nods and heads into the restored outbuilding and carries out four cold beers. Of course she does.

Cosima and Isabel seem to have developed a bond. A while later, Cosima returns to our table and tells us, "Isabel will give us one room we all four can share. Two double beds for 40€, or 10€ each."

"Perfect," I say.

We all agree to end our day here. Total distance walked: eight kilometers.

Now decided, Cosima messages Cameron to say we will not arrive in Sarria today.

Settled in the knowledge that we are here for the day, I relax. Only now I learn the food and drink here is all "donativo," simply pay what you want or are able.

Fewer people are passing by, and even fewer stop. I assume those who stayed last night in Samos have long since made their way past, and those to come will have started near Triacastela, taken the detour to visit the monastery, and continued.

As morning turns to afternoon, Max brings out the game Yahtzee, or more accurately, *Kniffel*, the German version he carries. Some of us play, while others take time to wander around this magical land and return to the table we have made our own. Every so often, Isabel brings out more food and asks, "Cerveza?"

We take a break from our leisurely afternoon and carry our packs up to our assigned room on the second floor. One by one, we shower. The house is larger than it appears from the outside. I count six bedrooms and one common bathroom upstairs. Four of the rooms are for guests, each with two beds. The lower level, at least what's visible, includes a huge kitchen, a bathroom, and a large living room. Cosima spends an hour in the kitchen helping Isabel prepare more food that arrives at our table, along with a bottle of wine.

Later, Cosima says, "Isabel gave me directions to a nearby property her family has owned for generations. Would you like to join me and explore the land?"

"Of course," I say with a huge smile.

As we are walking from the house, Isabel hands a padded comforter to Cosima.

We walk for a few minutes, then step over a chain blocking any vehicles wishing to enter an overgrown path in the woods. Exiting the trees into an open field, we find what looks like an abandoned house in the distance. We walk through a field of tall grass towards it.

It seems, long ago, a water wheel may have been attached to this old wooden house—sitting adjacent to a shallow stream. We can find no way into the house, but we climb over some dense vegetation and make our way down to a small, shade-covered beach—no sand, just pebbles. Across the water, we notice three cows relaxing in the shade. We have made our way to another magical place, which, again, we have (almost) to ourselves. Cosima lays out the comforter. We remove our shoes and wade into the shallow, almost still water.

Despite our drunken kisses in the shower, I am hesitant to do more than place my hand on her waist as we wade through the water under the cover of tall trees. Cosima and I lie down on the comforter and gaze up through the thick branches.

"Would you like a massage?" I ask.

"Yes, I would," she says and rolls onto her stomach.

I sit up next to her and start to awkwardly massage her back. I soon crawl over and straddle her. I massage her back and neck for long minutes. I massage her scalp through her thick red hair. Then one of her bare arms to the tips of her fingers, then the other. I move again to her back under her shirt, this time further down to her tail bone. I take my time on each part of her body. I slowly remove myself and start to massage her surprisingly soft feet and toes. I make my way to her calves and then back to her feet before returning up each leg, making my way ever higher along her bare thighs. I don't know if any arousal is building on her part, but I am reaching a particular state. I slowly massage her upper thighs and then her butt over her skort. There has not been a word spoken since I began, but now I whisper into her ear, "roll over." She does, sits up, and I peel off her shirt, and she lies back down.

I start the process over again and remain focused on each part of her body. Her soft white breasts, a contrast to the tan on the rest of her, are exquisite, and I spend extra time on her hardening nipples. I rub her stomach gently as it expands and contracts. Slowly, my hands reach just under the top of her shorts. I move to her feet and eventually her thighs.

I move back up her body, this time with my lips. I kiss her stomach, her breasts, my tongue circling. Her eyes remain closed. I slowly kiss her neck and then her lips. She returns the kiss, our tongues twisting. Our breathing becomes more pronounced. My hands begin again to explore her body, and my hand reaches for the zipper of her shorts.

She slowly shakes her head and whispers, "No … not here."

"Okay," I whisper, "roll back over." I lie next to her and lightly run my fingertips over her bare back. I hope to rub her to sleep. I don't know if I succeed, as I doze off.

I wake to Cosima under my arm, looking at me. "That was nice," she says, smiling.

We leave our hidden paradise and make our way back the way we came. The sun is blazing. The afternoon heat has arrived. We join the guys for an afternoon of cold beer and Yahtzee.

Isabel instructs us to go to a specific shady place in the garden. We watch as she carries a large round table to a surprisingly cooler spot. She checks in on us often as the afternoon passes. Walks are taken back along the mystical road that led us here.

I message Diana, "I stopped for the day before reaching Sarria. I am not sure I'll catch up to you again. I hope we meet up before I fly home."

Everyone must walk their own Camino.

While I am choosing to take this turn in mine, I am a bit wistful about probably not seeing Diana again, but I hope my journey brings me closer to the woman I have been chasing.

Throughout the afternoon, pilgrims occasionally stop to grab something to eat or drink, and as always, Isabel welcomes them with a smile and provides them with whatever they need. The most interesting of this afternoon's guests are a Polish couple and their five kids, ranging in age from seven months to nine years. They started their walk in Ponferrada a week earlier. They push (or sometimes carry) two strollers as they make their way to Santiago. This family of seven did not know they would be walking on the Camino even two weeks ago. The husband had wanted to walk the Camino as a family, but his wife was not convinced, telling him she would need "a sign from God." The sign arrived in the form of a T-shirt she spotted on a woman in Poland that referenced the Camino de Santiago. A week later, they arrived in Spain.

The husband, a teacher, is enthusiastic about their walk, while his wife, a homemaker, seems a bit weary. Isabel dotes over the kids and feeds the family until they refuse … that is, until popsicles arrive for the kids. She even helps repair one of the kids' shoes, the sole barely hanging on.

"Since there are no other guests tonight," Cosima tells us, "Isabel is giving me the adjoining room to sleep instead of having to share a room with three men."

At first, I am disheartened, as it was agreed earlier that I would be sharing Cosima's bed. Yes, in a room with her brother, but the thought of a night next to her was still thrilling.

A few minutes later, Cosima pulls me aside and whispers, "You will be sneaking into my room."

"Isabel has been on her feet all day," Till says. "I want to invite her to join us for a glass of wine … and I want to ask her in Spanish."

Between Cosima's Spanish and Google Translate, Till jots down his script on a napkin. The next time Isabel comes out, Till addresses her and repeats the words he has written, "Gracias por tu generosidad hoy Isabel. Por favor siéntate con nosotros y bebe una copa de vino." *Thank you for your generosity today, Isabel. Please sit with us and drink a glass of wine.*

Isabel's smile broadens and she sits down at the table. Till pours her a glass of wine. Isabel spots the napkin and nods. Till hands it to her. She reads it, then folds the napkin carefully as if it were a holy relic and places it in her apron. Her eyes blink back tears. "To Isabel," we toast as tears begin to well in our eyes. Using her apron, Isabel dabs her eyes.

While every day on the Camino will bring something new, today has been a wonderful surprise. Somehow, and for some unknown reason, we stumbled upon this place and Isabel—first deciding to stay for an hour, then two, and then the entire day. It's been an unforgettable day, and yes, being near a beautiful woman has enhanced my experience, but even without this aspect, today has been extraordinary. We are just passing through for one day; how unusual was today for Isabel and Enrique. Are they out with guests talking late into most nights? Do others help in the kitchen like Cosima? Or are they brought to tears by a pilgrim's sincere gratitude, like with Till? I have no idea, but they have created a life here that makes days like today possible for themselves and for those lucky enough to find it and embrace it.

The night sky is crystal clear, no ambient light anywhere; the Milky Way is visible above. Cosima goes into the house and brings back the comforter. She, Max, and I lie in the garden far away from the house, staring up at the night sky as Max points out the constellations. Other than Max's comments, the only sound is the chirping of crickets. Two shooting stars pass by, but somehow, I miss both. Till is wandering the property while he talks with his girlfriend back home. Eventually, Max says, "I am going back to the house." Cosima and I remain.

I roll towards her, and we kiss. My hands start to explore her body, but this time, when I reach for her zipper, I am not stopped. I slowly pull off her shorts and kiss my way up each of her legs. When I reach the top of her parting thighs, I finally enjoy the taste of her. My tongue teases, my fingers seek, and rhythmically I call her towards me. My other hand reaches to tease her nipples. Playful passion builds, then recedes, then builds again until she pushes my head away … squirming. After she's reached a crescendo, I lift my head and spot Max peering in our direction. I whisper to Cosima, "I think Max can see us." We continue anyway. My shorts come off, and we join together.

Afterward, we feel in the dark for our clothing, grab the comforter and head back. We turn around when we reach the spot where I saw Max standing. It's clear now; he could see.

We find Max sitting at the table with a large dog by his side. We sit down innocently at the table as if we had just returned from a walk through the garden. As Till finishes his call, Enrique and Isabel walk out of the house.

"One more bottle," Enrique says, a bottle of wine in his hand.

"To Isabel and Enrique and their little piece of heaven," I say, raising my glass.

"To Isabel and Enrique."

Upstairs, Cosima grabs her backpack and takes it into her room. As we all brush our teeth, Cosima tells Till she and I will be sharing her room because there are two beds, "so now we each have a bed to ourselves."

Isabel offered the room and the bed to Cosima, since she was the only woman, and though I don't want to dishonor the generosity they have bestowed upon us, I sneak into Cosima's room. We are quiet, so Isabel and Enrique won't know Cosima has a guest.

Cosima whispers, "It feels like high school, sneaking in my boyfriend."

She undresses and stands in front of me. I take in every inch of her beauty. She has been walking for months, and it shows. She looks at me with a coy smile on her radiant face, her long red hair pulled behind her ears.

"You will have to leave me on the Camino," she warns.

"Yes, I know," I reply with a smirk and nod. I take her hand and pull her into our bed.

DAY 24: SIVIL > FERREIROS

*What is a great life? It is the dreams of youth
realized in old age.*

~ Alfred de Vigny

Waking in the quiet of the countryside, in a private room next to a beautiful woman, is refreshing. Cosima opens the window and gazes pensively out, her topless body cast in a warm golden hour light. I stand behind, wrap my arms around her and look out to a gradient blue sky and two horses grazing in a bright green pasture under an early morning haze. I inhale the flowery scent of her hair. We have not even spent forty-eight hours together, yet it feels natural holding her.

Cosima leaves the room first to make sure the coast is clear, and I follow. Soon the four of us head down to 'our table,' where Isabel has coffee and a tortilla waiting for us. Cosima brings the guestbook to the table and we write our thanks to Isabel (and Enrique). Then we place our donations into the donativo box, grateful for the kindness and generosity we have received.

It is not yet nine o'clock, but Isabel walks out carrying two bottles in each hand. After a toast to "this amazing place," we slowly nurse our beers, finding it difficult to leave. Finally, we stand and toss on our packs. Isabel brings out something wrapped in aluminum foil and places it in the front pocket of Max's pack. We each hug Isabel, tears welling in our eyes. Isabel stands back and spreads her arms, and says, "familia." A few seconds later, "uno momento," and she heads back inside. She appears with four more beers and places one in each of our packs or shorts pockets—wherever she can find room.

We start walking, and I gaze again from side to side, thinking of these last twenty-four magical hours. The road slowly curves and gently climbs, and we find ourselves looking down on the backside of last night's home; one last glimpse of this unforgettable place.

Our walk into Sarria is easy and passes quickly, the four of us staying together in a tight pack. Sarria sits 116 kilometers, or roughly a five-day walk, from Santiago de Compostela and is the most popular starting point along the Camino Frances; with both train and bus service, it is an easy jumping-off point. Twice as many pilgrims begin their journey here than start out from Saint-Jean-Pied-de-Port. Most wannabe pilgrims cannot leave their lives back home for an entire month, but they can find one week to experience this treasure. Pilgrims debuting here will be issued a Compostela when they arrive in Santiago, meeting the requirement to walk at least 100 kilometers on any pilgrimage route.

We stop on a patch of grass alongside the Sarria River, which runs through its namesake. We unwrap the gift Isabel tucked into Max's pack, to find slices of tortilla, croquetas, and a large bocadillo. We spread our good fortune onto Cosima's sarong, take a selfie with all of us gathered around the feast, and Cosima emails the photo to Isabel.

Cosima's friend Lina, who has just finished walking her own Camino, is taking the train from Santiago to meet up with Cosima. Since her train won't arrive for a couple of hours, Till, Max, and I will keep walking and reserve beds in a village fourteen kilometers ahead, while Cosima waits for her friend.

Warnings of the walk after Sarria have been sounded over the past week by many an experienced pilgrim. The influx of pilgrims will bring changes, and finding a bed is expected to be even more challenging than even during my early days along the Way.

"Have fun, boys," Cosima says. "We will see you this afternoon," and waves as she watches us walk away.

A half-hour after leaving Sarria, we find ourselves on a long uphill through a beautiful forest of oaks. Till says, "You two can walk ahead. I was hoping to walk a part of my Camino alone; this afternoon would be a good time."

That's probably true, but I'm sure his knee is still bothering him, and he doesn't want to slow us down.

"Are you sure?" Max asks.

"Yes. I want some time to think," Till says.

"Okay, we'll see you in Ferreiros," I say.

Max and I keep walking at our previous pace as Till slowly falls back.

Max is a soft-spoken guy and somewhat reserved, but he opens up to me about his life and the struggles he's faced.

"Walking the Camino was my father's idea," he says. "We were walking together but separated after I met Till."

"Where is your dad now?" I ask.

"He's a couple of days ahead."

We talk about our lives back home as we move through the beautiful Galician countryside of gently rolling hills and an occasional patch of trees. When I learn Max has recently finished a carpentry apprenticeship back home, I ask. "Will you be starting work as a carpenter when you go home?"

"I am not sure. I really don't enjoy it,' he says, "at least so far. My training was hard, and I still have a lot to improve."

"Why did you study carpentry in the first place?"

"I needed to do something and thought I would like it," he says. "I had no experience with it before."

"If you don't get a job in your field, what else might you do?"

"I don't know," he says. "I will probably get a job doing it, but I am not excited about it."

"When I was your age, I didn't know what I wanted to do, either," I say, shaking my head. "Shit, I still don't know what I want to do with my life."

"What did you do before you started the Camino?"

"My career was in finance. A boring desk job I never loved, but it paid the bills," I say. "Now, I refuse to work another desk job, and I am trying to decide on what I'll do when I go back. Do you know what Uber is?"

"Yeah."

"I have been driving for Uber lately because it allows me to travel, but I don't see doing it forever."

"I haven't done much traveling," he says.

"I think it's great you're here on the Camino. I had dreams of travel and adventure when I was your age, but I didn't follow them."

"Why not?"

"I fell in love, I guess. I met the girl that would become my wife, and my priorities changed."

Our route continues along cobbled lanes, dirt tracks, and asphalt roads as we pass through hamlets every half-hour or so.

As we walk, I ask, "If you're not excited about carpentry, what would be your dream job?"

"I have no dreams right now," he says. "And I don't have a girl."

"There has to be something you dream about."

"I haven't thought about it. I have only worried about finishing my schooling," he says. "Right now, I'm just hoping to find a girlfriend."

"Have you had lots of experience with women?" I ask.

"I've only dated one girl, and it ended after a month," he says. "I don't understand them at all."

"A common problem," I say. "I'm not sure who does. Hell, I've only had two long-term relationships in my life, so I haven't had much experience with women either."

Max is quiet for a minute, then says, "I am not excited to return home. I am not sure what to do when I get back."

"I'm in the same boat as you," I say. "But if I tell you anything, it would be to really spend time thinking about what you want out of life now—before you get swept up in a life of responsibilities."

"You sound a lot like my father," he says. "He divorced my mom and still doesn't know what he wants. It has affected our relationship. I am trying to understand, and it's part of the reason I agreed to come."

When Max mentions his father, I question what my kids think of my choices.

After a minute of silence, I say, "I think as people get older, they start to think about things and question what they want to do with the rest of their life. People come up with all sorts of answers."

"I get that … I think," he says.

"What I find interesting is the dreams I had at your age are the same dreams I had decades later," I say. "So, some of the things rolling around in your head when you're young will always be there."

I share with Max that while I was on the Via Francigena a dormant memory popped into my head. I remembered when was I his age, I bought a book about travelling in Europe; I'd long ago forgotten the title, but I remembered the name Margolis. While I walked, I typed into Google Biking+Europe+Margolis. The top hit was *Susanna Margolis books,* and there it was: the cover of the book I had purchased thirty years earlier, *Walking Europe from Top to Bottom* by Susanna Margolis and Ginger Harmon. And there *I* was, doing precisely that.

Max and I arrive at our destination and find two options. We agree on the newer private albergue instead of the sad-looking municipal. We walk up a small rise to the most modern albergue I've come across, only to find a sign on the door instructing us to check in at the bar back down the hill. We order a couple of beers and hang out on the patio while we wait for Till.

Albergue Casa Cruceiro de Ferreiros is home for tonight. After our afternoon rituals, nap included, the three of us eventually find ourselves back at the bar.

An hour later, Cosima and Lina walk up to our table and throw off their packs. Lina has dark hair and a dark tan and is a few inches taller than Cosima.

"Hi Lina," I say, "It's nice to meet you. How was your walk?"

"It was beautiful," she says, sipping on Till's beer.

"We are famished. Can we order food, please?" Cosima says with a cheesy grin.

Ten minutes later, a variety of plates arrive at our table; pimientos (stuffed jalapeños), papas fritas (french fries), paella, croquettes, ensalada verde (green salad), cheese, and bread. We spend a couple of hours eating, drinking, and talking at a picnic table outside the bar before heading up to the albergue.

After the women shower, the five of us gather in a large common room with walls of glass looking out to the surrounding countryside. Sitting around a coffee table, the room empty except for us, we watch the sky slowly turn from blue to orange to black as we drink two bottles of Rioja the women carried in their packs from Sarria.

Lina is slowly making her way to Oviedo to start the Camino Primitivo and a return to Santiago. Speaking without much of an accent, she shares stories of her recently completed Camino. She is quick to laugh, especially when Cosima teases Till about his lifelong crush on her. The bottles empty quickly. Max says, "I'll head down to the bar and get more." Minutes later, he's back with two more.

The five of us find it amusing none of us have jobs to return to. Like Cosima, Lina left her job voluntarily before coming to Spain. Max and Till will be looking for jobs when they return home.

The only one of us certain of what they want to do in life is Cosima; the rest of us claim to have no idea what career path we will follow. Our thought-provoking conversation ends when the last bottle is emptied, and we head to bed.

My time with this group of younger Germans has been enlightening. Like me, they are all at a crossroads in their lives. I think of Diana and Jana, who are at a similar place. No one I have met on this walk is anxious to get back to their normal lives. Maybe it's simply the break from routine, a temporary escape, but I think there is something more. Life on the Camino seems to bring into the light something deep inside, at least to those who give themselves over to the experience.

DAY 25: FERREIROS > GONZAR

Don't come to the Camino looking for
answers, instead, come with an open heart
and you may be surprised by what you find.

~ Jane V. Blanchard, *Women of the*
Way: Embracing the Camino

Waking to the sound of rain, I peer out the floor-to-ceiling window next to my bunk—nothing but gray. No one is eager to leave the warmth of the albergue, so we take our time; our cadre is the last to leave. Rain jackets on, our legs bare, we head down to the bar, eager for our morning café con leche.

"It's not open," Till says as he pulls on the door.

"Really? There isn't anything else around," I say. I'm surprised it's not open. Almost every bar along the Way is open early to provide for those walking by.

"I need to eat something," Till says.

"I have some food in my bag," Cosima says.

"Everyone take out what you have," Lina says as she takes off her pack.

Max cranks open an umbrella at one of the tables. We stand under the partial shelter and root through our packs. We lay the results of our scavenging on the table: half a baguette, a hunk of salami, cookies, an open bag of chips. We spend a few minutes nourishing ourselves before we hit the road.

We pass an important milestone not a minute into our walk: a graffitied marker signifying we are exactly 100.0 kilometers from the cathedral in Santiago. Minutes later, a restaurant appears; a handful of soaked travelers are milling about, waiting to enter. We keep moving in what is now a steady stream of pilgrims, most having started this morning in the towns we passed through yesterday.

When walking behind my four friends, the color of their waterproof covers different from their packs, and with hoods covering their heads, not much is recognizable other than footwear and Cosima's hiking stick.

Rotating partners as we head to Portomarín, the landscape muted by rain and a heavy sky, we walk along asphalt and gravel pathways, past grazing brown cows with twisted horns. One such cow stands next to a barbed-wire fence and reaches up to munch on oak leaves. When I walk alongside Lina, we talk about our lives when we return home. She started a career in social work after her schooling years ago but is trying to decide if she wants to continue her chosen path.

"I'm open to whatever may come. I'm okay not knowing what I'll be doing when I return. I can easily find a job, and if I don't like it, I will find another," Lina says.

"That's a great way to think. I'd always followed what I thought the rules were and stuck with my chosen career. Because I had kids, I felt I needed to focus on the money aspect and support my family. I would dream of doing something new over the years but I never made an effort to change anything. When I started this walk, I was hoping for an epiphany and deciding on my thing for the next fifteen years."

"You're almost to Santiago. Did you have your epiphany yet?" she asks.

"Not even close," I say, shaking my head.

"Maybe I was hoping for the same. I came here to think about things in my life."

"That's probably one of the biggest reasons people of any age walk the Camino," I say. "I've read that seeking clarification is the most common response given by pilgrims when asked why they started out."

We continue among the scores of others walking under a gloomy sky, trying to avoid the puddles forming in the gravel track.

"What are some of the things you like to do?" she asks.

I think for a minute, then say, "Hiking, mostly. My dream job would be to share my love for the outdoors with young people, but I'm not sure how to turn that into a job at my age."

"Maybe not as a job, but you can find a way to do it as a hobby."

"Maybe," I say. "I am excited to share my love of the outdoors with my granddaughter as she grows."

Lina glances at me with raised eyebrows. "Cosima didn't tell me you were a *grandfather*."

"Yeah," I say with a smile. "What about you? Have you had any revelations on your Camino?"

"No. But it's been nice to leave everything behind. If you can't tell, I am dragging my feet about returning. Maybe I'll keep walking even after reaching Santiago for the second time."

"I don't blame you," I say. "Any time you can take a break from routine and think about your direction in life is valuable. I wish I had done something like that from time to time."

"I'm going to let the universe show me the way," she says.

"A little new-agey, but okay," I say. "I've been thinking too hard about what I should do next in life; maybe I should listen more closely to what the universe is telling me."

I lag behind and reflect on my conversation with Lina. Her philosophy of being open to what may appear sounds more appealing than being anxious about not knowing where my path will lead me. I remember the day I left Portland, the first day of my life on the road. I was joyous in the fact I didn't know where life would take me. Sometime during my journey over the past two years, my thinking has morphed into needing to decide on a long-term plan. I don't know why.

As I get closer to the end of my Camino, I understand that I had fallen back into my same old pattern: needing to find a path to follow, a new career, and, as I sought with Kelly, a routine—exactly what I had felt the need to escape from not so long ago.

Over the past year, I have been walking along, my eyes darting, searching for that elusive 'something.' As I get closer to Santiago, I start to see the light. I must walk with my head up and, as Thoreau said, "Go confidently in the direction of my dreams."

A light rain is still falling as the five of us walk across a long bridge over the Mino River and into Portomarín. We climb fifty-two steps leading to an archway that was once part of an ancient Roman bridge. That bridge now sits underwater, beneath the span we just crossed. This ancient arch acts as the pilgrims' unofficial entrance to the city.

Portomarín has an interesting history. In the 1960s, the entire town was moved to higher land when the government dammed the Mino River downstream to build a reservoir and flooded the old Portomarín. Nowadays, when the water levels are low, it is possible to glimpse some of the old buildings and the bridge submerged fifty years earlier. Before the dam's construction, many historic buildings were moved piece by piece up the hillside to the town's new location, including the twelfth-century Romanesque church, Iglesia de San Nicolás. The fortress-like church now sits in the center of the rebuilt town. Some of the numbers inscribed signifying the position of stones in the reassembling are still visible.

Lina is catching a bus here as she heads in the opposite direction of our quartet. The bus isn't scheduled to arrive for another hour, so we sit under an awning just across the cobbled street from the relocated church, drinking coffee and watching the rain. When her departure time nears, we walk to the nearby bus stop in a sputtering rain, a clearing sky visible to the west.

Our group, minus Lina, resumes our walk and agrees not to make any reservations despite the increased numbers. We plan to roll the dice and walk under the now blue sky until we find some place to stay the night. After a couple of hours of countryside walking, we reach the tiny village of Gonzar and stop for a beer at a stylish-looking restaurant, Casa Garcia.

With my cold beer in hand, I say, "Let's stay in this town tonight."

"What do you think, Till?" Cosima asks.

"Sure," he says. "I don't mind sitting here and drinking this afternoon."

Max stays quiet for a moment, then says, "I need to get to Santiago in two days, and it is eighty kilometers away, so I need to keep walking. I should have already been further ahead by now."

Max needs to meet his father in time for their flight home. After we finish our beer, we all stand and give Max a warm embrace.

"I will see you on the next Camino," he says as he tosses on his pack and trots off to put more distance behind him before stopping for the day.

Finding this restaurant is also a private albergue, I head inside and ask the cost of a bed here.

"It's pricy," I tell the others. "Fourteen euros for a bed." Far more than a typical albergue.

"There is a municipal down the street," Cosima says. "I want to check it out."

We walk over and find it doesn't open for another hour, but it is half the price. "The next round and the tapas are on me if we stay at the fancy place," I say.

They agree, and we head back and are happy to find we can check in and shower immediately.

Casa Garcia is a beautifully remodeled home centered around a lovely courtyard, a large bar at one end and a bathroom on the other. Inside are the restaurant's dining room and a common area for guests, along with two large bunk rooms. A few private rooms are upstairs, running along a balcony that looks down onto the courtyard. The semi-luxurious pilgrims' quarters are on the ground level. The walls and floor are made of stone, keeping the temperature cool; massive wooden beams run the room's width. The solid wooden bunks are more comfortable and quieter than the metal bunks found in most albergues. Tonight's accommodations are worth the extra cost.

There isn't much to this small village, and eventually, the three of us park ourselves at a table back along the street to relax and drink away the rest of the afternoon. It seems I will be walking with Cosima and her brother until we reach Santiago, and though it should perhaps feel a bit awkward, it doesn't. Till and I get along well; like his sister, he has a welcoming demeanor. While my relationship with Cosima is not obvious, he must know we have a physical connection, but it remains unspoken.

Casa Garcia does offer a pilgrim dinner, but given the cost of our beds this evening, we are content with a few plates of tapas. When the bar closes, we stay in the courtyard for a while longer before heading inside. Every bunk is filled, and most occupants are already asleep. A short time later, Cosima climbs down from her top bunk. Our eyes meet, and she motions with her head to follow.

Out in the courtyard, we talk quietly. Soon she says, "Follow me," and leads me into the small bathroom. We start kissing, and my hands run over her breasts and then between her legs as my heart races and my breathing quickens. Slipping my hand inside her waistband, I tease her, rhythmically rubbing my fingers against her. Cosima turns around and bends forward, pressing her hands against the wall. I pull her flowing pants down, and her legs spread. I pull down my shorts and enter her. It feels like I have entered an alternate reality. *Is this* my *life?* is what runs through my mind, clouded by an afternoon of drinking. I am aware the bathroom door is wide open, and if anyone were to enter the courtyard, they would witness us joined together. After I reach the ultimate moment, we quietly make our way back to our beds.

I lie still, staring at the wood slats above me; my mind races, still not sure my time with Cosima is real.

DAY 26: GONZAR > PONTE CAMPAÑA

*Memory is a way of holding on to the things
you love, the things you are, the things you
never want to lose.*

~ from the TV series, *The Wonder Years*

We sit sipping café con leche at the bar and again are the last to depart. We walk at a leisurely pace under a clear sky, in no hurry to reach Santiago. Birds flit about, chirping morning greetings as we pass. A light breeze blows as we follow quiet country roads through small hamlets dotting the Galician countryside. A couple of hours into our walk, we reach a historic stone cross near Ligonde. It was erected in the year 1670 and is one of the oldest still standing along the Camino. We stop briefly to examine the double-sided cross and find the crucifixion depicted on one side and a sorrowful Virgin Mary on the other. When we start walking again, I fall behind.

Today's date, August 26, has special meaning for me. It was forty years ago today that my father passed away; he was only thirty-five. I have often thought about my loss on this walk and how it changed me. This morning, when I think about the years after his death, I don't remember being unhappy; life was simply a new normal. Outwardly, I was a typical high schooler; in the top third of my class, I played varsity soccer and had a small circle of friends. I kept the pain of my loss buried, choosing not to think about it. At home, I was distracted by a television seemingly always on, hanging with my best friend, or playing board games with my brothers. I didn't dwell on the what-ifs, as that would have forced the pain to the surface.

I didn't feel I missed out, and for that, I owe everything to my mom, who did an incredible job raising her three boys alone. She never remarried; instead, she dedicated her life to the duty she felt, keeping Dad always high on the proverbial pedestal. She sacrificed much to give their sons the best lives possible. It was her way of honoring him. Even today, she devotes her life to her sons and grandkids. Her wanderlust gene, which she passed down to me, remains unfulfilled. Her selflessness is so much greater than mine. It is thinking about her sacrifices that brings tears to my eyes this morning.

Being more introverted than not, I'm curious now whether that may have been a consequence of my loss or just genetics; my mom is an introvert, while my dad was the life of the party. As my high school years progressed, I became moody, uncertain if it was typical teenage angst or a deep-rooted pain seeping out. How differently might my life have played out if our idyllic life continued, with my nuclear family intact? What guidance might my dad have provided?

It's impossible to know what person I may have grown into had I not lost him.

As the sun moves higher in the sky, Cosima reads the descriptions of upcoming albergues from a German guidebook. When I hear "private rooms," my ears perk up. Up to now, private rooms haven't been an option for us.

"There's one with rooms in a windmill," she says excitedly.

"What's the number?" I ask. If she wants to stay in a windmill *and* we'd have a private room, it would be perfect. I call the albergue. Luckily, the guy who answers speaks broken English.

"Do you have any rooms available?" I ask. After his response, I answer, "One ... and one bed in the albergue."

"What does it cost?" Cosima asks.

"More than usual," I say, "but since it was my decision, you just pay the cost of what a bunk would be."

"No! We will split the cost," she says.

"We will have one large bed to share," I say. "There were two rooms. I chose the one with only one bed."

Cosima shakes her head and smiles. Till, trailing behind, is unaware we have already found tonight's accommodation.

As we walk on, Cosima shares the story of Siete.

During her first week in Spain, she was walking with a group of others when a barely audible sound, just off the trail, led to the discovery of a tiny newborn kitten. All alone, its eyes not yet open, it was likely close to death. Cosima and those with her got the kitten to drink water from a water bottle cap. Using her sarong as a baby sling, Cosima carried the kitten the rest of the day and sneaked her into their albergue. She and the six other pilgrims named the kitten Siete, Spanish for seven. They found some milk to feed her, and that night the kitten slept quietly beside Cosima. The next day, they headed to an animal shelter in Logroño, only to find it closed. Instead, they brought Siete to a police station, where they met an officer who happened to volunteer at the shelter. He promised to care for the delicate creature until the shelter opened. Over the following week, they checked in with the helpful officer a couple of times and soon learned that Siete, her eyes now open, had been adopted.

"Wow, what a sweet story," I say.

She smiles.

I am savoring every minute with Cosima, this lovely woman with an 'old soul.' A word pops into my head, and I tell her, "I find you *enchanting*."

"I don't know that word," she says and pulls out her phone to translate it. She seems pleased with what she finds.

I am conscious Till is walking with his sister, and the Camino has been a good bonding experience for them. I often lag back or walk ahead, leaving them time to talk or simply walk together, not wanting to monopolize Cosima.

We reach the small town of Palas de Rei, and while it is what I've come to expect of a city this size along the Camino, there are many more places for pilgrims to sleep. We pass a handful of albergues, several small pensions, and a few small hotels, all needed to handle the recent influx of pilgrims. We stop to buy bread, cheese, and wine before heading to our windmill.

Up to this point, I have managed to avoid making more than a couple of reservations, enjoying the flexibility of stopping when it feels right, but this may not be the case with the increased traffic. Since having met up with Cosima, I am willing to spend a bit more, but I'm concerned Cosima is shelling out more than she has budgeted. Her continued travels are dependent on her savings.

Our destination tonight is only an hour ahead, making today a relatively short twenty-two kilometers. The three of us stroll on quiet country pathways and deserted roads under the cover of trees lining the narrow lanes. After crossing over a stream, we find ourselves in front of Casa Domingo, our home for the night.

"It's lovely," Cosima says.

We are not in a village or even a tiny hamlet; it's simply a home sitting in a beautiful rural setting. We approach the multicolored stone building, topped with wavy terra cotta, on a path paved with the same fieldstone and pass a ten-foot-tall scallop shell affixed to one of the stone walls. There is no windmill in sight.

Cosima tells Till that she and I are staying in a private room but doesn't share that it only has one bed. "The reason we are taking a room is the private bath. I want a long hot shower," she says.

We check in, and the host leads us out of the office. He assumes the two younger pilgrims will be sharing a room, so he says to me, "Your bed will be in here," pointing to the bunk room.

"Actually," I correct him, "Till is in the albergue." I feel a bit sheepish, my salt-and-pepper beard giving away our age difference.

The host shows Till to a room filled with bunks and then leads

Cosima and me across a field to a small house fifty meters away. When we walk inside, I say, "There's the mill." A plexiglass floor shows the water wheel's workings, using the small stream we just crossed, flowing outside. Cosima's guidebook must have just said *mill house* and not specified between wind and water. Exposed beams give this quaint house a rustic charm. On the upper level are three rooms, each with its own bath.

"This is amazing," Cosima says as she scans the room, her mouth slightly ajar. A queen-size bed and a small but luxurious bathroom— quite a bargain in my mind. We take turns showering and then head back to the main building.

Cosima is now wearing faded jeans, her hippie-ish top from San Anton, and New Balance sneakers. "My parents brought the jeans and shoes when I met them on the coast," she says.

"They are heavy," I say. "I wouldn't want to be carrying them."

"The comfort is well worth the extra weight," she responds. "After two months of walking, I barely notice." A cocky smile fills her face.

I head inside and order three beers from the bar and inquire about our dinner options.

"I vote for the pilgrim menu," Till says. "I have eaten enough bread and cheese." We place our reservation for dinner and have the afternoon to relax. I head off to read on the lawn, another bottle in hand.

There are only five others at dinner tonight: two couples and one older woman walking solo. As usual, dinner is served family-style. We all share a bit about ourselves and our Camino as we inhale our tasty and filling meal.

"We still have two bottles of wine in our packs," Cosima says.

After dinner we invite Till over to our place to relax on a small patio next to the stream. Cosima and I dust off cobwebs and wash the dirt from a table and chairs we find nearby. After we pour the first cups of wine, Till says, "I'm going to ask a guy I saw hanging out this afternoon if he wants to join us." A few minutes later, he returns.

"This is Jules," Till says.

Cosima and I shake his hand and introduce ourselves. Jules is over six feet tall and has a dark beard and thick, wavy hair.

"Nice to meet you both," he says in a rich baritone voice.

The four of us chat and laugh our way through the bottles; then Till and Jules head to the bar and bring back two more. We drink until somewhat late into the night. Eventually, Cosima and I say goodnight and head up our room, leaving them to finish the last bottle.

Within minutes, we are naked and in a passionate embrace. It is a long, romantic night, and I know we are not necessarily quiet in our lovemaking, but I am not sure how audible it may be in the other two rooms. It is late, so the other two couples from dinner may not have heard our headboard or sounds of pleasure. I lie next to Cosima and gently rub her back. Before we reach the tipping point into sleep, one of the other couple's beds starts knocking.

Cosima jokes, "We provided them the inspiration."

DAY 27: PONTE CAMPAÑA > ARZÚA

Whatever you can do, or dream you can—
begin it. Boldness has genius, power and
magic in it.

~ Johann Wolfgang von
Goethe, *Faust: Part One*

The sun is high in the sky when we wake. We hurriedly stuff our packs and head out to find Till. Surprised, we find him and Jules still asleep in their bunks, the only pilgrims still inside. "They must have been drinking well into the night," I say. Cosima wakes Till, and then the two of us head to the patio and drink café con leche.

"I enjoyed our night," I say.

"I did too," she says. "And not just the physical stuff. It's nice just spending time together. I have missed that since my breakup."

"How long after your breakup did you start your Camino?" I ask.

"Two months," she says.

"Why *did* you break up?" I ask.

"When he was definite about not wanting to have children, I knew I needed to end it," she says. "I still love him, but I want kids someday."

"I'm sure it was hard," I say.

"It still is," she says with a furrowed brow.

Till and Jules finally make it out, and our party is again the last to leave. We walk along cobbled lanes, views of lush countryside visible through the trees, passing through small settlements every few kilometers.

Thoughts of the last few days and nights drift. After chasing and then catching up to Cosima, I have pulled back the reins. The pace of my Camino has slowed. I was never in a hurry to reach Santiago, knowing it's the journey and not the destination, but the change has been dramatic. I am dumbstruck by the circumstance I find myself in here, walking with Cosima by my side.

Before noon we cross over an ancient Roman bridge, its four arches spanning the Furelos River, and soon enter Melide, a town famous for serving *pulpo* (octopus). For the last week, veteran pilgrims have raved about it.

"I want to try pulpo," I say. "It's supposed to be delicious."

Till makes a face, but says, "I'm game."

"If you want to try it, we will stop," Cosima adds.

We pass a dozen establishments proudly offering this local specialty before making it to Pulperia Ezequiel, where out front, we find enormous pots of boiling octopuses; caught off the coast, only an hour's drive away. The locals prepare it by boiling the whole octopus in large cauldrons, cutting it with scissors, and then seasoning the inch-square pieces with olive oil and paprika.

I bite into my first piece. It is firmer and chewier than I expected; the texture of the dozens of tiny suction cups evident with every bite makes it an interesting experience. However, it tastes nothing like rings of lightly fried calamari. "Well, it's not what I was expecting," I say at last.

"It tastes okay, but I can't get used to the tentacles," Cosima says with a scrunched-up face.

I can tell no one is a big fan. "Thanks for humoring me," I say. One platter of pulpo and sides of pimientos and fries easily feeds the four of us.

"You can at least check it off your Camino to-do list," Cosima says with a grin.

This afternoon we are walking with a destination in mind. The guidebook recommends the municipal albergue in Ribadiso, located along a small river. An afternoon swim sounds perfect. As municipals operate on a first-come, first-served basis, we can't call ahead, but we plan on an early enough arrival, since it is only twenty-two kilometers from today's starting point. We walk through a fragrant grove of towering eucalyptus trees and have a couple of steep climbs and descents as we approach our destination.

I have seen more pilgrims today than any day so far; solo walkers, pairs, and small groups. So I shouldn't be surprised when we find the municipal albergue full, yet I am. Cosima's lips turn, and there is sweat dripping from us all. We find a table at a bar next door. I remove my pack, which feels much heavier than it did this morning; it, too, soaked with sweat. There are cold drinks for all as we slump into our chairs. Our disappointment adds a few degrees to an already steamy afternoon.

On to Plan B. "I'm going to check what other places may have beds," I say and leave the others. I walk through this tiny hamlet overflowing with pilgrims and find a private albergue and a pension, but both respond to my inquiry with "completo." I walk back to the others.

"I have reserved three beds in Arzúa," Cosima says. "It is three kilometers ahead."

"I am going to walk further on," Jules informs me.

Thirty minutes later, we reach our albergue and say goodbye to Jules. The Albergue de Selma doesn't look like much from the outside; just a small sign above a door in a five-story residential building in a block of similar adjoining buildings; commercial spaces fill the ground level. A smiling, middle-aged man behind a small front desk greets us. "How was your walk today?" he asks enthusiastically. Marcial, the proud owner, checks us in and gives a tour of this seemingly brand new albergue. There's a large kitchen and dining area, a unisex bathroom with ten showers, and a ten-foot-long concrete sink. The lightly stained plywood construction gives the place an industrial yet rustic feel. The bunk room, separated from the rest of the space, is one cavernous room, but Marcial has created nooks of four beds, much like in Roncesvalles. Here a curtain hides each pod to provide added privacy, so it feels like the three of us are sharing one room.

Sitting at a long table in the dining area, I watch Marcial interact with those staying here. He lends a towel to a man after finding out he'd forgotten his at last night's albergue; he cheerfully directs others to the farmàcia, or to his favorite restaurant. I am impressed by what he's created, converting a vanilla box—a commercial real estate term—into the perfect place for weary pilgrims.

After I shower, I lie in my bunk, thinking of Marcial and how he has created a life he clearly enjoys and finds meaningful. During my days of quiet desperation, I was envious of those who had more control over their time, those not being forced to punch a clock. Here on the Camino, I have met pilgrims who live a nine-to-five life but have walked the Camino many times and tell me it's re-energizing. During my desperate years, as I searched in vain for a light at the end of the tunnel, my one- or two-week-long vacations were not enough to sustain a vigor for life.

I know that, back in the States, many manage the nine-to-five life just fine, like the Hedonist on the mountain. If I had taken a month-long break from routine each year to explore, would I have felt the need to blow up my old life? Back then, the idea of finding purpose wasn't even on my radar; I simply felt the urgency of escaping from a stifling corporate life. I didn't realize that a nine-to-five life filled with purpose might have also quieted that voice begging to break away.

Now I better understand that this life is mine to create. Knowing my material needs are few and having the time to explore the world as well as my deeper self is liberating. The only clock I'm on now is life's hourglass.

We walk to a market, then find a picnic spot in a field across from our albergue. We take turns playing songs, and Cosima and Till introduce me to their favorite German music. I share a few songs, including one I think Cosima would find meaningful after her breakup.

As the Darius Rucker song "Love Without You" plays, her green eyes glisten.

The sky turns pink as the sun drops below the horizon and talk turns to books we've enjoyed. Cosima suggests I read the Herman Hesse novel *Narcissus and Goldmund*. On my phone, I read a review of the book on Amazon. I am intrigued by the Goldmund character and his lustful wanderings and his search for purpose. I think, but don't ask … is this how she sees me? Or maybe herself?

Not long after the sun has set, we head back across the street and turn in for the night.

DAY 28: ARZÚA > O PEDROUZO

On the Camino, I have learned to live
day-to-day, not in the future.

~ Elana Franganillo Ortiz

The albergue's door closes at 8 a.m., so we are off to what now seems an early start. Not five minutes into our walk, Cosima stops and says, "I left the walking stick."

"Let's turn around," I say.

"No. You two keep walking. I'll catch up," she says.

"Are you sure?" I ask.

"Yeah, I'll hurry."

Till and I continue, but we slow our pace as we make our way on the sidewalks of a town much bigger than I suspected it was last night.

"Is the Camino what you expected?" I ask Till.

"Not really. I had no idea what it would be. Cosima told me last year I should walk it this summer, but I didn't think I'd like it. She had to convince me to walk with her for two days when we were at the beach."

"And you're still here, despite your knee," I say.

"I am sure I will be back. I am trying to get my girlfriend to come with me," he says.

Before we exit the city, we run across Jules.

"I got nervous about finding a bed in the next small village," he says. "I found it would mean walking another ten kilometers. I wasn't up for that last night."

The three of us move on together, and soon Cosima catches up as we're strolling along a quiet forest track. Our morning walk through the countryside is occasionally interrupted by hamlets composed of a handful of homes. Around ten o'clock, our route takes us through a small village and, after a bend in the road, an intriguing sight appears.

A dozen tables are scattered about beneath a small stand of trees, surrounded by literally thousands of empty brown beer bottles. The bottles are everywhere, hanging on pegs hammered onto every possible surface; on large boards on the edge of this oasis, on tree trunks, on logs standing upright like a coat rack, and a welcoming log archway. We have arrived at the Tia Dolores Biergarten.

"We are stopping!" Till declares.

Despite our early morning arrival, it is too enticing to pass up. A dozen pilgrims are enjoying a beer when we arrive. We take seats at a metal table covered in white graffiti and find white paint markers lying on each table. Every beer bottle placed on a peg has something written on it.

I walk into a small stone building and walk out with four bottles of the only beer offered, Peregrina.

"What a great idea this is," I say. "I'd think most pilgrims would stop and have at least one drink regardless of the time of day, but on a scorching afternoon, the cold beer must feel heaven-sent."

When we finish our beer, we each write something on our bottle. I write the names of those I've gotten to know best on my Camino—Jana, Diana, and Cosima—along with today's date, and find an empty peg.

Our walk this morning is filled with the refreshing scent of eucalyptus. We walk through forests of these trees, which stretch high towards the sky and past meadows stocked with grazing cows and through small hamlets along quiet country lanes. These pastoral landscapes make Galicia my favorite of the regions along the Way. When we reach A Brea, a small village, we hope for a market but only find a store selling cheese. We keep walking.

Not two minutes later, Cosima spots a large tree in a field twenty meters off our path and points. "That tree is the perfect place for a picnic," she says. "We have some leftover food with us; let's eat."

We all agree to stop and head to the shade of the massive oak.

Cosima's sarong again acts as our picnic blanket. We empty our packs of food and find half a baguette, some chorizo, half of both an avocado and cucumber, along with a sleeve of cookies Jules tosses on the blanket. "I'm going to run to the cheese shop and see what I can find," I say and walk across the field to where Google Maps says it is.

The cheese "shop" is actually where they produce the cheese, but a small office also sells the cheese they make. I buy a pointed, rounded mound of Queso Tetilla, *tetilla* being the Spanish word for nipple, and head back to the tree with my breast of cheese.

Lying in the grass this afternoon, talking and eating with friends, the pace of life measured only by the number of steps taken, I think about how precious such moments are. Remembering a book I read a decade earlier, *Living the Good Life: How to Live Sanely and Simply in a Troubled World*, I share the ideas it discusses and how they mirror life on the Camino.

"The authors lived in a rural setting on a parcel of land they gardened and worked to improve. They always welcomed like-minded people for extended stays. They spent the mornings working the land or on construction tasks, their afternoons free to enjoy each other's company and cook communal meals together," I explain. "Their limited material needs in life made this simple life possible."

I lie back on my pack and remember thinking that their days were peaceful and their life ideal. This book was my portal to learning the philosophy behind intentional communities. While I don't envision this kind of life happening for me anytime soon, I also don't envision returning to a nine-to-five life. Knowing my days in Spain are numbered, my mind touches on life after the Camino.

I am coming to terms with not knowing where my path will lead, but I hope for a life that allows for more moments like this: a connection with others and being outdoors in nature.

Being stationary for an extended period, we get a clear picture of the numbers walking the Camino.

"The amount of people is insane," Jules says. "I think over a hundred pilgrims have passed by in the hour we've been sitting here."

Cosima, Till, and I choose our destination, O Pedrouzo, five kilometers ahead, making today a short twenty kilometers. Jules, again, plans to walk on.

As we reach the outskirts of O Pedrouzo, yellow arrows and signs direct us to make a right turn, but the town and all the services lie straight ahead.

"Last year, I missed this turn," Cosima says. "We had reservations to stay here, but we didn't realize our mistake for a couple of kilometers. We kept walking."

"Where did you end up stopping?" Jules asks.

"We couldn't find beds anywhere. We tried to sleep outside, but couldn't, so we ended up walking through the night, even though my feet hurt with every step," she says. "We ended up walking fifty kilometers, all the way to Santiago."

"Wow, that's crazy," I say.

"We arrived at the cathedral just as the sun was rising. It was an amazing way to end my Camino. Unfortunately, my feet were in pain for months."

We say goodbye to Jules, then descend into the vibrant town of O Pedrouzo. We stop at one of the albergues recommended by Cosima's guidebook but find it full. The same goes for the second, and we start to get nervous. We have better luck on our third attempt, at Albergue Cruceiro, one of the larger private albergues, with close to a hundred beds. The woman behind the counter tells us, "There are beds available, but not near one another."

"That's fine," we say in unison. One by one, she takes our passports, credentials, and twelve euros. Once we're checked in, she leads us to the lower level and into one large room with fifty beds. There are also a few smaller rooms into which she peeks. "Ahhh," she says, "there are three available beds in this room." We each stake our claim.

When evening arrives, the three of us walk back to the main drag to shop for dinner. The temperature is perfect as we stroll along busy sidewalks, past many restaurants and more albergues, pensions, and small hotels. "There are a ton of people here tonight," I say.

"My guidebook listed sixteen places to stay," Cosima says. "The walk into Santiago is going to be a crowded one."

"I need to find the farmacia," Till says.

"I need an ATM," Cosima says.

Spotting a bench across the street, in front of a yellow municipal building with three flags hanging out front, I point and tell them, "I'll wait for you there."

Leaning back, I watch dozens of smiling people pass by; I assume most are pilgrims, reason enough to be smiling. My phone pings. I pull it out to find a message from Diana, a photo of her smiling face in front of the Cathedral in Santiago de Compostela: *I made it! I am headed home in the morning.*

Congrats! I am still twenty kilometers away. I'm sorry I won't get to see you again. It was great getting to know you, I respond.

As Cosima lays out her golden sarong in a grassy field on the outskirts, we find ourselves with the same problem as a few nights ago: we have nothing to drink from; our well-worn plastic cups are back at our lodgings. I walk back to an albergue we just passed, and a kind woman behind the desk locates three plastic cups and generously offers them to me. I will add a collapsible cup with a carabiner to the packing list for my next long walk.

The three of us watch the sun fall towards the horizon as we enjoy another typical evening. Talk turns bittersweet as we discuss our walk soon coming to an end. Walking to "the end of the world"—the coastal town of Finisterre—is mentioned. It would mean three more days walking to the ocean, but things remain up in the air.

Another day comes to an end, and we head back to our albergue in near-darkness. We stop to grab our clothes from the clothesline and enter the back entrance on the lower level. We walk through the large bunk room filled with groups of high schoolers milling about as a cacophony of chatter fills the space while the time for lights-out approaches. After we brush our teeth and are headed back to our room, Cosima says, "Come to my bed once everyone is asleep."

I lie in bed for twenty minutes. When I think everyone in the room is sleeping, I crawl out of my lower bunk and make my way to her. I gently tap her shoulder. When I get no immediate response, I head back to my bunk and dream of Cosima, on what may be our last night together.

DAY 29: O PEDROUZO > MONTE DE GOZO

*People grow through experience if they meet
life honestly and courageously. This is how
character is built.*

~ Eleanor Roosevelt

"Why didn't you join me last night?" Cosima asks.

"I tried to wake you, but you didn't respond."

"I wish you had tried a little harder." She smirks.

We walk out into a misty fog, and I throw on my lightweight fleece for the first time in a week. We stop at a bar just before leaving town for what may be my last café con leche on the Camino. We sit under a bright blue awning, sipping our coffee and watching a never-ending flow of pilgrims heading uphill to rejoin the Way.

We have been dragging our feet for the past week, not wanting our walk to end—delaying starts and shortening the distance walked each day. It's the same this morning, slowly sipping our coffee until we finally stand to go.

We throw on our packs and head off into the morning haze. We are soon walking silently through yet another large grove of eucalyptus. A short time later, the quiet is gone, replaced by the singing and chanting of a pack of teens. This small band is walking as a part of much larger group, easily identified by their matching T-shirts. A pained expression comes over Cosima's face, her mood matching the gloomy weather.

"Let's stop to let them pass," she says.

We do, but they are soon replaced by others singing and chanting, this time in Italian. I am surprised to find these school-age Italians walking so far from home.

"There should be a rule which says the last day of the Camino must be walked in silence," Till says. "A time for reflection."

"I agree. This is crazy. We are walking through a big party," Cosima says. "I'm sorry I'm in such a terrible mood. I don't want to enter Santiago like this. I want to stop for the day before we get there."

"That sounds good to me," I say. "I'm not looking forward to this ending."

"Fine with me," Till adds.

While I was not necessarily in a bad mood, the idea of stopping gives a lightness to my steps and brings a smile to my face.

Our route heads towards a busy highway, and when it takes a turn, I am surprised to find we are walking next to the runway lights for the Santiago Airport. We are getting close. As we pass through the small hamlet of Vilamaior, we spot Casa de Amancio, a relatively modern-looking, single-story stone building. *Modern* meaning it looks like something built in the last fifty years.

"I need to stop," Cosima says.

There haven't been many facilities on our route this morning, so we stop for something to drink and to use the restroom. We squirm through a swarm of pilgrims, past long lines in the small lobby (clearly, we're not the only ones needing to pee) and onto a patio out back, where we find an open table.

We sit drinking beer, my fleece now back on, under a gray sky, and take turns waiting inside. Cosima consults her guidebook and says,

"There is an albergue in three kilometers."

"Perfect," Till says.

After our break, we continue along relatively quiet roads; no more singing, but still surrounded by many others. As we walk through yet another aromatic forest, I am startled when we pass a stand selling Camino T-shirts and other souvenirs.

After a short climb, we stand beside a massive monument constructed to commemorate a visit to this hill by Pope John Paul II thirty years earlier. Turning from the memorial, I catch my first glimpse of Santiago de Compostela's cathedral, its three spires visible from five kilometers away, even on this dreary day.

Almost every other pilgrim who stops to take in this view continues back along the Camino's official route, while we head in the opposite direction, downhill to our albergue. We arrive just past noon and find a few people waiting outside the Centro Europeo de Peregrinación. We drop our packs and join them.

I smile when I spot a shirt from Loras College, a small Catholic university in Dubuque, Iowa.

"Did you study there?" I ask.

"Yes, last year," he says. "But I'm back at university in France."

"My father went there," I say, happy for this small sign of my dad being out here.

While we wait outside, the Frenchman asks, "Have you seen the Monument to the Pilgrims?"

"No. Where is it?" I respond.

"Just down the road," he says, pointing in the opposite direction from which we came.

Cosima, Till and I leave our packs, and minutes later, we find two somber-looking pilgrims cast in bronze, the green patina hinting at their age. Each ten-foot-tall pilgrim has one arm outstretched, pointing towards the cathedral, the other hand grasping a walking staff, gourd attached.

After the doors open, I peer out from walls of glass as I wait my turn to check in to this albergue run entirely by volunteers from Poland. A green lawn spreads out from the back of the building, and now patches of blue peek from the clouds. There is a large dining room with a posted bill of fare for a typical pilgrim menu, which seems our best option for dinner tonight. The sleeping arrangements tonight are either a bunk for a donation or a private room for 20€. I consider taking a private room with hopes of a late-night rendezvous with Cosima but say, "Bunk, please," when asked, not wanting to upend the easiness the three of us have created.

A volunteer leads us along a paved path, past a long, narrow building housing a dozen individual rooms; on the opposite side, a tree-lined lawn. Our accommodation tonight is in one of two identical buildings, and it has the feel of the barracks on an army base. Three more facilities are nearby; one building houses a kitchen, and the other two are bathrooms, one each for men and women; an outdoor laundry area is on the backside of one of the bathrooms. While our bunkroom is common, the whole of this place is not; it is the perfect place for a relaxing afternoon.

After a shower, I hand-wash every item of clothing in my pack, then lay everything on a low stone wall to dry. Later, I lie down in the grass to read in the shade of a tree. On this quiet afternoon, my destination visible in the distance, I think of what an incredible time it's been since I started this journey twenty-eight days ago.

I think of the many friends I have encountered: Jana, Victoria, Olivia, Birte, Julie, Diana, the group of Italians, Annika, Jerome, Cosima, Till, Max, Jules, and the many who've created a life here on the Camino. Looking back, I can see the connections that led me here, grateful for crossing their paths.

Being open to whatever may come is an important lesson I've learned here on the Camino, but more important is being open with those I meet. I don't think that, before the Camino, I was being my most authentic self; I held back my childlike wonder, dreams, and fears, afraid to be me. Here I've been brutally truthful about my flaws and mistakes.

In my past incarnation, I wasn't open to possibilities. I lived a relatively small life, confining myself to what I knew. This idea will be one of the most valuable lessons I'll take from this journey. I have lived more adventurously the past couple of years, but here on the Camino, I've become more myself. I am more confident in my life's direction, despite not knowing where it will lead me.

Once my mind clears, I continue reading about Larry Darrell and the end of his journey. Later, a smiling Cosima strolls across the lawn and sits beside me. I reach out and touch the soft skin of her calf.

"Whenever we are ready to eat, I have our dinner!" she says proudly. "Two guys were cooking in the kitchen, and they made way too much food and offered us their leftovers—enough to feed all three of us. All that's missing is the wine."

"Awesome!" I say, before quickly correcting myself and saying, with a smirk, "I mean, *fantastic*. So what are your plans for tomorrow and the days to come? Are you heading to Finisterre?"

"Yes, but I'm not sure what Till is going to do."

"I am definitely going to continue, since my flight isn't for another week. I'd love to walk with you, but if you'd rather continue with Till or by yourself, I'll understand."

"Of course I want to walk together; if I didn't, I would have told you," she says, a bit irritated. "Till and I are planning to stay two nights in Santiago, and he's going to let me know his plans once we get there."

I smile. "Okay. I'm happy to hear that." Walking to the end of the world with Cosima is an exciting prospect, with or without Till.

Only a handful of others are in this beautiful compound. Someone has set up a small tent at the far end of the lawn, and a couple of others roam the grounds. As the afternoon turns into evening, the three of us head into the kitchen, where there are two pots, one filled with mushroom risotto and the other with spaghetti, tomato sauce, and green olives. Cosima starts to warm up the food; Till heads out to set up the picnic in the grass; I head to the main building's dining room, hoping to find some wine.

I approach a long counter, which I imagine also serves as a bar, but find it empty. A few seconds later, a lovely Polish woman walks from the kitchen and asks, "How can I help?"

A couple of minutes later, I walk back across the green, a bottle in each hand, to find our dinner laid out on a familiar tapestry.

After washing our dishes, we sit outside under a tangerine sky, drinking wine, when a woman traveler walks by. "Join us," Till says. She does.

Till fetches another cup from the kitchen. The woman, who is also German, is on a solo trek from Saint-Jean. When the last of the wine is gone, Till goes and buys two more bottles. Much of the conversation switches to German, as our guest's English is limited, with Cosima translating.

After dark has fallen, two Spanish men stop briefly to chat and offer Till to take a drag from a cigarette. "Hashish," one of the men says. Till takes a toke and passes it to me; I draw in and inhale whatever is in the cigarette. Both Cosima and the German woman shake their heads; the men gesture to keep the cigarette before they disappear in the dark.

Along our walk, with every new experience, Cosima has said "check" to mark something off a to-do list. Days earlier, the three of us listed things we still wanted to do; I said I hoped to get high at some point. Cosima now says with a smile, "Check," and motions with her finger as if to mark it complete.

Cosima walks off, then turns and motions for me to follow. I walk into the dark and find Cosima standing in front of the laundry area. We kiss passionately and grope each other before I lift her onto a narrow table and reach for her underwear. She slowly shakes her head before she lowers her hand and then raises it and sticks her finger in my mouth to tease me with a taste of herself. She jumps down and walks away. I'm left speechless.

I make my way back to our late-night picnic in the dark; the combination of wine, a few drags from the cigarette, and arousing play have me in a euphoric state. Eventually, Cosima and I say goodnight, leaving Till with his new friend, and head back to our bunk room. We enter to find it half full of dozing pilgrims. Soon, we, too, are asleep.

DAY 30: MONTE DE GOZO > SANTIAGO DE COMPOSTELA

A mind that is stretched by a new experience
can never goes back to its old dimensions.

~ Oliver Wendell Holmes

This morning, Cosima, Till, and I take our time. It's only five kilometers along this historic trail to the Cathedral of Santiago de Compostela, where a Pilgrim's Mass is offered every day at noon. We reach the outskirts of Santiago in fifteen minutes. We walk along city streets, past modern buildings as cars zoom past and the bustle of modernity reappears. I scan ahead for yellow arrows to ensure we are heading in the right direction.

As we wait at a stoplight, Cosima says, "I would like to walk alone to the cathedral. I will meet you guys on the plaza out front."

"Sure, we'll see you there," I say.

After we cross the street, Cosima slows her pace. Till and I follow a stream of backpacks through streets that grow narrower as the well-kept buildings lining these cobbled lanes grow older. As we approach a covered archway, the sound of bagpipes grows louder. Descending a few steps along the paved pathway, I find a young man playing beautifully, his red velvet case open for alms. I reach into my pocket and toss what coins I have into his case.

We walk through the passageway towards the light—and it opens onto a grand plaza. Over a hundred people are scattered about; excitement fills the air. Pilgrims pose in front of the Romanesque cathedral; others are splayed out on the age-old stones. Till and I walk towards the arcade of the building opposite the cathedral and turn to take it all in. It's stunning.

"There's Caroline," Till says, pointing at the young German woman we walked with on our way out of Samos. She's resting alone against the stone base of a pillar.

We walk towards her. "Can we join you, Caroline?" Till asks.

Caroline looks up and smiles. "Of course."

Taking off our packs, we sit down, facing the cathedral's intricate carvings and its three soaring spires.

"Would you like to join us for the noon mass?" Till asks.

"I would love to," she says.

I haven't gotten to know Till as well as I have the many others on my Camino—but his welcoming nature inspires me. He's befriended Max and Jules; he's invited Isabel in his humble Spanish; last night he opened his arms to the woman. And now here he is, putting Caroline at ease with his broad smile and generous spirit.

Till had initially planned on walking with his sister for just two days, but the Camino has charmed him. I watch Till and Caroline chat and nod my head. The life of a pilgrim fits his open and kind disposition perfectly.

Cosima approaches us, and a smile washes across her face. She pulls out three Peregrina beers from her pack.

"Perfect," I say.

"Grab your cup, Caroline," Till says, "we'll share."

Cosima opens the bottles and hands Till and me one each. Caroline removes a metal cup attached to the outside of her pack. We each pour a bit of our beer into it.

We raise our drinks: "Prost," we say in unison.

As we sit talking, a butterfly lands on my knee. We watch it for a few seconds before it flies away.

"Wow!" Caroline says. "How symbolic."

"It is." It reminds me of the Nathaniel Hawthorne quote, I say: "Happiness is as a butterfly, which, when pursued, is always just beyond your grasp, but which, if you will sit down quietly, may alight upon you."

"Are you the butterfly?" Cosima asks.

"No. For me, it symbolizes contentment."

I'd arrived in Saint-Jean-Pied-de-Port in pursuit of something, though I didn't know what. As I walked day after day, my mind quieted. Pursuing an elusive epiphany was no longer my focus. I simply enjoyed whatever came my way. Things had changed a bit after Cosima messaged me the first time. The chase—getting to know her—has been an important part of my journey, but even so, it's only a part. I feel connected to the Camino—the places, the experience—in a way that I haven't felt about anything before. I'm amazed by how a simple path across a sometimes desolate landscape can have such a profound effect on one's mind, body and soul.

Till glances at his phone. "It's getting close to noon."

"In case you didn't know, the cathedral is closed for renovation," Caroline explains. "Mass will be held nearby at Iglesia de San Francisco. It's only a short walk away."

I think we are all disappointed the cathedral is closed. I wanted to witness the flying censer—the massive incense burner shown in *The Way*. We arrive late; it's a little past noon. Packs are forbidden inside, so we place ours alongside the hundred others lining a stone wall opposite the entrance.

When we enter the church, we stand in the back, as the pews are full. As usual, I don't understand a word spoken. Restless, I shift my weight from foot to foot as the service continues methodically. When standing still becomes too uncomfortable, I lean against a massive stone column. Mercifully, it comes to an end. Muted chatter fills the nave as hundreds of pilgrims rise and flow out of the church.

The church sits below street level, and as I reach the top of the stairs, I run into Lorenzo and Leonardo. We share hugs.

"I have thought about what you shared with me in San Anton," Lorenzo tells me. "I appreciate your wise words."

I am not sure what he is referring to, but I am grateful for his kindness. "Thanks," I say. "I hope you both had a meaningful journey."

"Yes, yes, it was amazing," he says.

"Where are you two staying in Santiago?" I ask.

"We are staying at the seminario," Leonardo says. "You?"

"I don't know yet. My friends and I need to find a place," I say. "Hopefully, I'll see you two again."

I find Cosima and Caroline, who have begun calling albergues listed in her guidebook to find one with four beds for tonight. On their fourth attempt, they succeed. Once tonight's accommodations have been secured, we search out the Pilgrim Office to collect our compostela. Conveniently, it is only one hundred meters from the church.

We enter the Pilgrim Office, actually a large two-story building, and a uniformed man at the door says, "You can collect your number on the lower level."

We head down an open stairway to the basement and find many pilgrims milling about. An automated screen prints out our numbers in line; they are in the 500s. A large monitor nearby displays the number 320.

We head to a courtyard at the back of the building and join those waiting to be called. We take seats in the grass under a sunny sky and continue our conversation. When we find out the wait will be hours, Cosima says, "Let's come back in the morning. I need food."

"Fine with me," I say.

"Maybe we can meet up later," Caroline says. "I fly out tomorrow, so I am going to wait."

While discussing where to meet Caroline, I get a message from Jana: *Have you made it to Santiago yet?*

Yes, this morning. I'm at the Pilgrim Office now, I reply.

Me too.

I wander past the warren of rooms to meet Jana. She is standing in front of an office with information on walking to "the end of the world."

We chat briefly and agree to meet for a drink later. It feels good to see her again.

I find the others still sitting in the courtyard. "I spoke to Pablo," Cosima says. Pablo, the owner of Cosima's walking stick. "We are all going to meet for drinks this evening."

"Sounds fun," I say. "I am going to meet my friend for a drink this afternoon. You're invited."

Cosima, Till, and I leave Caroline and head off in search of something to eat. We end up enjoying a store-bought picnic on a patch of grass along a busy walkway leading to a nearby park. Next to our picnic spot is a colorful statue of two women walking arm in arm. We find these vibrantly painted figures have been placed here to honor two elderly sisters who strolled through this park every day for decades; it's known as *The Two Marias.*

After lunch, we have only a two-minute walk to Mundo Albergue, our home for tonight. "This is convenient," Cosima says. "The cathedral is only a few minutes away.'

After I shower, Cosima says, "I may meet you there." I head off to meet Jana at a bar on the backside of the cathedral. The bar pours onto a wide terrace which spills down a long flight of steps into another large plaza, this one not as grand or as lively as the one opposite. We order glasses of wine and find a table outside. "That's the Holy Door," Jana says, pointing down to a passage blocked off by a wrought-iron gate. Ornately carved walls surround the entrance and there are dozens of intricate statues—the largest, centered on top, representing, I assume, the namesake himself.

"What is it used for?" I ask.

"It's only open during Holy Years. The years when the feast of Saint James falls on a Sunday," she says. "And if you walk through the Holy Door, the church grants absolution, washing away all your sins."

"Sounds like a bargain for us sinners," I say.

Jana takes a sip of her wine and asks, "Sooo … why did you keep running from me?"

"I don't think I was running," I say, shaking my head. "The day we split up, I had every intention of meeting up that evening. After that, I had trouble slowing down."

"It sure felt like you were," she says. "You told me you tended to run from things. I thought we were getting closer—then you were gone."

"It wasn't intentional," I say as I shake my head.

"Were you afraid something might happen between us?" she asks.

"I don't think so. But, if you remember … when we first met, you said you were going to honor your vows until you were certain of your decision. So I wasn't going to test you," I say.

"I remember," she says, nodding.

"I guess I did want to walk alone for a bit," I admit. "Then in Burgos, when I was going to wait for you, I decided to walk with an Italian because I thought it would be interesting to get to know someone from a different country."

"I get it. I met someone, too. A guy, another American, after you walked ahead," she says and takes another big gulp of wine. "We walked together for about a week. I think we both had a bit of a crush, but neither of us made a move."

"I'm surprised," I say, raising my brows.

"I think I wanted something to happen, but we parted ways," she says with a shrug. "I think once anything romantic starts on the Camino, you're going to be connected until the end. I am not sure either of us was ready for that."

"I know," I say. "I've been walking with a German woman, and we've been together for about a week. I agree, once that line is crossed, you feel attached and will continue together till the end."

We exchange stories of our walks, and I share the story of meeting Cosima. "She may come and meet us at some point," I say.

"I told you I am headed to Finisterre tomorrow. I would love it if you'd join me," Jana says.

"Honestly, Jana, I would love to, but I've planned to keep walking with my German friend. I want to see where it goes." I would enjoy walking with Jana again, but I will not leave Cosima.

"I understand. You're thinking with your dick," she says and laughs.

"That may be true," I reply. "But we have gotten close on our Camino romance."

Jana and I agree returning home will be challenging, both uncertain about what awaits us back in the reality of our day-to-day lives.

I glimpse Cosima walking across the plaza below. I stand and wave my arms.

"This is Jana," I say. "This is Cosima."

They shake hands. "Nice to meet you."

"You too," Cosima says, still standing.

"Have a seat," I say. "Can I get you a glass of wine?"

"No thanks," she says. "I will leave you two to talk. I want to explore a bit. We'll meet up later."

Cosima walks away.

"Well, I can see what the attraction is for each of you," Jana says. Then she confides she had a fling with someone older while in college, so she understands Cosima's interest in an older guy.

"Really?" I ask. "I'm surprised. I assumed you had always kept those urges buried."

"One thing I like about you, Mike," she says. "You're honest. You don't play games."

"Good to hear," I say. "In the past, I kept too many things inside. It's one of the many things I am working on."

We talk a while longer and then wish each other well on our walks to the ocean.

"I am glad we were able to meet up. I hope we stay in touch once we are back in the States," I say.

"Me too," she says.

We stand and share a long embrace before heading off in different directions.

It seems from our conversation that Jana hoped she and I would have moved past the friend stage, and perhaps I did run from that possibility. When a man and a woman are close for an extended length of time, I think a feeling of intimacy may naturally develop and can lead to crossing a line into something physical.

With Cosima, it was different. There was an immediate connection with her, then a long period of anticipation, which fanned the initial spark. As soon as we reconnected, there were already embers ready to ignite.

At the time agreed, the four of us meet across the street from our Albergue. Cosima has Pablo's walking stick in hand.

"I am not going to be able to join you," Caroline says. "I agreed to meet up with a group I had walked with the last few days. Maybe I'll see you later tonight."

"Have fun!" Till says.

The pedestrian-only streets around the cathedral are teeming with people, a combination of locals and pilgrims. Tantalizing smells flow from the many bars and restaurants we pass. The tables are packed. Cheerful voices fill the narrow streets. I imagine Santiago always having a festive feel to it, with this constant influx of pilgrims bringing joy and energy with them.

We find the bar tucked into a small nook in a maze of tight alleyways—the patio just big enough for a half-dozen tables. Cosima spots her friend. Pablo is fit, handsome, clean-shaven, with dark wavy hair, and appears to be in his early thirties. His white linen shirt sets off a dark tan. He rises from his chair to greet Cosima and Till with hugs.

"It is great to see you again," Cosima says with a big smile.

"You too," Pablo says. Cosima hands Pablo his well-used wooden stick.

"This is Mike," Cosima says.

Pablo and I shake hands.

"Nice to meet you," I say. "I've heard great things about you."

Pablo smiles and says, "You too. Now, let's get everyone a drink."

The three Camino friends reminisce about their time walking together and share their Camino stories since they separated. For the most part, I sit back and listen. I learn Pablo has spent most of his life in Santiago, growing up here, where his parents still live. Pablo has walked many of the different routes to Santiago. This summer, he combined a family reunion with a couple of weeks on a Camino. He is headed back home to Madrid tomorrow.

When Pablo mentions heading to another bar, Till says, "I have been dreaming about the restaurant you talked about."

It doesn't seem Pablo was expecting to go out to dinner tonight, but, being a generous host, he says, "Sure, if you want. But it will cost about thirty euros each. If that's okay?"

I sense Cosima is hesitant, but Till says, "Yes!"

The decision has been made.

Pablo calls and makes a reservation for eight o'clock, the restaurant's opening time.

We have plenty of time before dinner, and Pablo says, "Instead of going to another bar, we should walk to Parque de la Alameda. It is not far."

Pablo leads the way. We pass *The Two Marias* and are soon strolling along a tree-lined path through a sixteenth-century park with views of the city on one side and the cathedral on the other. A golden-hour light enhances the park's beauty. Towering oaks and fragrant eucalyptus envelop the park. We find many locals here, but it's not crowded. It seems we have found a hidden gem in the city, of which most pilgrims are unaware. We stop in front of a large stone fountain with the sun setting directly behind it. The silhouette of Cosima gazing towards the city below will stick in my mind.

The restaurant, Asador Gonzaba, is outside of the touristic part of town near the cathedral, but still only a short walk away. It is elegant, with modern finishes throughout. Large slabs of meat hang in a sleek, refrigerated display case, like a piece of art. The first to arrive tonight, we are seated at a large, round table in a room with a barrel ceiling constructed of red brick. As we inspect the menu, Cosima and I glance at one another and think the thirty-euro estimate is way too low.

"I've been excited about this place for weeks," Till says.

His excitement is understandable, after weeks of primarily picnic meals. "Pablo, will you order for us?" Till asks.

"Of course," he says.

The waiter arrives, and Pablo orders in Spanish. "You will enjoy it," he tells us.

While we talk of life and the Camino, the waiter brings out the wine. Not too much later, and sooner than I expected, two waiters carrying covered platters arrive at our table. They unveil two huge cuts of meat, still on the bone, resting on cutting boards. Till's eyes widen, as do mine.

"It looks amazing," Cosima says.

"One cut is beef, the other veal," Pablo tells us.

"I will serve everyone," Till says, his eyes bulging as he grabs a knife.

We feast.

Along the Way, we passed so many cows. Beef is a staple in the north of Spain, though not necessarily for pilgrims. While the two slabs are more than enough to fill us, Cosima and Till both laughingly gnaw on the large bones.

When the bill comes, I'm surprised the total comes to just under thirty euros each. While this was the most I have paid for a meal on my walk, it is about what I would have paid for dinner and drinks at a Chili's back home.

After ten o'clock, we leave the restaurant and say our goodbyes to Pablo, after he—once again—almost forgets his walking stick, left at the door. He heads to his parents' home, and we head back towards our albergue.

There is no curfew, and as we get near, we spot Caroline standing under a streetlight.

"How was your night?" Till asks her. The two begin to talk.

"Would you like to take a walk through the park?" I ask Cosima.

"I would," she says with a grin.

We saunter along a gravel pathway, past old-timey streetlights casting a warm yellow glow. I wrap my arm around Cosima as we move in silence next to the park's edge overlooking the cathedral, still visible in a hazy light. We make our way into the heart of the park, where we take a seat on a bench. Cosima rests her legs over mine. I stare into her eyes, a solemn expression on her face, and lightly brush her cheek with the back of my hand before gently placing my lips on hers.

As we head back, we discuss plans for exploring Santiago tomorrow and agree to set our alarms so we can make it to the Pilgrim Office early and avoid a long wait.

DAY 31: SANTIAGO DE COMPOSTELA

As you move towards a dream, the dream
move towards you.

~ Julia Cameron, *The Artist's Way*

It's twenty minutes before eight when we get to the Pilgrim Office. We join a handful of others and sit beneath a hazy sky with our backs against a wall, waiting. When the doors open, we enter in single file. "Good morning," says a man as he hands out slips with a number—mine is 11. We line up outside of a room to wait. Shortly after Till and Cosima enter, my number appears on a screen above the door.

I hand my well-used credential filled with colorful stamps, a visual documentation of my journey, to one of four volunteers behind a long counter.

"Where did you start your Camino?" he asks while unfolding my credential to inspect the stamps.

"Saint-Jean-Pied-de-Port," I respond with a smile. I glance over at

Cosima as she chats with her inquisitor.

"Did you walk the entire way by foot?" mine asks.

"Yes," I say.

"Congratulations on completing your Camino," he says as he writes my name in Latin by hand on my official Compostela. "As one of the first twenty-five pilgrims of the day, there is a voucher here to visit the Portico de la Gloria this evening." It's an area closed off to the general public unless a guided tour is purchased. I am surprised, having thought the entire cathedral was closed for renovations.

He nods as he hands me my compostela, voucher, and credential.

"Thank you," I say.

I find Cosima and Till waiting outside the office. Cosima, her lips pursed sideways, hands me a certificate with her name and the word *lunch*—one I didn't receive.

"The first ten pilgrims were given a certificate for lunch at a nearby restaurant," Cosima says. "I explained there were three of us and tried to get an extra, but couldn't."

"No worries," I say. "It will be good for the two of you to celebrate together."

"We are not going unless we all go," Cosima says.

My brows furrow, and I say, "No, no, please go."

"No!" she says, giving me a look.

"Maybe I can go and just pay my way," I say.

"Okay, we will split the cost of the third meal, but if we cannot all eat, we will give the vouchers away," she says.

"I can live with that," I say.

We meet Caroline in front of the cathedral, and together we walk a few blocks to a local market Pablo recommended. Mercado de Abastos is bustling with locals. We pass several stands offering fruits and vegetables and then enter one of many identical stone buildings.

"Wow, that is powerful," Till says.

The scent of raw seafood permeates the air. We stroll through the well-lit space; a barreled ceiling bordered with windows rises high overhead. We navigate through the crowd, making our way past a dozen small stalls with glass display cases lining each wall—merchants selling fresh seafood of all kinds and every possible cut of beef and pork.

"Imagine the delicious meals that will be prepared," I say.

The stalls in the next building are overflowing with breads of all kinds and countless delicious-looking sweets. In another, we find a woman holding a platter of cheeses. We each sample the four she has. After agreeing on one variety, a soft cheese with a buttery aroma, we buy a large round to enjoy later. The last building we enter is a food hall with a seating area squeezed in the middle of the dozens of options lining the walls. The smells are tempting, but we want to save room for our hoped-for meal.

After our market exploration, we set a time and place to meet up with Caroline later this afternoon, before she leaves.

Cosima, Till, and I meander through the streets and arrive at the designated restaurant, Enxebre, the entrance on a sloping pedestrian-only street that descends from the cathedral's main plaza.

It is a little before noon, and the restaurant has yet to open. We stand outside, along with familiar faces from the morning's line. Cosima says to one of the others, "We will give our tickets away if we all three can't dine." A younger man approaches her.

"I am here to offer my meal, too. I must leave the city soon," he says. "You are welcome to it." He hands Cosima his voucher. "Since it has my name, I will wait with you for the restaurant to open and explain."

"Thank you," we all say to this smiling, bespectacled young man.

The Camino is still providing.

After introductions, we chat with Jean René, a Frenchman wearing a wide-brimmed green felt hat that reminds me of the 'lemon squeezer,' a hat worn by the Kiwis during the First World War. Soon the doors open, and Jean René explains to the hostess.

"It is not a problem," she says.

Cosima hugs Jean-René. He nods and raises his hand in farewell.

We, ten pilgrims, are seated at one long table. A sign explains that this meal is a tradition offered by the Parador, the luxury hotel that sits above the restaurant, and is exclusively for ten pilgrims each day.

We chat with those gathered while enjoying a delectable four-course meal, accompanied, of course, by fine red wine. After a week of subsisting primarily on bread and cheese, I feel spoiled by my last two meals here in Santiago.

After lunch, standing in the cathedral's plaza, Cosima calls the Albergue Seminario Menor and reserves beds for tonight. We three split up and set a time to meet back here and walk together to the seminary.

I wander the cobbled streets under a clear blue sky, searching for a small souvenir to bring back home. I pass several tattoo shops as I stroll the narrow lanes around the city's historic center. I have seen countless tattoos of scallop shells along the Way, on the arms and legs of those repeating their journey here. I seriously consider marking my body, not only to commemorate my journey but as a reminder to keep the spirit of the Camino alive in me. But I don't pull the trigger on getting my first tattoo.

While the cathedral doesn't offer the daily mass, and the main doors are locked, I find a side door granting access. Upon entering, I find the interior covered in plastic sheeting, the nave empty of pews, and scaffolding set up in all corners of the sanctuary. Hushed conversations and footsteps echo through the chamber, and a line of solemn pilgrims wraps around the altar, waiting to view the crypt which houses Saint James's remains.

The story of how one of Jesus's disciples ended up buried here is quite a tale. It is believed James came to Spain after Jesus's crucifixion to spread the word. He later returned to Judea, where King Herod II had him beheaded in 44 A.D. because of his faith. His body was sailed to the Galician Coast and buried there. In the year 814, a hermit found his remains, and his bones were carried inland and buried on a hill under a large oak tree—the same site where, 200 years later, the church built this cathedral. Like any legend, it serves a purpose; I, for one, am happy it led me here.

On the ceiling twenty meters above is anchored the pulley system used to swing the famed Botafumeiro, Galician for smoke expeller, the largest censer in the world. The Botafumeiro hangs typically above the altar; today, it's visible nearby in a glass case, and a thick rope descending from above is tied to one of the massive pillars. The censer weighs well over a hundred pounds, and it takes eight people to swing it. These *tiraboleiros* pull down on eight individual ropes attached to the much beefier one. This massive censer travels at over forty miles per hour when it reaches its maximum arc within the transept—the swinging of the Botafumerio serving the same purpose as that of a priest's small censer. When the cathedral is open, this massive censer is typically flown once a week, at noon Mass on Sunday, as well other meaningful dates throughout the year. After seeing this spectacle in *The Way*, I was hoping to witness it in person. Maybe next time.

These massive renovations are in preparation for the next Holy Year. The last holy year was 2010. Over the past few years, the cathedral's exterior has undergone a detailed restoration to prepare for the 2021 celebration, in anticipation of swarms of Catholic pilgrims desiring absolution descending on Santiago.

I find Cosima and Till sitting on the smooth flagstones across the plaza, where the same jubilant atmosphere continues as new pilgrims arrive every few minutes. "Hey there," I say. "Shall we go?"

"Yes, I want to check in before we meet up with Caroline," Cosima says.

We head across town towards the seminary. After first mistaking a large convent for the seminary, we eventually locate the massive four-story brick seminary, built high on a hill overlooking the city, with three garden labyrinths below. I'm surprised to find it is still an operating seminary. At the reception desk, we are given the option of a bed in a dorm, or, for ten euros more, a private room with a single bed. "I'm taking a private room," I volunteer—and the thought of a night lying next to Cosima races through my head.

"I will as well," Till says.

"Okay, I will, too," Cosima says.

We make our way through a labyrinth of stairways and hallways to find our rooms. Our three rooms are next to each other. "Let's meet out front in forty-five minutes," Cosima says.

"Sounds good," I say. We are to meet Caroline in an hour.

The room is spartan, with white walls decorated with only a single small cross at the head of my bed, but it feels spacious, with high ceilings, a sink, a small desk, and a closet. I open my window and peer out across a courtyard into what I assume are similar rooms, and to my left, the city's red-tiled roofs.

Sitting in the shade of a tall evergreen, we open a bottle of wine and toast to our time on the Camino.

"I have to be back at work in two days," Caroline says, frowning. "Two weeks wasn't enough."

"Will you come back?" Till asks.

"I hope so," she says. "I would like to start in Saint-Jean-Pied-de-Port if I return."

"I will be back for sure," Till says.

"I know I will," I add.

"I am going to begin heading back home in the morning," Till says. "I will make an adventure of it."

This is news to me, and I feel a surge of excitement. "How's that?" I ask.

"No planes or trains. I will hitchhike or use BlaBlaCar (a rideshare app)," he says. "I am in no hurry."

"You don't want to reach the ocean?" I ask.

"I want a reason to return," he says. "I will walk to the ocean from Saint-Jean-Pied-de-Port someday—maybe next year."

I glance at Cosima and raise my eyebrows, flashing her a quick smile. She purses her lips and scrunches her nose, a look I have grown to treasure.

We sit in the grass talking until Caroline says, "I need to get to the bus station." We all stand and say our goodbyes.

"It was fun," Caroline says as she hugs each of us goodbye.

We plan for a simple evening—a picnic dinner near the seminary—and head to a nearby shop to pick up a few items to add to the tasty cheese from this morning.

As night approaches, we find a gazebo near the front of the seminary, the perfect place for late dinner. We eat while watching the sun set over the city; loud fireworks explode overhead, reinforcing what I had learned earlier about the Spanish love of setting off fireworks for no reason. A chill in the air forces us to retrieve an extra layer from our rooms.

Till wanders off, cell phone in hand, talking to his love back home; Cosima and I walk down the hill and along a path, hand in hand. We enter one of the garden mazes, the hedges standing a good seven feet tall, and start necking in a hidden nook.

Later, Till joins us as we lie in tall grass on the hillside, staring up at the stars, reminiscent of our night at Isabel's. "I would like to attend a German mass at a small church in the morning," Cosima says.

"Sure," Till says.

"I'd like that," I say.

We head to our rooms well before the 12:30 a.m. curfew. I practically skip through the halls, excited for a late-night rendezvous. Tomorrow it will be just me and Cosima walking towards the end of the world, but I have no idea what the sleeping arrangements will be over the coming days and think this may be our last night sharing a bed.

Five minutes after the three of us say goodnight, I join Cosima. We gently and quietly make love for what seems like hours, uncertain if our activities in this room, where future priests once slept, are considered sacrilegious. Late in the night, I leave Cosima and head back to my room to sleep.

DAY 32: SANTIAGO DE COMPOSTELA > A PENA

*Each one of us has our own evolution of life,
and each of us goes through different tests
which are unique and challenging. But
certain things are common. And we do learn
things from each other's experience. On a
spiritual journey we all have the same
destination.*

~ A.R. Rahman

We hurriedly walk along empty streets through an ethereal mist on our
way to a small chapel for the 8 a.m. mass. Inside this quaint chapel, we
find the pews empty and twenty people of all ages sitting in a semicircle
of benches and chairs on the altar. The small congregation greets us in
German, and I manage a simple "guten morgen" as three chairs extend
the arc. We are handed lyrics to a couple of songs, and the simple service
led by a smiling, middle-aged German woman resumes. Like most of the

masses I have attended on this pilgrimage, I am uncertain about what is said; this morning, the only difference is the language, still foreign to me.

The sound of something crashing to the floor is followed a split second later by a piercing scream. Everyone turns and looks towards the commotion at the back of the altar. An older woman is bent over a young girl who has fallen backward off a bench onto the tiled floor. Cosima joins a couple of others who approach to see if they can be of assistance. The girl is unresponsive, and the woman I assume to be her mother is doing her best to rouse the girl. Shocked looks are on all our faces. I fear the worst.

After a couple of nerve-wracking minutes, the girl is conscious, able to sit up. She is carried to a pew. Like everyone else here, I am relieved. A couple of minutes later, the service continues. Afterward, Cosima shares, "She has diabetes and passed out due to low blood sugar. She will be fine." Quite a start to our day.

On the plaza in front of the cathedral, we say goodbye to Till. He has arranged for a ride on BlaBlaCar, an app popular in Europe whereby people driving longer distances offer up available seats for a nominal charge. His ride this morning will take him a few hours east as he starts his homeward adventure, while Cosima and I will continue walking westward. Cosima and her brother share a long embrace; I give Till a quick hug.

"Be safe," Cosima says.

We turn and head out of the city at a relaxed pace. Almost immediately, we pass a familiar mileage marker: a yellow shell on a field of blue, a yellow arrow pointing the way, and not one but two brass plates. No longer marking the kilometers to Santiago, these plates read *Fisterra 89.568 km* and *Muxia 86.482 km*. The countdown has just been reset. The markers are now counting down the distance I have left to walk with my enchantress. But in actuality, it's not the distance left to walk but the ticking clock that will determine when we must part.

The crowds are now gone, and the sun is starting to peek out from behind the clouds. Our walk to Finisterre should take three days, but it will require long days of walking, more than we have grown accustomed to. After a bit of an uphill climb, we turn to find another beautiful view of Santiago and its cathedral—and we say our farewell.

"I need to find a new walking stick," Cosima says. "I have gotten used to walking with one."

Eventually, she finds one as we walk through a patch of trees. "It's too long and too heavy," she says, "but it will have to do until I find something better."

We have expansive views of rolling Galician hills as the trail gently rises and descends. Late in the morning, we stop at a bar in a small town to find some food and café con leche. We sit on the patio of the nearly empty bar and meet Eliza, yet another German, resting with her leg elevated on a chair, her knee tightly wrapped.

"How long have you had that problem?" Cosima asks.

"A couple of weeks," she answers. "I saw a doctor in Léon, and he gave me some meds and said to rest it for a week."

"Did you?" I ask, already knowing the answer.

"I took one day off and then started again at a much slower pace," she admits sheepishly. "I did spend three days in Santiago to rest it."

"You are determined," I say.

"I guess," she says. "I am not sure when I will have a chance to walk the Camino again."

We all share a bit of our journey before Cosima and I stand to leave.

"Good luck in reaching Finisterre," Cosima says.

"You too."

After passing through the village of Aguapeseda, we find ourselves with a long climb on a path that meanders through a thick, green Galician forest. By the early afternoon, we are crossing an old stone bridge, the Ponte Maceira, when a sporty black Alfa Romeo drives onto the ancient span from the other side. The bridge is maybe a foot wider than the car. A pilgrim walking ahead of us climbs onto the old stone guardrail.

"Let's back up," Cosima says. We turn around and let the car continue unimpeded. I am surprised to find any car even attempting this, but clearly, it's allowed.

On our second attempt, we stop at the bridge's apex to find one of the more beautiful scenes of my entire Camino. A natural dam about five feet high arcs across the Tambre River, water falling in white streams over the stone ledge. The backdrop: gently rolling hills of green and puffy white clouds drifting above through a vivid blue sky. Huge gray boulders speckle the water, which pools below the dam before flowing under this eighteenth-century stone archway.

We peer westerly off the other side of the bridge. "That's a perfect place for a picnic," she says. We walk back in the direction from which we came and follow a dirt path to a somewhat flat patch of grass, next to the river, beneath a large oak tree. We dig through our packs for food and the bottle of wine we purchased from the bar this morning.

"How do you feel about being back home in a few days?" Cosima asks.

"I'm eager to see my family," I say, "but otherwise, I'm not sure. How much longer do you think you'll keep walking?"

"A month … maybe longer. It depends on money and if I am still enjoying it."

"I'd like to keep walking," I say. "It's such a simple existence. And of course, I love spending time with you."

"Me too."

"When will you find out if you're accepted to medical school this time?" I ask.

"October," she says.

I can sense a sadness about not yet having been accepted and frustration about not moving closer towards her goal.

"I know you're hoping to get in and move to that phase of your life, but have you thought about what you'll do if you don't?"

"A little. I will probably get a nursing job, save up and travel again," she says with a shrug.

Cosima is living her life in six-month increments while praying she's eventually accepted, never able to commit to anything while she continues her efforts to become a doctor.

"I love that you have a dream, and you find purpose and meaning in it," I say. "Caring for others is clearly what you should be doing. I've seen that side of you often. I wish I had something like that."

"Thanks," she says, looking me in the eye, and smiles. "What are your dreams now?"

"You know I dreamt of travel for years, so I've been living that. Now I hope to find a purpose, one not so selfish."

"It's not selfish to follow your dreams of traveling."

"Maybe," I say. "But it's not a selfless as yours."

"I am afraid my dream might not happen," she says as she leans back against her pack. "If it doesn't, I'll have to find something new."

We sit quietly, and I pour the last of the wine into our cups, the only sounds that of the flowing river and chirping birds.

We are walking again and unsure where we will stop—finding a private room will be my aim. I took a picture of a small sign planted along the trail earlier in the day, which mentioned private rooms.

"May I see your guidebook?" I ask, wanting to check if the albergue will work out logistically. I am happy to find the Albergue Alto de Pena lies twenty-seven kilometers from Santiago and will put us on pace to reach Finisterre.

"I found the perfect place," I say.

I call ahead.

When we reach the city of Negreira, we find the main road blocked off to cars. Long strands of pennants in burgundy and gold, along with flags depicting various coats of arms, are strung across the street for two blocks. The town is celebrating some sort of medieval festival. Dozens of booths line the street, offering food and crafts, but it seems most are closed for siesta.

The savory smell of cooking meat wafts in the air as we pass by a massive circular grill covered with various meats and sausages. Despite the temptation, we keep moving and soon pass through the gates of the Pazo do Coton and leave this old walled town behind.

Our route climbs, and we pass a quaint stone church weathered over the centuries, Iglesia de San Julián, and find a funeral underway. From a distance, we witness twenty or so mourners dressed in black. They are gathered in the courtyard of the cemetery amongst several columbaria, the walls filled with the remains of those who have finished their life's Camino.

Shortly after, we leave the pavement and enter a forest.

"What kind of life do you think he had?" I ask.

"Are you sure it was a man?" she responds.

"Yes, in my imaginings, he is a man," I say, "and he lived in this small Spanish town his whole life."

"Okay," she says. "Maybe he did, but he also fought in the war, and traveled the world."

"Was he a kind man or a grumpy old man?" I ask.

"Definitely a kind man," she says. "And he was married to his wife for sixty years and had many children."

"Will he be missed?" I ask.

"Of course."

"I wonder how I will be remembered," I say as I think of my funeral. "I have thought about what my kids and granddaughter will think about me when I'm gone."

"I think they'll say you were a kind and loving man who lived his dreams."

"I hope so," I say. "But, with my choices the last few years, I don't know."

"You have to live your life," she says.

"Yes, but I knowingly gave up my grandkids coming over to their grandparents' house to celebrate special occasions," I say. "Those are the times from my childhood I look back on and smile."

"It doesn't matter. They won't have the same memories as you."

"I guess so," I say. "I am hoping to share adventures with my kids and grandkids … and as you said, they will know he followed his dreams."

"There are trade-offs, but seeing a happy old grandfather is the best any grandchild can hope for."

"I'll take that," I say.

We leave the forest and rejoin a quiet roadway under a hot summer sun, and soon we need to find water. Finally, after passing through a farmer's field on a small dirt track, we enter a small village and take a rest break after finding a fountain. Our elevation has steadily increased since Negreira, and after our break, we continue uphill until we reach our albergue around six o'clock.

We check in and are assigned a room on the second floor with two single beds.

"This won't work," Cosima says as she starts to push them together. She soon heads down to the woman's bathroom to shower. She's back before I finish organizing my pack.

"I am going to write a letter. I'll meet you on the patio," she says.

"I'll be down soon," I say.

There is only one shower for each gender, and I must wait. When I finally make it back to our room, I find a missed message from Cosima on my phone: a picture of two glasses of wine. I hurry down and join her on the patio.

"There is a pilgrim dinner in the restaurant," she says. "But I am not that hungry."

"Me neither," I say, and we order two small plates and another bottle of wine.

We sit outside as the hours pass, the temperature drops, and the stars appear. When a woman begins putting chairs on tables, she says, "The main door will be locked in a few minutes." She kindly allows us to bring our half-full bottle and glasses back to our room.

We are greeted with "Hello!" as we enter the albergue's foyer and turn to find Eliza, from this morning, sitting at a small table, her knee covered by a bag of ice.

"Wow, you walked a long way with that knee," Cosima says, shaking her head.

"Yes, I just got here fifteen minutes ago," Eliza says. "It was a long day."

"Where did you find the ice?" I ask.

"The man who checked me in."

I find an empty mug in a cabinet, and the three of us finish the wine while we talk. Soon Eliza says goodnight and hobbles to the bunk room. A few minutes later, Cosima and I head upstairs to top off what has been a perfect day, filled with beautiful scenery, easy conversation, and good wine.

DAY 33: A PENA > O LOGOSO

Why did you deceive yourself that you are
powerless to change your life?

~ Unknown

We walk out onto the patio with coffee in hand. A low-hanging fog at this elevation brings a chill; I dig out the fleece from my pack. We sit looking towards the rolling hills, our view softened by the haze. We are in no hurry this morning. Sipping our second café con leche, we watch others toss on their packs and start off. We soon find ourselves the only pilgrims left. Finally, we walk down the steps from the albergue and onto the Camino Finisterre.

"I am not the one normally who gets worn out from too much sex," Cosima jokes. "But I was last night."

"I must admit, that isn't typically the case," I say. "You bring something out in me."

"That's nice to know," she says with a grin.

Shades of green continue to dominate the Galician landscapes, and our walk this morning is mainly along quiet country lanes, through lovely landscapes of gentle hills and crop-filled fields. Tractors with waving farmers pass on occasion as we make our way. We walk long stretches in comfortable silence.

In a small village, we stop in a small market to buy the makings for yet another picnic lunch. An hour later, our route passes by a tree-covered hill that looks out onto a scene of vast green fields, and in the distance, undulating hills. We find it an ideal spot to enjoy our picnic fare. As we sit side by side, I constantly reach out and touch Cosima, her hand, her arm, her leg. Pilgrims pass by every so often, and we exchange the required "Buen Camino."

I lean back against my pack and close my eyes. My thoughts take me back to my old life of convention, when I was an overweight, clean-shaven businessman daydreaming of a more rugged life. I knew what I wanted to look like physically, but it seemed an impossibility. My imagined exterior was modeled after a picture on the back cover of a book: a guy was hiking out of the Grand Canyon; lean, tan, bearded, wearing a backpack and a smirk. Eventually, to my surprise, I became the man I had envisioned, down to the sandals the guy in the picture was wearing; adventurous and fit enough to climb mountains.

What I didn't think about back then was the man inside. I had changed my body and sought out adventures to distract myself from the real work that needed to be done. As my daughter, a grad student in psychology, tells me, "Our interior landscape is filled with difficult terrain. All the real work we must do is in our minds."

Over the past months, this has become my focus. On the Camino, I have inched closer to an idealized version of myself.

"I think it's clear why I like you ... you're beautiful, compassionate, and you know what you want in life," I say to Cosima. "What is it that attracted you to me?"

"That's easy. You're attractive and sweet, and the fact you are living a life you have dreamed of is very sexy."

While I feel good about my life's direction, I wasn't aware it showed.

I'm happy knowing I have become a different man, but I know I am still nowhere near the peak.

Our midday break lasts for over an hour, and I even doze off for a bit, lying on this shady hillside.

Our walk this afternoon leads us higher. To the north lies a cerulean lake, to the south a small mountain. "We must be getting close to the ocean. I can almost smell it," I say. "If we keep climbing, we may be able to see it."

Cosima stays silent; her expression changes, and she looks away.

Ahead there is a less defined pathway going towards the summit of the mountain we are climbing, but as we get nearer, a marker points to the right, avoiding the steep climb. As the route turns, Cosima hastily throws off her pack and takes off uphill at a fast pace. I am unsure why, but I drop my pack and follow. I give her space and don't catch her immediately; I wait until we near the top. Together we climb the last few meters in silence. We tramp through tall, prickly grasses. I scrape my legs as we move towards a ten-foot-tall concrete obelisk.

Cosima steps up on the base of the marker and gazes to the west. I join her atop the marker and enjoy a 360-degree view of the area. The blue tentacled lake to the north, much green and a few small villages to the south and west, and lines of wind turbines to the east. Cosima seems relieved when the ocean is not in sight.

Though we haven't spoken of any serious feelings towards each other, a connection has formed.

We hug and share a passionate kiss, her cheeks wet from tears. I step down from the concrete marker and stroke her leg as she stands atop the marker on our mountain. My face at the height of her waist. I find myself exploring her, and we are soon making love. Twenty minutes after reaching the summit, we slowly walk down, gather our packs, and continue on our way.

It is getting hot and much of this afternoon's walk is uphill. We pass through the town of Olveiroa, which is the more common stopping point for pilgrims on this leg, but our bed is still four kilometers ahead, putting us over thirty for the day. Walking along a paved pathway, we pass by a few nameless but familiar faces from last night, wading in a gently flowing stream. "Hola," we say in response to their raised hands. We push onward and start another climb before reaching a ridge exposed to the sun, which is still blazing hot despite having started its descent hours earlier. Cosima is now using her multipurpose sarong as a hijab to keep the sun's rays from her head. We stop on the trail to take in a stunning view. I look at her and simply say, "Beautiful."

Soon the trail flattens out, and the sun falls behind the ridge of a mountain to the west. Two hundred meters straight ahead, I see a small building. As we get nearer, I can make out *O Logoso* on a narrow yellow building. We've arrived at our albergue, here on the side of a tree-covered mountain, directly on the trail.

Outside, a couple of pilgrims drink beer at a long, heavy wooden table that can seat ten. A large building under renovation is off to the left, and we check in at the small bar. We are shown to our room upstairs in the building under construction, where there are two newly completed rooms.

"There's a bathroom!" Cosima says.

"That's a nice surprise," I say.

We shower and change before heading down for a drink. The only option for food is either the pilgrim menu or a couple of tapas options. Not ready for dinner, we sit talking with other pilgrims, wine in hand, at the large outdoor table.

Later, Cosima says, "We should have a romantic dinner on our final night together."

"That sounds perfect," I say.

The two of us are seated at a table for four, inside the small bar filled with large windows. We make our choices from the options given, and soon, a bottle and glasses are delivered. Before the food comes out, Eliza arrives. I glance at Cosima, and she gives a quick nod.

"Please join us," I say.

"Thanks," she says, taking a seat. The host comes and takes her order.

As we talk about our day and our lives over dinner, Jules, whom we haven't seen in a week, arrives with a new friend. They, too, join our table. The five of us drink and share stories until long past dark.

As the night comes to a close, everyone else heads towards the dormitory. Eliza's eyebrows rise when she sees we are headed in a different direction, to a private room upstairs.

As we make love, the moon's glow seeping in from the window lights Cosima's face. I stare into her emerald eyes, and we share a melancholic smile.

It's late ... I'm exhausted ... sleep begins to call ... I drift off ... with Cosima lying in my arms.

DAY 34: O LOGOSO > THE WATER

Happiness (is) only real when shared.

~ *Into the Wild*, quoting
Christopher McCandless

The alarm on my phone quietly wakes me at five. I spoon Cosima, and my hands start to caress her silky, bare skin. I kiss her neck, inhaling the scent of her shampoo while my hands rub every part of her. I enter her from our spooning position, and we move rhythmically until Cosima gets up on her knees, our bodies moving with the same aim.

Afterward, she lies in my arms for a few reflective minutes before she whispers, "Happy Birthday." I turn fifty-three today. While we lie in bed, she removes a bracelet that matches her gemstone necklace and places it on my wrist. She has not removed it since I first met her, and I am taken aback by her gesture. I peer into her eyes. "Thank you," I say, and we kiss.

Soon after our morning 'wake-up,' we head downstairs and out the door. It is our earliest start together, and we head towards "the end of the world" and the end of us.

It is still dark, but a hint of the sun's rise is evident, as silhouettes of wind turbines lining a mountain ridge to the east are visible. Fifteen minutes into our walk, we reach a bright yellow building painted with a large map of the routes from Santiago to Finisterre and Muxia. This information center appears brand new but is not yet open for the day. A few hundred meters on, the route splits at a large traffic circle; to the right, Muxia, and to the left Finisterre, just under thirty kilometers away. Finisterre is where I will catch the last bus to Santiago.

We head left and pick up our pace; we have a long day ahead of us.

The sky brightens, and a gentle breeze chills my bare arms. A while later, I ask, "Do you find it strange we have grown so close in only thirteen days?"

"It hasn't been that long," she says with a quizzical expression.

"I know; it doesn't seem that long to me either, but today is our thirteenth day together," I say.

"I am surprised, and *no*, I did not expect to get so attached," she says. "How do you feel?"

"I'm extremely happy," I say. "It's so easy being together. But I remember what you said on our night at Isabel's … I'll need to leave you on the Camino." Then I say, "It's going to be hard."

"For me, too."

"I don't want to rush our final day," I say. "I am not walking to reach a destination; I am walking to be with you and enjoy our time together. Let's stop in Cee, and I will catch the last bus there."

"That is fine with me, but I thought you wanted to reach the ocean."

"It would be nice to see it, but I would rather spend a quiet afternoon with you."

"Cee it is," she says with a smile.

Cee is a city that sits on a narrow bay and is only a couple of hours away. Based on the satellite view on Google Maps, it seems like a nice place to spend the afternoon. Once that's decided, our pace slows.

Since the information center, we haven't passed anything on our route; no bars or shops. The yellow arrows have kept us on a gravel path most of the morning. The trail runs through open patches of land, over rocky terrain next to evergreen trees, whose growth seems stunted as we near the coast.

"Have you seen the movie *Before Sunrise?*" I ask as we walk side by side.

"No. I don't think so," she says, shaking her head.

"It's a story about a boy and a girl who meet while traveling and create a deep connection quickly—like the two of us, but their time together only lasts one night and ends at sunrise."

"I'm sure I would like it," she says.

I get overly excited when I remember the sequel and start talking faster. "There are actually three movies with the same characters. In the second movie, *Before Sunset*, an American male character writes a book about their time together. The next time they meet is a few years later, after his book becomes a best seller. So ... I'll write a book, which will be turned into a movie, and you must be my date at the premiere."

Cosima, laughing, says, "Okay."

I had mentioned to her before that I wanted to start writing. As we walk, I tell her, "The Camino has given me something to write about."

After a gentle bend in our path, a sliver of blue becomes visible on the horizon; the water Cosima has been dreading is now in sight. We have a steep descent on the gravel path; slowly, we make it to our final destination.

Having not eaten a morsel of food all morning, we decide finding food will be our first objective. As we enter the city, we pass a woman walking out of her house. In halting Spanish, I ask, "Donde hay un supermercado?"

Noticing our packs, she asks with a smile, "Do you speak English?"

"Yes," I say.

"Come with me. I am headed that way," she says.

She and Cosima engage in lively conversation while I follow behind. En route down a narrowing street, the kind woman says, "Please wait. I will be right out." She runs into a shop.

"What a kind woman," Cosima says.

Not a minute later, she's back, and we continue.

I am amazed how Cosima brings out the friendliness in others. There is something special in her demeanor, an intense empathy I've rarely witnessed. Her personality seems perfectly aligned with her life's ambition. All along the Way, I have seen her sincere caring for others, from their feet to their souls.

The lovely Spanish woman points out the grocery store. "Enjoy your day," she says and continues on her way. "Thank you," we say.

As is only appropriate, we get what we need for a picnic lunch and then head towards the water.

We find a large green space that looks out onto the bay and a small beach. Beyond our view, the bay opens onto the ocean. While it is not the broad panorama I would have found in Finisterre, it is still a stunning sight—a half-dozen boats out on a calm sea under a bright blue sky. We find a spot next to one of the many trees lining a promenade that circles the green and set up for a leisurely afternoon.

Sitting in the shade, we talk of our days to come. Cosima will head to Finisterre in the morning, where she plans to spend a couple of days, then a walk up the coast to Muxia, before making her way to Oviedo and the Camino Primitivo. Her walking adventure will continue before returning home to what she hopes is the start of medical school. I will be on a plane over the Atlantic twenty-four hours from now, heading home to a life that is yet to be determined.

We sit drinking wine, eating, and talking as the sun continues its climb. In the afternoon heat, we head off on a quest to find ice cream. Successful, we return to our spot in the shade.

"Can you grab your earbuds?" I ask.

"Of course," she says.

We walk to the empty beach and wade into the water, and each put in an earbud. I play Darius Rucker's song "Hands on Me." Our arms around each other, we sway knee-deep in the sea and gently kiss.

When the time comes that I must head to the station, I ask myself, and not for the first time, *Why am I leaving her today?* The inadequate answer: *A nonrefundable ticket.*

We sit on a bench holding hands. The heartbreak I feel is reflected in her watery eyes.

Along the Way, I have found the Camino helps form deeper connections between people than is common in my 'real life,' but Cosima and I are simply a Camino romance. I must leave her here, just as she said.

When two people meet and spend almost every moment together for two weeks and feel a passionate connection, what happens when it ends? I guess only time will tell.

Too soon, the bus arrives. We remain holding hands until the driver makes his final call. We share one final hug. I pay the driver for my ride back to Santiago de Compostela and find a seat on the nearly empty bus, one that gives me the best view of Cosima. She stands on the sidewalk, our eyes locked as the bus pulls away.

This story is not one of a man meeting a woman and living happily ever after, but simply the story of my Camino.

Gazing out the window, passing many of the places I walked through the past few days, I reflect on my amazing journey: the people I've met, the places I've been, all now pieces of the mosaic that is me.

When I arrived in Saint-Jean-Pied-de-Port, I was looking for direction. A quote by Thoreau reminds me, "Not until we are lost ... do we begin to understand ourselves."

Was I lost before I started this walk? I was, but only because I felt I needed to find the single route to follow for my last act. I was roaming the foothills, hoping to stumble upon a trail that would lead me higher, to a life of meaning.

I started the Camino hoping for some insight directing me towards such a path. I had no such epiphany. There are no yellow arrows in life. However, I know *now* that simply doing what feels right at the moment is okay. If something changes, I can veer onto yet another path, just as I did when stepping off the well-beaten one not long ago. The proof lies in the fact that my new path led me here.

While I didn't complete the physical journey to Finisterre, 'the end of the world,' just as I haven't finished my inner journey of becoming the person I want to be, I am grateful for the substantial strides I have made along the Way. This walk has brought me closer to myself.

I will leave Spain with wonderful memories, certain I will return. Maybe I will run back after a painful episode in my life, or maybe I will bring a loved one here to share this magical and meaningful experience. I do know, whatever path I may be headed down in life, I will always walk a bit easier simply knowing The Camino will be here … waiting.

ULTREIA (ONWARD)

My struggles are not unique to me, but like you, I suffer in silence,
tormented by a voice inside.

Luckily, *Hope* is not lost;
Like the setting sun, it casts the shadow of my burdens behind as I journey closer.

Glancing back, the challenging terrain I've crossed is illuminated.
I keep moving towards a dream ... my mind on fire.

Alone, I reach a cabin in the woods.
Once loved, it now sits in ruins ... waiting to rise again.
I linger. I consider.

Finally ... the mountain calls, and a storied trail beckons.
I answer.

Friendly faces and glorious places,
Evenings full of connection and memories shared.

Flanked by others along the Way,
My thoughts dovetail as we stroll along.

This journey transforms, but not into something new.
The layers built up since 'that' day-start to fall away.
It's me at the core.

In getting lost, a bit of grace has been found.

My walk ends, but my story continues...a new ending to write.
A smirk reappears, I have a life to live...
Before the long sleep calls and I gently fall.

Two roads diverge, and you, you alone, must choose.

By Michael Burnett

*The Camino is God's dream for how people
should be when they are with each other.*

Found on the website:
withoutbaggage.com

EPILOGUE

As I made my way across Spain, I stopped thinking I would find any answers along the Way. The Camino, I decided, would not point me to the meaning and purpose I was seeking.

It turns out I was wrong.

The Camino did give my life direction … in the form of this book. I fell in love with writing. It became my passion, my new "something to be enthusiastic about." In the weeks after my return from the Camino, a feeling of urgency to write this book took hold. I started writing a little every day and committed to seeing the project through. I even signed up for a personal enrichment class in creative writing at my local community college.

Since this book was my first writing project of any length, progress was slow. I have always been a dreamer, but I have not been so great at putting in the hard work needed to see my dreams come to fruition. I had vision but no follow-through, so completing this book was no sure thing.

Then, six months after I returned home, Covid-19 hit. During lockdown, I sat at the kitchen table in my childhood home, and writing this book became my full-time job. As the book began to take shape, I was surprised by how much I was enjoying the process—and impressed with myself for keeping my commitment to write each day.

My purpose was now clear: to share my love of the Camino with those who don't yet know it and be a light to those who might be struggling to find that perilous "something more." I hope my story makes a difference for those who read it.

Where my path goes from here, only time will tell, but I'll be walking with my head up, excited for whatever is to come.

ABOUT THE AUTHOR

Michael Burnett was born and raised outside of Chicago. He spent most of his life in the Midwest before a move later in life to Portland, Oregon. There his love for being outdoors in nature grew, as did his passion for hiking. His evolution to a writer was slow. It wasn't until he escaped a nine-to-five life and started living a life filled with adventure that he put pen to paper.

Michael is a father of two grown children and is back living in the Chicago area, where he enjoys spending time with his three grandkids. When he's not traveling, Michael can be found enjoying time outdoors or planning his next adventure with his significant other. They are now making plans for a life on the road and their next long walk.

For more information about Michael and his current project, visit his website: walkingandwriting.com.

If you enjoyed this book, please leave a review on Amazon.com. Thanks!

Coming in late 2022 from:

Michael Burnett's next book:

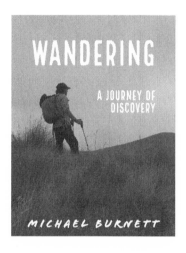

Jack Dufour, like many nineteen-year-olds, is feeling lost. He just failed out of college and is uncertain of his next steps in life. While visiting a friend in Madison, Wisconsin he finds what he thinks is a sign. Two weeks later he is on a plane to Europe.

On his journey he unearths a passion for life that he had been missing. Jack learns to find joy in the unknown, experiences an openness and kindness of those he meets, and revels in the simplicity of a life without the expectation of material success.

Follow Jack as he walks across a continent and becomes the man he didn't know was within his reach.

Made in the USA
Monee, IL
23 September 2021